KNOW YOUR RIGHTS!™

FIFTH EDITION

Richard M. Alderman
"The People's Lawyer™"

KNOW YOUR RIGHTS!™

FIFTH EDITION

Answers to Texans' Everyday Legal Questions

Gulf Publishing Company
Houston, Texas

KNOW YOUR RIGHTS!™

FIFTH EDITION

10   9   8   7   6   5   4   3   2   1

Library of Congress Cataloging-in-Publication Data

Alderman, Richard M.
    Know your rights! / Richard M. Alderman. — 5th ed.
      p. cm.
    Includes index.
    ISBN 0-88415-420-3
    1. Law—Texas—Popular works. I. Title.
KFT1281.A37 1997
349.764—dc21   97-13340
                                                      CIP

*This publication is designed to provide accurate and
authoritative information with regard to the subject matter
covered. It is sold with the understanding that neither the
publisher nor the author is engaged in rendering legal advice
to specific individuals.*

*IF LEGAL SERVICE OR OTHER EXPERT ASSISTANCE
IS REQUIRED, THE SERVICES OF A COMPETENT
PROFESSIONAL SHOULD BE SOUGHT.*

To my grandparents

CONTENTS

PREFACE TO THE FIRST EDITION

YOU may not think about it, but nearly every day you have to know the law. Not only must lawyers make decisions based on knowledge of the law, but people like yourself must apply basic legal principles in daily life. And if you do not know the law, you are making decisions partially uninformed.

The Texas and federal legislatures have passed scores of laws designed to protect you in your everyday transactions. Most of these laws are considered self-regulating. This means the laws are supposed to work because you know about them, and your knowledge keeps merchants from trying to violate the laws. The breakdown in this system is apparent: Because most people do not know their legal rights, the laws often do not work.

This book is designed to ensure that our laws do work by helping you learn about them. The book covers a wide variety of topics ranging from credit card rights, to landlord-tenant relations, to the legal aspects of warranties and wills. The choice of topics and the format of the book are based on my personal experience as "The People's Lawyer™" for a Houston television station.

As "The People's Lawyer™," I have received thousands of letters about the most common legal problems. This mail has led me to two conclusions: First, many of you share the same everyday legal problems to which you do not know the answers; and second, there is no readily available source of information. This book was written to address both problems.

But this book is not designed to make you a lawyer, nor is it meant to encourage lawsuits. Instead, it is designed to make you aware of the choices and rights you have under the law. Whether you are dealing with a store that will not replace a damaged television set, a neighbor whose barking dog keeps you awake all night, or perhaps a landlord who deducts too much from your security deposit, you must know your legal rights to reach a fair, equitable solution.

Once someone knows you know your rights, he is usually quick to try to work something out. Compromise and settlement—not litigation—should be the goals of any legal system. They are the goals of this book.

Richard M. Alderman

PREFACE TO THE FIFTH EDITION

As I noted in the original preface to this book, my goal in writing *Know Your Rights!*™ was to help everyday people understand the law, enabling them to better stand up for their rights. The book has been even more successful than I imagined. Now, 12 years after its initial publication, I find I must add to the book to keep up with the increasing number of legal questions I have received and the changes made by the courts and legislature.

The format of this edition remains the same. What has changed is the coverage. In the first edition, I discussed what I believed to be the most common legal questions people had. In subsequent editions, I added several new chapters and expanded many of the existing ones. For example, divorce, immigration law, and employment were all added. In this edition, I have expanded the coverage of nearly every chapter, added a new chapter about lawyers, and updated the answers to comply with current law.

Also, as you might expect, some of the material in the earlier editions has become out of date or incorrect because of action by the courts and legislature. A problem with any book about law is keeping it current. With the publication of this edition, you now have the most up-to-date information available. It is unavoidable, however, to prevent even this edition from being dated. The material is based on the law as it existed in June 1997.

Those of you who are buying this book to replace your fourth editions already know how valuable a resource it can be. If this is your first purchase, let me emphasize what I said in the first edition. *Once someone knows you know your legal rights, he is usually quick to try to work something out.* I hope you find this book is one of the best investments you have ever made.

Richard M. Alderman

KNOW YOUR RIGHTS!™

FIFTH EDITION

CHAPTER ONE

Applying for Credit

FOR most of us, credit is an essential part of life. Our homes, our cars, and much of our personal property are all purchased on credit. Just imagine what it would be like if we had to pay for everything with cash. Yes, America is truly a land of consumer credit; together we owe hundreds of billions of dollars.

Because of the importance of obtaining credit, Congress has passed three laws to protect people who are trying to get it:

First:
> **The Equal Credit Opportunity Act** ensures that all credit applicants start off on the same foot by prohibiting discrimination based on color, age, sex, race, or marital status.

Second:
> **The Truth-in-Lending Law** protects individuals from paying too much for credit by requiring that all relevant information be disclosed before a contract is signed and, more importantly, that the information be provided in an understandable manner. In other words, you must be given enough information to permit you to shop around for credit.

Third:
> **The Fair Credit Reporting Act** requires that you have a full opportunity to find out what information is in your credit report. It also gives you the right to correct any errors that might exist in that information.

When you apply for credit, you should know the law. You should also know what factors are important in obtaining credit and what information your creditors cannot use to deny you credit. As you will discover in the following letters, there are legal solutions for some of the more common problems you may experience while trying to obtain credit.

Why can't I get credit?
"You must be told why."

Dear Mr. Alderman:
I need your help. I can't figure out why no one will give me credit. I
have applied for two credit cards, and both times I was turned down.
I have a good job, and I have never had financial problems. What
can I do to get credit?

If you have been turned down for credit and have not been told why,
someone has violated the law. Under the Equal Credit Opportunity Act,
you must be notified of the decision within 30 days after your application
was completed. *If credit is denied, you must be notified in writing. The*
notification must explain the specific reasons for the denial or inform you
that you may request a full explanation.

If you are denied credit, be sure to find out why. In your case, reread
the letter you received and see if it tells you whom to contact for an
explanation. If it does not, write the creditor and demand to know the
specific reasons it denied you credit. You should also consider contacting
the Federal Trade Commission to report that the creditor is not comply-
ing with the law. The FTC has a regional office in Dallas:

Federal Trade Commission
1999 Bryan St.
Dallas, TX 75201
(214) 979-0213

After you find out why you were denied credit, you can take steps to correct the problem. It may be that the creditor thinks you have asked for too
much money or that you have not been employed or lived in the community
long enough. Once you know why, you can discuss these reasons with the
creditor and attempt to work it out. Sometimes you will discover the creditor simply had incorrect information. As you will see in the next letter, credit reports may be wrong, and when they are, you can correct them.

How do I get a copy of my credit report?
"A new law may help."

Dear Mr. Alderman:
I have had problems getting credit because of prior debt problems. I
have had a good credit history for the past eight years, and I now

want to make sure that my credit report is accurate and that the negative information has been removed. How do I get a copy of my report?

Under a new Texas law, a credit bureau must provide you with a copy of all information contained in its file concerning you. The copy must be provided within 45 days of your request.

I suggest you immediately call the credit bureau and request a copy of your file. The bureau may ask for some identification information to ensure you are the person you claim to be. Under prior law, the bureau could also charge you a small fee unless you had been turned down for credit within the past 30 days. As I understand the new law, the report must be provided at no charge.

If you find any inaccuracies in the report, you can take steps to have them corrected. The next letter explains how to do this.

What can I do if my credit report is wrong? "You have rights."

Dear Mr. Alderman:

I was just refused a credit card. I was told the reason was that I had missed several payments on my motor home . . . but I don't even own a motor home. When I asked where the company obtained this information, I was told it was in my credit report. What should I do? I am sure all my creditors believe I am living in a motor home I'm not paying for.

A law protects you from having inaccurate information in your credit report. It is the Fair Credit Reporting Act. This law protects you from inaccurate reporting of credit information by giving you the right to find out what is in your report and allowing you to require that the reporting agency correct any errors. Because of the importance of having an accurate and up-to-date credit file, I suggest you contact the credit reporting agency immediately and assert your rights under this law.

The Fair Credit Reporting Act applies to any "consumer reporting agency." The most common type of consumer reporting agency is the credit bureau. Information gathered by a credit bureau, called a "consumer report," is sold to creditors, employers, insurance companies, and other businesses for the purpose of evaluating your credit-worthiness. If you are denied credit because of information contained in such a report, the creditor must give you the name and address of the credit reporting agency. I assume that, in your case, the creditor supplied you with this information.

The next step is to contact the credit reporting agency and request a full report of the information in your file. Under a new Texas law, the agency must provide you with a copy of the report within 45 days. If you have been denied credit, you must be given a copy at no charge. The law is unclear as to whether a charge may be imposed in other cases. In my opinion, however, a charge may not be imposed.

Under the law, the credit reporting agency must tell you about every piece of information it has concerning you. You also must be told the names of everyone who has been given a copy of the report within the past six months.

If you disagree with any of the information, you have the right to demand that the agency reinvestigate the items in question. If the new investigation reveals an error, the agency must send a corrected version of the report to everyone who received the old report within the past six months.

In your case, demand that the credit bureau reinvestigate. If the credit bureau discovers you do not own a motor home, it must renotify your creditors and give them a copy of the accurate report. Sometimes, though, the credit bureau will stand by its original report.

For example, a creditor may have reported that a consumer was late in paying some bills. The consumer paid late only because he did not receive the bills on time. The credit bureau may refuse to change the report because the creditor still says the consumer paid late. If this happens, you have the right to include a brief statement containing your version of why you paid late. This statement will become part of your file and will be sent whenever a creditor requests a credit report.

You should also be aware that there is a time limit on how long credit information can be reported by a consumer reporting agency. Generally, after seven years information is considered obsolete and may not be reported. However, a few exceptions to this rule exsist:

- Bankruptcy information can be reported for up to 10 years.
- No time limit exists for information reported for a prospective job with a salary of more than $20,000.
- No time limit exists for information reported on more than $50,000 worth of credit or life insurance.

If you have ever applied for a charge account, a personal loan, insurance, or a job, someone probably has a file on you. This file might contain any information that creditors use to determine your credit-worthiness. Everything, including how quickly you pay your bills, whether you have ever filed bankruptcy, and whether you have ever been sued, may be written into your credit report.

Because a good credit report is so important, it would be a good idea to check your file before a problem arises. It is quite easy to call your nearest credit bureau (see list below) and arrange for an interview.

Amarillo

Amarillo Credit Association, 912 S. Taylor St., P.O. Box 470, Amarillo, TX 79184; (806) 374-1611 and 374-3758.

Austin

Merchants and Professional Credit Bureau, P.O. Box 140675, Austin, TX 78714; (512) 346-4305.

Corpus Christi

CSC Credit Services, 5350 Staples, Suite 425, Corpus Christi, TX 78411; (512) 980-4070.

Dallas

CSC Credit Services, 1503 LBJ Frwy., Suite 250, Dallas, TX 75234; (972) 243-7255.

East Texas

CSC Credit Services, 320 North St., Suite 313, Nacogdoches, TX 75961; (409) 564-7341.

El Paso

CSC Credit Services, 1200 Golden Key Cir., Suite 331, El Paso, TX 79925; (915) 590-4700.

Houston

CSC Credit Services, 652 N. Sam Houston Pkwy. East, P.O. Box 674402, Houston, TX 77060; (713) 878-4840.

Laredo

Credit Bureau of Laredo Inc., *see Corpus Christi.*

McAllen

CSC Credit Services, *see Corpus Christi.*

Midland-Odessa

Credit Data, 1004 N. Big Spring St., Suite 507, Midland, TX 79701; (800) 392-7816.

Port Arthur

Trans Union Credit Bureau of Port Arthur, 3830 Highway 365, Port Arthur, TX 77642; (409) 721-8701.

San Antonio
CSC Credit Services, 85 N.E. Loop 410, Suite 307, San Antonio, TX 78216; (210) 979-8621.

South Central Texas
See San Antonio.

Victoria
Credit Bureau of Victoria, 2001 E. Sabine, Suite 206, Victoria, TX 77901; (512) 573-9161.

How can my ex-spouse's debts appear on my credit report?
"They were your debts as well."

Dear Mr. Alderman:
My former common law husband and I bought a car and financed it through his credit union. He was the buyer. I just co-signed the note. After he missed two payments, they repossessed the car. They asked me to pay, but I told them that as far as I was concerned this was his debt. Now they have put this on my credit report. Can they do this?

Basically the answer is yes. As I discuss on page 40, co-signing a note is a very serious undertaking. You are agreeing to the same obligation as the other person. If he doesn't pay, you have to. If there is a default, it is your default as well. The information will appear on both your credit report and his.

Remember, you have the right to add your own statement to your credit report explaining information contained in it. You may want to add a brief statement indicating this is your ex-husband's debt.

How can I shop for credit?
"Truth-in-Lending."

Dear Mr. Alderman:
I am in the market for a new car. I know it's important to get the best interest rate, but it is all so confusing. There are all kinds of ads with different rates, and every time I call to ask about interest, they tell me about the APR. What is an APR? How can I compare interest rates as well as price? It seems that you can't find out the interest rate until after you buy something.

(text continued on page 8)

A credit sales contract should be written in standard language and should clearly reveal all costs involved in the transaction.

Big Wheel Auto   Alice Green

ANNUAL PERCENTAGE RATE The cost of your credit as a yearly rate.	FINANCE CHARGE The dollar amount the credit will cost you.	Amount Financed The amount of credit provided to you or on your behalf	Total of Payments The amount you will have paid after you have made all payments as scheduled	Total Sale Price The total cost of your purchase on credit, including your downpayment of $ _1500 –_
14.84 %	$1496.80	$6107.50	$7604.30	$9129.30

You have the right to receive at this time an itemization of the Amount Financed.
☐ I want an itemization.   ☒ I do not want an itemization.

Your payment schedule will be:

Number of Payments	Amount of Payments	When Payments Are Due
36	$211.23	Monthly beginning 6-1-97

Insurance
Credit life insurance and credit disability insurance are not required to obtain credit and will not be provided unless you sign and agree to pay the additional cost.

Type	Premium	Signature	
Credit Life	$120 –	I want credit life insurance.	*alice green* Signature
Credit Disability		I want credit disability insurance.	Signature
Credit Life and Disability		I want credit life and disability insurance.	Signature

Security: You are giving a security interest in:
☒ the goods being purchased.
☐ _____ .

Filing fees $ _12.50_   **Non-filing insurance** $ _____

Late Charge: If a payment is late, you will be charged $10.

Prepayment: If you pay off early, you
☒ may   ☐ will not   have to pay a penalty
☒ may   ☐ will not   be entitled to a refund of part of the finance charge.

See your contract documents for any additional information about nonpayment, default, any required repayment in full before the scheduled date, and prepayment refunds and penalties.

I have received a copy of this statement.

alice green   5-1-97
Signature   Date

_____
e means an estimate

(text continued from page 6)

Until recently creditors were free to confuse consumers by using all sorts of language when they loaned you money. Interest rates could be quoted as "add on," "discount," or "simple." Terms of an agreement, such as down payment, total price, and penalties, could be hidden throughout the contract, and it would take a lawyer to figure them all out.

But under a law known as Truth-in-Lending, all this has changed. Under this federal law, creditors must use standard language to disclose terms and must let you see a completed copy of the contract before you sign. *The purpose of Truth-in-Lending is to let you compare rates and shop around.*

On the previous page is a sample credit sales contract. Under the law, if you went to three different car dealers, they would each have to use a substantially similar form so you could compare how much you would pay and at what interest rate.

Under the law, interest rates must be disclosed as an annual percentage rate (APR). This is a mathematical formula that lets you compare rates, no matter how creditors compute them. Why should you compare? A difference of only a few percentage points in the financing of a car could save you hundreds of dollars.

If you would like a copy of the Truth-in-Lending Law and all the regulations passed to enforce it, write or call the Board of Governors of the Federal Reserve System, Washington, DC 20551, (202) 452-3000, and ask for "Regulation Z Truth-in-Lending."

Are credit laws different for women?
"No! Equal credit opportunity exists under the law."

Dear Mr. Alderman:

I am a recently divorced 26-year-old woman. I have worked for the past five years as the manager of a small baking company, and I think I make a good salary. The other day I went to my bank to borrow some money for a home improvement loan. The bank refused to give me the loan and told me a single woman with two children might get married, leave town, and not pay back the loan. Even though I assured the loan officers this would not happen, they insisted I get a co-signer. This doesn't seem fair. I know that one of my male employees who makes less than I do just obtained a loan at this bank. Can they do this?

It is difficult to tell if you have been illegally discriminated against, based on your brief letter. However, a law that protects people from credit discrimination does exist. If after reading this you believe you have been the subject of discrimination, I urge you to contact the appropriate federal agency and file a complaint.

Because of the importance of credit in today's society, Congress has enacted the Equal Credit Opportunity Act. *This law prohibits discrimination against an applicant for credit on the basis of sex, marital status, race, color, religion, national origin, or age.* The law does not ensure that any one person will be given credit, but it does require that the same standard of credit-worthiness be applied to all applicants.

Under the Equal Credit Opportunity Act, a creditor may not turn you down for credit just because you are a woman or single. To protect you from such discrimination the law specifically limits what a creditor may do when you apply for credit:

- A creditor *may not* ask your sex on a credit application—with one exception. If you apply for a loan to buy or build a home, a creditor is required to ask your sex to provide the federal government with information to monitor compliance with the act. You do not have to answer the question.
- You *do not* have to choose a courtesy title (Miss, Ms., Mrs.) on a credit form.
- A creditor *may not* request your marital status on an application for an individual, unsecured account (a bank credit card or an overdraft checking account, for example), unless you live in a community property state (Texas is a community property state) or rely on property located in a community property state to support your application.
- A creditor *may* request your marital status in all other cases. But you can only be asked whether you are married, unmarried, or separated (unmarried includes single, divorced, or widowed).

To make sure you are treated fairly once you apply, the creditor may not do certain things when deciding whether you are credit-worthy. Specifically, the creditor

- *may not* refuse to consider your income because you are a married woman, even if your income is from part-time employment.
- *may not* ask about your birth control practices or your plans to have children. A creditor may not assume that you will have children or that your income will be interrupted to do so.

- *may not* refuse to consider reliable alimony, child support, or separate maintenance payments. However, you don't have to disclose such income unless you want to in order to improve your chances of getting credit.
- *may not* consider whether you have a telephone listing in your own name, because this would discriminate against married women.
- *may not* consider your sex as a factor in deciding whether you are a good credit risk.
- *may not* use your marital status to discriminate against you.

But some closely related questions are permitted. To estimate your expenses, a creditor may ask how many children you have, their ages, and the cost of caring for them (including your obligations to pay alimony, child support, or maintenance). A creditor may ask how regularly you receive your alimony payments or whether they are made under court order, for purposes of determining whether these payments are a dependable source of income. You also may be asked whether there is a telephone in your home.

Finally, a Texas creditor may consider your marital status because, under the laws of this state, there may be differences in the property rights of married and unmarried people. Such differences may affect the creditor's ability to collect if you default.

The law says a woman has the right to her own credit if she is creditworthy. A creditor may not stall you on an application and must inform you why credit was denied. If you are not given an explanation, you are entitled to request specific reasons for the denial.

If you are denied credit, find out why. If you have been discriminated against, the law allows you actual damages plus a penalty. The following agencies are available to assist you if you have been the victim of credit discrimination.

Federal Enforcement Agencies

Retail stores, department stores, consumer finance companies, all other creditors, and all nonbank credit card issuers:
Federal Trade Commission, Equal Credit Opportunity, Pennsylvania Ave. at Sixth St. NW, Washington, DC 20580; (202) 326-3761.
Regional office: Federal Trade Commission, 1999 Bryan St., Dallas, TX 75201; (214) 979-0213 (call 8 a.m.–5 p.m., Mon.–Fri.).

National banks:
Comptroller of the Currency, Administrator of National Banks, Washington, DC 20219; attn: Consumer Affairs Division, (202) 874-5000.

State member banks:
Federal Reserve Bank, 2200 N. Pearl St., Dallas, TX 75201, (214) 922-6000.
Branch banks: Federal Reserve Bank, 1701 San Jacinto, Houston, TX 77002; (713) 659-4433; and Federal Reserve Branch Bank, 126 E. Nueva, P.O. Box 1471, San Antonio, TX 78295; (210) 224-2141.

Nonmember insured banks:
Federal Deposit Insurance Corporation, 550 17th St. NW, Washington, DC 20429; (202) 393-8400.
Regional office: Federal Deposit Insurance Corporation, 1910 Pacific Ave., Suite 1900, Dallas, TX 75201; (214) 220-3342.

Savings institutions insured by the FSLIC and members of the FHLB system (except for savings banks insured by FDIC):
Office of Thrift Supervision, 1700 G St. NW, Washington, DC 20552; (202) 906-6000.
District office: Federal Home Loan Bank of Dallas, 5605 N. MacArthur, Irving, TX 75038. P.O. Box 619026, Dallas-Fort Worth, TX 75261-9026; (972) 714-8500.

Billing: *Creditors subject to Packers and Stockyards Act:*
Office of the Administrator, Packers and Stockyards Administration, Room 1094 South, 1400 Independence Ave. SW, Washington, DC 20250-2800; (202) 720-0219.

Small business investment companies:
U.S. Small Business Administration, 409 3rd St. SW, Washington, DC 20416; (202) 205-6770.
Hotline number to ask questions: (800) 827-5722.
Regional office: U.S. Small Business Administration, 4300 Amon Carter Blvd., Suite C, Fort Worth, TX 76155; (817) 885-6581.
Field offices:
4300 Amon Carter Blvd., Suite 114, Fort Worth, TX 76155; (817) 355-1933;
100 E. 15th, Suite 400, Fort Worth, TX 76102; (817) 871-6002 (score office);
9301 SW Frwy., Suite 550, Houston, TX 77074-1591; (713) 773-6500;
1611 10th St., Suite 200, Lubbock, TX 79401; (806) 472-7462;

10737 Gateway W., Suite 320, El Paso, TX 79935; (915) 540-5676;

222 E. Van Buren St., Suite 500, Harlingen, TX 78550; (210) 427-8533;

606 N. Carancahua, Suite 1200, Corpus Christi, TX 78476; (512) 888-3301;

North Star Executive Center, 727 E. Durango, Room A-527, San Antonio, TX 78206-1204; (210) 472-5900;

Federal Building, Room 967, 300 E. 8th St., Austin, TX 78701; (512) 916-5288.

Brokers and dealers:

Securities and Exchange Commission, 450 Fifth St. NW, Washington, DC 20549; (202) 942-8088.

Regional office: Securities and Exchange Commission, 801 Cherry St., Suite 1900, Fort Worth, TX 76102; (817) 978-3821.

Federal land banks, federal land bank associations, federal intermediate credit banks, and production credit associations:

Farm Credit Administration, 1501 Farm Credit Drive, McLean, VA 22102-5090; (703) 883-4000.

What happens when I turn 65?
"Don't worry."

Dear Mr. Alderman:

I am 64 years young, and I have no intention of retiring. I hope to stay at my present job for at least another 10 years. I am worried that it will become harder for me to get credit, now that I am approaching what many think of as retirement age. I have even heard some companies will cancel your charge cards if they discover you have reached age 65. Is this legal? It shouldn't be; I am just as financially responsible as I ever was.

The same law that protects the woman in the previous letter from sex discrimination protects you from discrimination based on your age. *The Equal Credit Opportunity Act makes it illegal to discriminate against an applicant for credit based on his or her age.* The law does not prohibit a creditor from considering your age, nor does it guarantee that you will obtain credit. It simply prohibits a creditor from using age as an arbitrary basis for denying or decreasing credit if you otherwise qualify.

In your case, the creditor cannot arbitrarily cancel your credit cards just because you turned 65. This would violate the Equal Credit Opportunity Act. However, if you retired at 65 and your income substantially decreased, this fact could be a sufficient basis for a creditor to deny or limit credit. *The law is clear that a creditor cannot require you to reapply, change the terms of your account, or close your account just because you have reached a certain age.*

I must emphasize, though, that age can be a factor in extension of credit. For example, if you are age 62 and you apply for a 30-year house mortgage, the bank can consider the fact that your retirement income will be less than you presently earn and that your earning potential will decrease. If you were denied the loan based on these considerations, the creditor would not be violating the law.

So how do you determine why you were denied credit? Under the law a creditor must notify you within 30 days of its action and give you specific reasons for its denial or tell you how to get an explanation. You have the same rights if the creditor closes your account. If after you receive this information you think the real reason was age discrimination, you have the right individually to sue for damages, or you can seek the assistance of a federal agency. Numerous federal agencies oversee the Equal Credit Opportunity Act, and they are listed earlier in this chapter.

What about these credit repair services? "Be careful."

Dear Mr. Alderman:

I recently saw an ad for a credit repair service that guaranteed it would fix my bad credit. I called, and the company wants $500. My credit is so bad that it seems worth it. I just want to make sure this is all legal. Is it?

Based on what you said, it may not be. Because of the recent flood of complaints concerning companies offering to fix bad credit reports, the Texas Legislature and Congress recently enacted laws to try to limit abuse. The new laws do not permit payment in advance. Additionally, companies must post bonds to protect you in the event you are misled or deceived. Credit repair services are not allowed to charge for getting you credit that's available to the general public or to misrepresent what they can do. The company also must have available a copy of its registration statement that lists any litigation or unresolved complaints against the company. If you sign a contract for services, you can cancel that contract within three days. Finally, any violation of the credit service organization also violates the Deceptive Trade Practices Act.

The bottom line: The Fair Credit Reporting Act, discussed on pages 3–6, gives you the right to require that your credit file be accurate. There is no way anyone can have accurate but negative information removed from your file. In my opinion, anything the credit repair service can do, you probably can do for yourself for a lot less money.

Can I be charged more if I use a credit card?
"Not under Texas law."

Dear Mr. Alderman:
The other day I went shopping for a new microwave oven for my wife. I found one I like, but when I went to pay, the store told me I would have to pay a 5% surcharge if I paid by credit card. The manager told me the credit card company charges him a surcharge and he was simply passing it on to me. As he explained it, he only gets 95 cents on a dollar from the credit card company, and therefore he has to charge me more to make the same profit. I paid the extra 5%, but now I don't think it was right. The store advertises it takes credit cards, and it doesn't seem fair that I have to pay more. Is this legal?

In simple terms . . . no! Texas law says a merchant, with the exception of a governmental body, may not charge a customer more if he uses a credit card instead of cash. Of course, the law doesn't require that merchants take credit cards, but once they do they may not charge you more. I suggest you let the store manager know that he didn't have the right to charge you the extra 5%, and that if he doesn't refund it, you will take the store to small claims court. In my opinion, charging this illegal extra amount also violates the Deceptive Trade Practices Act, and you could be entitled to up to three times the amount you paid if you show the merchant acted knowingly. You also may want to let the attorney general's office know about this practice.

If credit surcharges are illegal, how can a store
give a discount for cash?
"They are not the same."

Dear Mr. Alderman:
I don't understand. I heard you on TV, and you said it was illegal in
Texas to charge more if someone uses a credit card. The next day I
went to a gas station, and it had two prices, one for cash and one for
credit. The credit price was higher. Isn't this illegal? What should I
do about it?

I know this is confusing, but charging more for credit is illegal, while giving a discount for cash is not. Let me give you an example. Suppose a store sells a TV with a list price of $100. If it charged you $104 when you used a credit card, that would be illegal. But if you paid cash and only had to pay $96, this discount would be legal and logical. Here is why:

When you pay with a credit card, the credit card company does not give the merchant 100 cents for every dollar you charge. It discounts the amount it pays the merchant. For example, the credit card company may only give the merchant 96 or 97 cents for every dollar you charge. *In other words, a merchant pays for the credit when you use a credit card.* By giving you a discount for cash the merchant is simply recognizing that it saves money when you pay cash, and it passes that savings on to you. That is what the company is doing.

Because the merchant doesn't know who is going to pay cash and who isn't, the price of any item includes the cost of the credit (the amount the credit card company will deduct). If a merchant doesn't give you a discount for cash, the merchant is in effect charging you for credit you didn't use. As far as I am concerned, every merchant should have two prices: one cash, one credit. If it doesn't, the cash customers are paying more to subsidize those who use credit. (Of course, the bottom line, whether you pay cash or credit, is to always shop for the best price.)

The credit card company didn't tell me how high the interest rate was. Is that legal?
"No."

Dear Mr. Alderman:

Not too long ago, I got a slick offer in the mail for a new credit card. It guaranteed me a high line of credit and no annual fee. It sounded like too good a deal to pass up, so I signed up. The first month, I paid half my bill, expecting to pay the other half, with interest of course, the following month. I couldn't believe it when the bill arrived. I was charged 24% interest! Is this legal? How come I was never told that in exchange for no annual fee, I was going to pay a ridiculous interest rate?

The good news is that what happened to you should never happen again. The bad news is you probably are stuck with the high interest rate. The best advice I can give you is to cut up the card and shop around for a new one.

Under a law that took effect in August 1989, banks and department stores are required to disclose key financial terms of their credit cards in all their solicitations. This allows you as a consumer to shop around for the best rate, instead of being misled into accepting a high rate by a slick promotion. The **Fair Credit and Charge Card Disclosure Act of 1988** amends federal law and applies to bank cards, department store cards, and other charge cards, such as American Express and Diner's Club. The law requires that solicitation mailings must "clearly and conspicuously" disclose key financial terms, such as interest rates, fees, grace periods, minimum finance charges, purchase transaction charges, and balance computation methods. You also must get this information when your account is about to be renewed for another year. The only time this law does not apply is when a solicitation is through an ad in a magazine, newspaper, catalog, or "take one" application displayed in a store or restaurant.

This law is designed to let you shop around for the best rate when you get a credit card. You will be surprised how much money you can save by getting a card with a 16% interest rate instead of a 24% interest rate.

CHAPTER TWO

Bankruptcy

IT is hard to pick up a newspaper these days without reading that someone or some company has filed bankruptcy. Since the enactment of the new bankruptcy law in 1978, bankruptcy has flourished.

Bankruptcy is one of the most misunderstood areas of law. To many, bankruptcy means failure: "Throw in the towel and try something else!" But, under what is known as Chapter 11 or Chapter 13, bankruptcy can let you stay in business instead of ending it. As with Continental Airlines, bankruptcy may not have any outward effect on the way a company does business. In fact, many businesses are much more successful after their bankruptcies.

Because bankruptcy is so complicated, I can only begin to cover this subject. The questions chosen, however, should provide a basic understanding of the types of bankruptcies and the effect bankruptcy may have on you.

What is bankruptcy?
"There are two types."

Dear Mr. Alderman:

I just read that the company that was supposed to remodel my house filed for bankruptcy. Yesterday, the workers showed up to do the job. I told them I didn't want a bankrupt company working on my house, and they told me we had a contract. The thing I don't understand is how all these companies are still in business if they filed for bankruptcy. I always thought when you filed for bankruptcy you had to sell everything. Am I wrong? Why would a business file bankruptcy and then stay in business?

You are not entirely wrong because two very different types of bankruptcy exist. Under the **Bankruptcy Code**, a business or a person can either file to liquidate assets, pay creditors what is owed, and start all over, or the Bankruptcy Code can help the business or person reorganize financial affairs so it or he can stay in business and try to pay off the debts. In the first type of bankruptcy, known as a Chapter 7 bankruptcy, a company usually goes out of business. This is what most people think of when they hear the word "bankruptcy." But in the second, known as Chapter 11 for a company and Chapter 13 for an individual, the business continues to operate. Most of the recently publicized bankruptcies have been Chapter 11 bankruptcies, designed to give a company time to pay off its creditors and make a fresh start. For example, Continental and Braniff airlines filed under Chapter 11.

So what happens when someone or some business files bankruptcy? First, bankruptcy is controlled by federal law, and all bankruptcies are filed in a special federal court. When a debtor (that is what a business or a person is called upon filing bankruptcy) files for a Chapter 7 bankruptcy, he or she agrees to give up all "non-exempt assets" in exchange for a discharge from his or her debts. In Texas this usually means a person gives up everything except his home and about $60,000 worth of property in exchange for the release from his debts. (To learn more about exemptions, turn to page 56.) The creditors split whatever money there is among them. All the creditors must stop collection efforts, and in most cases the money is divided prorata, based on the amount of the debt. *After the Chapter 7 bankruptcy, the debtor usually doesn't owe any money to anyone.* Of course, if you had liens on your property, for example, your house, you would either have to continue to pay or lose the house. And some debts, primarily taxes, are still owed even after bankruptcy.

When a corporation files a Chapter 7 bankruptcy, it usually gives up everything and goes out of business. The creditors split whatever there is and that is the end of it. The corporation no longer exists, and the debts are considered satisfied.

But under the other type of bankruptcy, a company (or individual) may use the bankruptcy court to get time to reorganize its affairs and try to work things out. Two bankruptcy proceedings let you do this: a Chapter 11 and a Chapter 13. They are very similar. Under either, once the debtor files, all the creditors have to stop trying to collect and wait for the debtor to propose a payment plan to attempt to pay everyone back. Basically what happens is the bankruptcy court gives the debtor protection from hungry creditors, while the debtor tries to figure out how to work things out. The main difference between Chapters 11 and 13 is that Chapter 11 is for anyone, corporations and individuals, while Chapter 13 is only available to people with regular incomes. A Chapter 13 is sometimes called a wage-earner proceeding. Chapter 13 is the type of bankruptcy you may see in newspaper advertisements with headlines such as "Stop Creditor Harassment . . . File for Protection Under the Federal Bankruptcy Laws."

So to get back to your question: If the company is still in business it must have filed a Chapter 11; or if it is a sole proprietorship, a Chapter 13. This means the company has the right to continue in business, and in fact, its contract with you is still enforceable. I suggest you let them finish the work. If you trusted the company before, there is no less reason to trust it now.

Bankruptcy has taken on a new significance lately. With the assistance of the Bankruptcy Code, debtors can gain valuable time to try to remedy their financial affairs. But bankruptcy laws are very complicated, and some attorneys specialize only in bankruptcy. *If you are considering bankruptcy, make sure you consult with a specialist. Look for an attorney who is Board certified in consumer bankruptcy.*

What happens when I file?
"That depends . . ."

Dear Mr. Alderman:

I really can't believe I'm writing you this letter, but I need your advice. For 20 years I have been a hard-working citizen, and I've never even been late in my payments. I own a house, with a mortgage of course, and two cars. My wife and two children have most of the things they need. Now I am suddenly in trouble.

About six months ago my employer told me I had to take a substantial cut in pay or be fired. Any job is better than none, so I agreed to work for less. The following week, we discovered my wife needed surgery. The bills are already more than $13,000, and my insurance only covers a very small amount. I am behind in all my other bills, and the credit card companies are beginning to hound me.

I would like to pay off what I owe, but I don't see how I can do it. Everyone wants to be paid at the same time. I never thought bankruptcy was right—a man should pay his bills; but now it seems to be all that is left. What would happen if I filed for bankruptcy?

First, as I pointed out in the previous letter, you should know two different types of bankruptcy exist. In your case, as an individual with a steady income, the choices are a Chapter 7 or a Chapter 13. I will tell you about each in order.

If you file a Chapter 7, all your creditors must stop trying to collect, you lose all your non-exempt property, and you start all over again, usually not owing anyone a cent. The purpose of a Chapter 7 is to free you of debt and let you begin fresh. In exchange for being free of your debt, you have to give up non-exempt assets. In Texas this means you can keep your home and up to $60,000 of personal property. If you have anything else, it goes to your creditors. After you file bankruptcy, your creditors share whatever money there is. *After the bankruptcy is over, your creditors cannot try to collect anything from you.* The only significant exception to this would be the bank or finance company that loaned you money to buy your house and car. Because they have a lien on your property, you either have to give it up to pay off the lien, or agree to continue paying after the bankruptcy. One other exception is money owed for taxes or alimony. These debts must still be paid even after bankruptcy.

A Chapter 7 bankruptcy is a serious matter, and you should discuss your particular case with an attorney. If you feel you are so hopelessly in debt that the only way to get going again is to clear up all your bills, Chapter 7 may be the thing for you.

But if what you think you need is just more time to work things out with your creditors, you should consider a Chapter 13. In simple terms, a Chapter 13 is a court-supervised repayment plan requiring all your creditors to leave you alone and let you pay them off over a longer period of time, usually three years. *The first benefit you get from filing a Chapter 13 is all your creditors must immediately stop trying to collect.* All harassing calls, letters, and even lawsuits must stop, and everything goes to the bankruptcy court to be worked out. After you file a Chapter 13, the next step is to come up with a plan to pay everyone back. Usually what you try to do is pay all your creditors less than you are paying now but over a longer period of time. *You should consider a Chapter 13 only if you think that with additional time you will be able to pay everyone off.* If you know that even with an extra three years you are still too much in debt to pay everyone what you owe them, use a Chapter 7, not a Chapter 13.

To file bankruptcy you will need the assistance of an attorney. Talk with him or her before you file, and make sure all your options are considered.

One more thought: Some organizations help consumers restructure their debt without the need for bankruptcy. These groups are usually called "consumer credit counseling services," and one of them might be able to give you the assistance you need.

Here is a list of consumer credit counseling agencies throughout the state of Texas. They usually don't charge for their help.

Consumer Credit Counseling Service of Southeast Texas, 4600 Gulf Frwy., Houston, TX 77023; (800) 873-2227, (713) 923-2227.

Child and Family Services, CCCS Division, 1221 W. Ben White, Suite 108A, Austin, TX 78722; (512) 447-0711.

Consumer Credit Counseling Center of South Texas, 1706 S.P.I.D., Corpus Christi, TX 78413; (512) 854-4357.

CCCS of Greater Dallas Inc., 8737 King George, Suite 200, Dallas, TX 75235; (214) 638-2227.

CCCS of Fort Worth, 6100 Western Place, Suite 550, Fort Worth, TX 76107; (817) 732-2227.

CCCS of North Central Texas Inc., 1600 Redbud Blvd., Suite 300, P.O. Box 299, McKinney, TX 75069; (800) 856-0257.

CCCS of Greater San Antonio Inc., 6851 Citizens Pkwy., San Antonio, TX 78228-1312; (210) 921-2227.

What happens when someone else files?
"You may be out of luck!"

Dear Mr. Alderman:
I bought a house for more than $70,000 from a local builder. The house was never finished properly, and I had problems from the day I moved in. I was finally forced to hire a lawyer, who sued under the Texas Deceptive Trade Practices Act. We won! The court awarded me $36,000, but the builder never paid, and now he has filed bankruptcy and gone out of business. What happens next? Am I ever going to get my money? I have since heard he is back in business, using a different name. Can he do this?

Unfortunately, I don't have any good news for you. If the builder has filed a Chapter 7 bankruptcy, he will be discharged from all his debts, including the money he owes you, and all you get is a pro rata share of his non-exempt assets. What all this legal jargon means is the builder doesn't owe you anything and you get to share whatever extra money he had when he filed bankruptcy.

To make sure you do get whatever is coming, you should file a "proof of claim" with the bankruptcy court. Because you are one of the builder's creditors (anyone he owes money to), you should receive notice from the court of how and where to file your claim. Once you file this simple notice with the bankruptcy court, you will be included in any settlements and get whatever money you are entitled to. But don't expect to receive much. On the average in bankruptcy, creditors receive only a few cents on the dollar. I should point out that if you are not listed with the court, an unlikely event because of the amount of money you are owed, you are not affected by the bankruptcy.

After the builder has filed bankruptcy he has the right to go back into whatever business he wants, under whatever name he wants. The purpose of bankruptcy is to clear up one's debts and get a fresh start. The builder is now free of his debts and can begin all over. This may not be the way you would want the system to work, and it is often unfair to people like you, but bankruptcy is becoming a more and more popular alternative for people who find they just have to get out from under their debts and see no other way to do it.

From your letter it appears that the builder filed a Chapter 7 bankruptcy—the type designed to liquidate his assets. However, if the builder filed a Chapter 11, you stand a good chance of being paid, but you should have your attorney help you collect.

Will bankruptcy clear up my student loans?
"Probably not."

Dear Mr. Alderman:
I recently graduated from college. I owe more than $25,000 in student loans, in addition to my other bills. I am having trouble making ends meet, and I am considering filing bankruptcy. How will this affect my student loans?

Until recently, student loans were not "discharged" in bankruptcy. This means that even after you filed bankruptcy you would still owe the money for your student loans. The law, however, has changed.

The Bankruptcy Code now states that student loans are not discharged, *unless*—

the loan first became due before five years before the filing of the bankruptcy; or requiring payment will impose an undue hardship on the debtor.

In other words, under the law your debt probably will not be affected by the bankruptcy if it is less than five years old. For example, if you have a student loan that just became due, you probably shouldn't file bankruptcy because you will still owe the loan after the bankruptcy. But if the debt is more than 5 years old or it is unusually large in comparison to your income, the bankruptcy will wipe it out just as it does most other debts.

Can a farmer file bankruptcy?
"Yes. There is a special law."

Dear Mr. Alderman:
I am a small farmer who, like most others, is having problems making ends meet. The other day I heard there was some special bankruptcy law for farmers. Is this true? If it is, can you tell me about it?

Because of the special hardships faced by farmers, Congress enacted a bankruptcy provision just for them. The law, called Chapter 12, can help stave off farm liquidations and give the farmer more flexibility than ever before.

Chapter 12 is a special section of the Bankruptcy Act just for "family farmers." These are individuals with debts of less than $1.5 million; and 80% of that debt and 50% of their income must come from farming. Corporate and partnership farmers also qualify if one family owns the corporation or partnership.

If you qualify as a family farmer under this law, you can file a petition that immediately stops all your creditors from taking any action. This is similar to what happens in a Chapter 11; however, Chapter 12 gives you more leeway to determine how your debts will be handled.

The bottom line is Chapter 12 gives farmers the flexibility needed to rearrange their debts and at the same time continue in business. If you are having serious financial problems, I suggest you speak with an attorney about filing a Chapter 12.

What happens if my ex-spouse files bankruptcy?
"You may not be out of luck."

Dear Mr. Alderman:
I was divorced two years ago. Under the divorce decree, my husband is supposed to keep paying the mortgage on the home that our children and I live in. He is now threatening to file bankruptcy if I don't agree to reduce the amount of child support he has to pay. Can he do this? He has more than enough money to keep up his end of the bargain.

The answer depends on the financial status of your husband. Generally, if a person files bankruptcy he is discharged from his debts. This means he no longer has to pay them.

Some debts, however, are not affected by bankruptcy. For example, a debt or obligation regarding child support of alimony may not be discharged. Other debts arising out of a divorce, however, may or may not be discharged.

Other marital debts may be discharged in bankruptcy, but only if the debtor does not have the ability to pay the debt or if discharging the debt would benefit the debtor in a way that outweighs the hardship imposed on the spouse or children.

What this means is bankruptcy would not change your ex-husband's obligation to pay the mortgage unless he really cannot afford to make the payments. If he does have more than enough money, like you say, he will have to continue making the mortgage payments even after he files.

CHAPTER THREE

Banks & Banking

FOR most people, checks are considered the same as cash. When you go into a store and the clerk asks, "Cash or charge?" you say cash if you are using a check.

Today nearly everyone who spends money has a checking account. And most of us know the benefits of using a check instead of cash: You have a record of your transactions, and if the check is lost or stolen, you will not bear the loss the way you would if it had been cash.

Banks handle billions of checks each year and transfer untold amounts of money between accounts. For most of us these transfers go smoothly, and we have little need to know or use our legal rights against a bank. But we do have substantial legal rights, and when something goes wrong you may find that the bank, not you, has to pay.

A thief has been using my checks. Do I have to pay?
"Not unless it was your fault."

Dear Mr. Alderman:
About two weeks ago my purse was stolen in the parking lot of the supermarket. I immediately reported it to the police and then went home and made a list of everything in my wallet. I remembered how important you said it was to notify everyone as soon as possible, so I contacted all my credit card companies. I also called the bank and was told to come in, close the account, and open a new one. The next day I did that and learned the thief had written three checks to himself, signed my name, and cashed them that morning. The bank told me I was responsible for these checks because the forgery was so good there was no way for the bank to know. This doesn't seem right. Before I go and ask to see the president of the bank, I would like to know what you think. What are my legal rights?

Under the law, a bank generally has no right to pay checks on which your signature was forged, and if it does it must recredit your account or be responsible for damages. A bank may only pay a check that is "properly payable," and checks with forged signatures are not properly payable. In simple terms, properly payable means in accordance with your instructions; and you did not tell the bank to pay that check—the thief did.

A few exceptions to this rule exist, but none seems to apply in your case. For example, if your negligence was what made the thief's forgery possible—let's say you carelessly left a signature stamp in a public place—then the bank may not have to pay. Also if you wait too long to report the forgery, and because of that the bank suffers a loss, you can't complain to the bank.

Basically, the law is straightforward: A bank may not take your money to pay a check on which your signature is forged. Your account must be recredited and it is up to the bank either to bear the loss or find the thief and try to collect. If your bankers still refuse to give your money back, take them to small claims court or see a lawyer.

P.S. If your check is stolen, quickly report the loss to the bank. But there is no need to pay the bank for a stop-payment order. As I just explained, it is the bank's loss if it pays.

My check was signed by someone other than the person I gave it to. Do I still have to pay?
"Probably not . . . . You are entitled to the signature you asked for."

Dear Mr. Alderman:
I owed my next door neighbor $150 for a fence we put up. I gave him a check, which he put in his desk. When he went to cash it he realized it had been stolen. My neighbor asked me to give him another check, but I am worried about what will happen if the thief cashes or deposits my old check. What are my legal rights if the thief forges my friend's name and my bank pays the check?

Under the law, a bank that pays a check with a forged endorsement has no right to take your money to cover the check. If it does, you have the right to require the bank to recredit your account.

For example, suppose your check was made out to Bob Neighbor. The thief turns over the check and endorses it "Bob Neighbor pay to Tom Thief." Thief then takes the check to his bank and deposits it by signing "Tom Thief." His bank gives him credit for the check and sends it to your bank. Because your bank has no way of knowing the signatures are not genuine, it will probably pay the check and debit your account. When you get your statement you discover the check has a forged signature. In the meantime, Thief has taken his money and gone.

According to the law, once you show the bank the endorsement is forged, it must recredit your account. The bank then has the right to get the money back from the other bank, and that bank must try to recover from the thief.

What you should do now is contact your bank and ask if the check has been paid. If the check has been paid, explain what happened and ask the bank to recredit your account. The bank probably will want you to prove your neighbor didn't endorse the check and may ask for him to sign an affidavit to that effect. Once the bank is certain the signature is a forgery, it will probably recredit your account. If it does not, you have the legal right to compel the bank to do so.

If the check has not been paid, the bank will probably ask you to put in a stop-payment order. This will ensure the check is not paid.

As for your neighbor, once you get your money back from the bank, give him another check. Your obligation to pay him still exists.

As I said in the answer right before this one, a bank may take the money in your account only to pay checks that are properly payable. Checks with forged endorsements are not properly payable, and the bank has no legal right to take your money to pay them.

How can I be responsible on a forged signature?
"The law imposes time limits within which you must act."

Dear Mr. Alderman:

I run a small business. I recently discovered my signature had been forged on one of my checks. I contacted my bankers and asked that they recredit my account. They told me that because it happened more than one year ago, I was responsible for the loss. I thought I read that a person has no liability based on a forged signature. Who is right?

You are both right. A person has no liability on a check that has a forged signature. For example, if someone steals your check and forges your signature, you have no liability on that instrument. If your bank pays the check, you have the right to have the bank recredit your account. In other words, when a bank pays a check with a customer's forged signature, the bank must bear the loss.

All laws, however, have time limits within which rights must be asserted. For example, if you were injured in a car wreck, you have the right to sue the person who caused the accident. The lawsuit must be commenced, however, within two years. If you were to wait longer than that, your claim would be barred. We call these time limits "statutes of limitation."

Our banking laws also have time periods within which claims must be asserted. Under the law, you must notify the bank of the forged signature within one year. If you wait longer than that, you are precluded from asserting a claim.

Knowing your rights is important. Asserting them in a timely manner is essential.

How do I stop payment on a check?
"In Texas, it must be in writing."

Dear Mr. Alderman:

Hello again. I am the same person who wrote you before about the check I gave my next door neighbor that was lost or stolen. I called the bank and was told I had to stop payment. I said to go ahead and was told I would have to come down to the bank to do it in writing. The bank also told me I would have to pay a fee if payment was stopped. Is this the law, or is my bank just making things difficult? You know how inconvenient it is to go to a bank during the middle of the day.

In most states a customer can stop payment over the telephone. Under Texas law, though, an oral stop-payment notice is not binding on the bank. This means the bank may let you stop payment over the phone but is not obligated to do so. As a practical matter most banks will only honor a written stop-payment order.

As to whether your bank may charge you for doing this, the answer is probably yes. Although at least one state attorney general (Michigan's) has stated that stop-payment orders are part of the obligation owed a customer and that an additional fee may not be charged, there has been no similar ruling in Texas. *I suggest you consider the cost of stop-payment orders when you shop for a bank. The cost can vary greatly between banks.*

The store charged me $30 for a check that bounced. Is this legal?
"Probably not."

Dear Mr. Alderman:
The other day I bought a CD at my local record shop. It cost $15.95.
I paid for it with a check. Unfortunately, I don't balance my check-
book as well as I should, and the check bounced. The store called me
and told me I owed $15.95 for the check and $30 for the fact that it
bounced. When I went to pay, the clerk showed me a sign over the
cash register that said All Returned Checks Will Be Charged $30! Is
this legal? Thirty dollars is a lot of money.

Based on what you say, the store probably acted unlawfully. Under the
law a store may charge you up to $25 for a returned check. The store prop-
erly posted notice that it would charge a fee for returned checks. Because
the amount is more than $25, however, the store acted unlawfully.

My bank charged me $20 for a bounced check. Is this legal?
"There is no specific law governing service charges."

Dear Mr. Alderman:
I know it isn't right to bounce checks, but not everyone is an accoun-
tant, and sometimes I don't balance my checkbook the way I should.
The other day my bank sent me a notice that I bounced a $19 check
at a local store. I went right down to the bank and deposited my pay-
check, and the check that bounced was paid. Now the bank has
charged me $20 for bouncing a $19 check. This is crazy. Does the
bank have the right to do this?

No specific law governs what a bank may charge for the services it performs. The cost of the services a bank performs, such as checking accounts,
stop-payment orders, and NSF (non-sufficient funds) checks, is governed by
basic principles of contract law and the Deceptive Trade Practices Act. *The*
$20 fee is valid if you voluntarily agreed to pay it—unless the bank deceived
or misled you, or the price is unconscionable. A fee would be unconscionable if it were grossly in excess of the value you received.

For many banks, fees paid for bounced checks, represent a substantial
source of income, and different banks charge vastly differing amounts—
fees as low as $10 or as high as $30 are not unusual. Lawsuits have been
filed in other states challenging a bank's right to charge a high fee, but to
the best of my knowledge there are no such suits in Texas.

The best advice I can give you is practical, not legal. Shop around for the bank that has the fairest fees for the services it performs, and in the future try to balance your checkbook.

Can a bank require a credit card ID before it cashes a check?
"Yes"

Dear Mr. Alderman:

A store recently told me it wouldn't take my personal check unless I showed the clerk a driver's license and a major credit card. I refused, and the clerk made me pay cash. What purpose is served by showing a credit card? My driver's license proves who I am. Is it legal to require a credit card to cash a check?

Basically, a store isn't required to take a personal check unless it wants to. Therefore, it can place whatever requirements it wants on the customer. If the store wants to require you to show a credit card, I see no reason why it can't.

I cashed a check for a friend. How am I liable?
"When you sign a check, you become responsible."

Dear Mr. Alderman:

A friend asked me to cash a $1,000 check he had been given by someone else. I gave him the cash and then deposited the check in my account. My bank gave me credit for the check, and I thought that was the end of it. It was not. My bank now has taken $1,000 out of my account because the check bounced. Why am I responsible for this? It wasn't even my check. What are my rights?

Unfortunately for you, the bank had the right to do just what it did. You now will have to try to recover the $1,000 from either your friend or the person who wrote the check to your friend.

When someone makes out a check, the check is merely his or her promise to pay the money. The bank on which the check is drawn has no liability on the check. It simply takes money out of the person's account to pay what that person promised. If there is no money in the account, the check will be returned, and the person who wrote it will be responsible, not the bank.

But the person who wrote the check is not the only one responsible. Anyone who endorses the check also promises to pay. Therefore, when your friend endorsed the check to you, he became liable to you. When you endorsed the check to your bank to deposit it, you became responsible to the bank.

When the check bounced, three people were responsible to your bank: the person who wrote the check, your friend, and you. The bank chose to collect from the easiest person, you. Now you have the right to try to collect from your friend or the person who wrote the check.

Cashing a check for someone is like making them a loan. You are giving that person money that you hope will be reimbursed by the check you deposit. Unfortunately, as you found out, signing your name to the check also makes you responsible and can be very expensive.

How can my bank pay a post-dated check?
"The law allows it."

Dear Mr. Alderman:
I recently gave someone a post-dated check. At that time I didn't have enough money in my account to cover it. I assumed it would not be paid until after the date on the check. Instead, the person I gave the check to deposited it, and my bank paid it. This caused many of my other checks to bounce. The bank charged me $20 for each of these checks. How can this happen?

A post-dated check is a check that you date sometime in the future. Many people believe, as you did, that this means the check may not be paid until the date that appears on the check. Unfortunately, this is not the law.

A bank is allowed to pay a post-dated check whenever it is presented to the bank. It may pay the check even if it is presented many days before the date on the check.

If you want to make sure a post-dated check is not paid before the date on the check, you must notify the bank that you have written a post-dated check. If you do this, the bank has no legal right to pay the check early.

I should point out that even though you have no claim against the bank, you do have rights against the person you gave the check to. If the check was given with the understanding that it would not be deposited until the date on the check, the person you gave the check to should be responsible for the fees you incurred when your other checks bounced. I suggest you let him know you expect him to reimburse you.

CHAPTER FOUR

Contracts

IN a certain sense, there is no such thing as a contract. You can't buy one, you can't hold it, and you can't pick one up and tote it around. A contract is simply a legal term for a promise that the law will enforce. Sometimes this promise will be evidenced by a piece of paper, but that paper is not a contract; the legally enforceable agreement is.

Any agreement you enter into may be legally enforceable and may become a contract, no matter what words you may use, and regardless of whether it is oral or written. For example, suppose the neighborhood boy comes by your house and yells, "Hey, lady. Want your lawn cut?" A nod of your head will result in a contract, and after he finishes the task, you will have to pay.

So you see, your life consists of one contract followed by another. When you buy gas for your car or groceries at the store or have your laundry cleaned, you enter into a contract. Some basic knowledge of contract law should help you with your everyday problems.

As you will find in the next few letters, you don't need very specific language, and you usually don't need anything written to enter into a binding contract.

Must a contract be formal?
"Just an agreement."

Dear Mr. Alderman:

I own a house at the lake that's about 20 years old. The fence needed repairs, and my neighbor told me he would split the cost if I would have the fence repaired. We talked about it awhile, and ultimately I agreed to have it fixed, and he agreed to pay half. The bill amounted to $350, and now my neighbor refuses to pay. The price, I feel, is very reasonable, but my neighbor says we didn't have any kind of a formal arrangement, and there is nothing I can do. Is he right?

The law of contracts is not as complicated as many people think. If you agree to do something in exchange for someone's promise to do something else, there probably is a legally enforceable agreement. To put it simply, if you intended to be legally bound, you probably are.

In your case, each party made a promise to the other. You promised to fix the fence, and he promised to pay you one half the cost. Based on your letter, it seems that at the time of the agreement you both thought you had entered into a contract. Your agreement is probably legally enforceable.

Contract law long ago dispensed with the need for any formalities before an agreement could be enforceable in a court of law. The modern trend is to enforce every agreement that the parties intended to be binding. You can't get out of a contract by simply saying, "I know what I said before, but it wasn't really a formal contract." If your neighbor doesn't pay you the money he owes, I suggest you take him to small claims court. Maybe the judge can convince him he has entered into a legally enforceable agreement.

What if she doesn't give me the gift?
"There's not much you can do about it."

Dear Mr. Alderman:
For the past five years my grandmother has been ill. Weekly, I would go to her home, help with her chores, and buy her groceries. Last month she told me she really appreciated everything I had done for her and she wanted me to have her diamond pin. Yesterday, I went to her house and asked about the pin. She said she had changed her mind and given it to my sister. My dear sibling has never done anything for my grandmother. Is there any way I can make my grandmother keep her promise?
P.S. I even have a written promise that reads, "In exchange for the love and affection shown to me by my granddaughter, Betsy, I promise to give her my diamond pin before the end of the year."

The fact that you have a signed, written promise does not mean you can force the person to do what she promised to do. *As a general rule, promises to make gifts are not enforceable.* This is because of the legal doctrine known as "consideration."

Under the law, a promise is enforceable only if given in exchange for something. In legalese there must be a "quid pro quo"—something for something. For example, suppose I promise to pay you to paint my house. What we have actually done is exchange promises. I have promised to pay you in return for your promise to paint. We have each given something in exchange for something else. The promises are enforceable, and we have a contract. The exchange, however, must be for something in the future. If you promise to pay someone for something that has already happened, the promise is not enforceable—it is a promise to make a gift. For example, if you paint my house without my asking, and after you finish I say, "You did a good job. I promise to pay you next week," the promise would not be enforceable because it was not made in exchange for performance. For every enforceable promise there is a quid pro quo, something exchanged for something else.

So what does all this mean to you? Your grandmother promised to make you a gift for what you had done in the past—and such promises cannot be enforced in a court of law. Even though your grandmother may be morally bound to give you the pin, there is no legally enforceable obligation. Things would be different, though, if your grandmother had said, "If you help me with the groceries, I will give you my pin." In that case there would be a legally enforceable promise because she would have made her promise in exchange for yours.

The bottom line is not all promises, even those in writing, are enforceable. If someone promises to give you a gift and doesn't, you usually can't force him to pay.

There is, however, one exception to this that you should know. If you rely on the promise and suffer a loss, you may be able to force the person to compensate you for your loss. For example, suppose your grandmother told you she was going to give you $500 to buy a coat, and relying on this you put down a $50 nonrefundable deposit. If your grandmother changed her mind, you couldn't force her to pay the $500, but you could collect the $50 you spent in reliance on her promise.

Is a contract valid if I don't sign?
"It probably doesn't matter."

Dear Mr. Alderman:
My driveway needed repair, so I called a contractor to fix it. We discussed what he would do, and he sent me an estimate of $1,500. I phoned him back and told him to go ahead and begin work. The next day, when he arrived with his crew, I informed him I had changed my mind and was going to fix it myself. He was very mad and told me he

was going to lose $100 because he had to pay his crew for showing up. I told him I was sorry, that it wasn't my fault, and besides, we never had a real contract because I never signed anything. I have now received a letter informing me he is planning to sue me in small claims court for the $100. Since I didn't sign anything, do I have to pay?

Most people are surprised to find out they usually don't have to sign anything to have an enforceable contract. In your case, your contract was for the performance of a service, and such contracts do not require a signature *unless they can't be performed within a year.* Your contract clearly was to be performed in less than a year, and you are responsible for any loss the contractor incurred.

Under the law, most contracts do not have to be in writing or be signed to be enforceable. But some contracts are considered more important than others, and there is a law called the **Statute of Frauds** that requires certain kinds of contracts be "evidenced" by a signed writing. The most common types of contracts that need a signed writing are contracts for the sale of land, contracts that cannot be performed within one year, contracts for the sale of goods that cost more than $500, and contracts to pay the debts of another. To enforce these types of contracts, there must be sufficient writing to show a contract has been made, signed by the person against whom the contract is being enforced. A brief example will show you how this law works.

Suppose I agree to sell you my house. Because contracts for the sale of land are covered by the Statute of Frauds, the agreement is not enforceable unless we have a writing. We orally agree to the sale, and I then go home and write you a letter telling you how excited I am about the deal, and discussing all the details. I sign the letter and mail it to you. At this point there is an enforceable contract against me because I signed a writing, indicating we made a contract and giving the important terms. But the contract probably would not be enforceable against you because you did not sign anything. *If you are worried about the enforceability of an agreement, protect yourself: Put it in writing.*

The Statute of Frauds is designed to prevent one person from forcing another into contract by falsely stating they had an agreement. Without the writing, the agreement is not enforceable. But the law does not like people to use the Statute of Frauds to get out of contracts that they made and other people relied on. For example, suppose you agreed to buy a custom-made boat from me for $2,500. After I build the boat, you change your mind and say you won't pay. The contract is for the sale of goods that cost more than $500, so I need a signed writing to sue you. Am I out of luck? Not in this case. There are many exceptions to the law that require a writing, and this is one of them. Because the goods were specially manufactured, I can sue you even without the writing. All I have to do is prove you orally agreed. The same rule applies whenever one party has performed his part of the deal and then the other party tries to get out of the contract.

Remember, most contracts do not require a writing. Even when a writing is required, the requirement may be waived if it is unfair to one of the parties. Best advice: If you make an oral contract, be prepared to keep your promise.

Does an agreement to split lottery winnings have to be in writing? "Probably not."

Dear Mr. Alderman:
Several of my friends and I buy lottery tickets each week. Each of us puts in $2, and we buy 10 tickets. We have agreed that if we win we will split the winnings. I know it is unlikely, but if we did win, could I force everyone to split the money? Do we have to have a written agreement?

You have the right to force everyone to divide the money, provided you can convince a court that you really did make the agreement. Basically, you and your friends have entered into a contract. The terms of the contract are that each of you will provide part of the proceeds to buy the tickets and, if you win, you will divide the proceeds equally.

This agreement is enforceable without any form of a writing. As I stated in the prior letter, most contracts do not have to be in writing to be enforceable. This contract, because it could be performed in less than one year, is an example of one type of contract that does not have to be in writing. You would need a writing, however, if your agreement to buy tickets was for more than one year and did not end even if you won the lottery earlier.

This does not mean, however, that it would not be a good idea to put your agreement in a written form. Even though your agreement is enforceable, there still may be problems proving it if you were to win. The best way to avoid any future problems is to write an agreement and have everyone sign it.

Can I share lottery winnings with my children?
"Yes, but prepare a contract."

Dear Mr. Alderman:
I know I may be dreaming, but I have a question about what happens
if I win the lottery. Is it legal for me to share the winnings with my
children? Can I give them a share of what I won without paying any
extra taxes?

There is nothing illegal about giving some or all of you lottery winnings to your children. However, how you structure the transaction will determine the tax ramifications. Obviously you will be taxed on any winnings you receive. You cannot avoid being taxed on those winnings by transferring part or all of the money to your children. Your children, however, pay no taxes on the money you give them. However, if you were to give too much, generally a total of more than $600,000, you may fall victim to what is called a "gift tax." This could be where you got the idea about paying an extra tax.

Alternatively, you could enter into a contract with your children to share the winnings. An agreement between you and your children to split the winnings of a lottery ticket that any of you purchase, assuming they are old enough to participate in the lottery, is an enforceable contract. This agreement should be in writing, That way if you do win, checks will be issued to you and your children. With this arrangement, ordinary income tax would be owed individually by each person receiving a check. In other words, you would pay taxes at your income tax rate, and your children would pay their tax rates.

Finally, you may want to speak to an attorney who specializes in estate planning. He or she will let you know the best way to structure any lottery winnings.

What if he doesn't do what he promised?
"There's no punishment."

Dear Mr. Alderman:
I signed a contract to purchase a stereo from a local store. When I
went back the next day to pick it up, the manager told me he had just
sold the stereo to another customer and that he couldn't get another
one for several weeks. I was really mad . . . since I knew the manager
didn't like me and had sold it just for spite. I went to another store,

right around the corner, and I bought the same stereo for a much bet-
ter price. Now I want to know if I can do anything about the fact that
the store manager didn't sell me the original stereo. I have a written
contract.

The law of contracts is designed to do one thing: ensure that you get the benefit of your bargain. If someone breaches a contract, you are entitled to money damages to put you in the same place you would have been in if the contract had been performed. *It is very rare that punitive damages are awarded for breach of contract. All the law requires is that the breaching party put the other party in as good a position as he would be in if the contract had been performed.*

In your case, you were better off after the store breached the contract than you would have been had the store performed, so you are not entitled to any damages. If you had to pay more for the stereo at the other store, you could recover the difference in price. But in your case, you saved money. Even though you have a written contract, you cannot get any kind of penalty from the merchant for not living up to his part of the bargain.

The damages for breach of contract can be demonstrated in this way:

    market price   (what it will cost you to get the same thing
                                  somewhere else)

    − contract price   (what you would have paid)

    = damages

    + consequential loss (whatever else you lost because of the breach)

    = total recovery

For example, suppose the stereo cost $100 more at every other store and you had to drive an extra 50 miles to find one. You would then be entitled to $100 (the difference between the market price and the contract price) plus a reasonable amount for your mileage (a consequential loss). In your case, though, the formula results in a negative number, and even though you don't owe the store, it doesn't have to pay you any damages.

The law requires that you perform any contract you enter into, but
damages are designed to compensate, not punish. If the other party's
breach didn't hurt you economically, you are probably not entitled to any
damages.

I couldn't afford to pay for my layaway.
Don't I get my money back?
"It depends."

Dear Mr. Alderman:

A few months ago I saw a great dress at a little store near my house. I asked if the store did layaways, and the clerk said yes. She gave me something to sign and told me I had to pay $5 a week and that in 12 weeks the dress would be mine. The dress was marked $60, so this seemed fair. I paid for seven weeks and then lost my job. When I went back and told the clerk I couldn't make the payments anymore, she said, "Fine. We'll keep your money and the dress." Then she showed me the paper I signed that said the store could do this. I know I should have read it before I signed, but I just assumed that if I stopped paying I would get my money back. Can I do anything?

You asked a good question, and I was surprised I couldn't find a Texas law dealing directly with the area of layaways. It is a matter of private contract between you and the store. Whatever you agree to is enforceable, as any other contract would be. *It is very important that you carefully read the agreement before you sign it.*

Nevertheless, this does not mean the store has the right to do whatever it wants. It is still subject to the Texas Deceptive Trade Practices Act. Under this law, the store would be liable if it misrepresented the terms of the agreement. For example, if the clerk told you you would get your money back, the store could not hold you to a written agreement that said otherwise. In that case, by keeping your money the store would violate the Deceptive Trade Practices Act, and you could get up to three times your damages. (Read Chapter Ten.)

This law also prohibits the store from doing anything "unconscionable." This is defined as an act that takes grossly unfair advantage of a customer's knowledge, ability, experience, or capacity. In your case, the conduct of the store—charging $35 and giving you nothing in return—could be considered unconscionable if you lacked the ability to protect yourself from such a bad deal and the store took advantage of you. A court would make this determination. However, in my opinion, the store seems to have taken advantage of you, and this act could be considered unconscionable.

If you think you were deceived or that the store acted unconscionably under the Deceptive Trade Practices Act, you should consider letting the store know and going to small claims court, if necessary. Remember, though, before you use this law, you must do certain things, so read Chapter Ten carefully.

Who owns my dental records?
"Your dentist."

Dear Mr. Alderman:
I recently changed dentists. To avoid taking additional X-rays, I asked my former dentist for the X-rays he had. He refused to give them to me. Can he do this? I paid for the X-rays; aren't they mine?

Under the law, what you paid for were the services of the dentist. The records of the dentist, including X-rays, belong to the dentist. If he or she does not want to give them to you, you have no right to them.

I understand your desire not to have additional X-rays taken, and many dentists will allow patients to take their X-rays to another dentist. I suggest you speak with your dentist once more and explain why you want the X-rays. Perhaps you can work something out.

Should I co-sign a note for my friend?
"Being a co-signer can be dangerous."

Dear Mr. Alderman:
A good friend of mine is having a problem getting credit because of financial problems she had more than two years ago. She is now back on her feet but still has a bad credit report. She has asked me to co-sign a note to buy a car. I fully trust this person and know she will pay.
Recently, however, someone told me that if my friend doesn't pay, it could hurt my credit. Is this true? Can her default show up on my credit report?

Being a co-signer may seem like the nice thing to do, but unfortunately the old saying "No good deed goes unpunished" often applies to co-signers. When you co-sign or guarantee someone else's signature, you are in effect agreeing to the same obligation that person is. If that person does not pay, you must. And if you do not, your credit report will reflect it. In other words, don't co-sign unless you are willing to bear full responsibility for the obligation.

I should point out, however, that you are not without recourse if you must pay. If you as a co-signer pay, you are entitled to seek recovery against the person primarily responsible on the note. For example, if your friend didn't pay and you had to, you would be entitled to reimbursement from your friend.

How long do I have to change my mind after I sign a contract? "Usually no time!"

Dear Mr. Alderman:
Last week I went to buy a new car. It was late at night, and after a very hard sell, I signed a contract. The next morning I thought about the terms and decided they were more than I really could afford. When I called the car dealer to cancel, he said I couldn't. I thought you had three days to get out of a contract after you signed it. Isn't that the law in Texas?

No. In fact, as far as I know, it isn't the law anywhere. In most cases, once you sign a contract you are obligated by its terms. Unless you were tricked, deceived, or defrauded into signing the agreement, you are usually bound. (Read the material in Chapter Ten if this is the case.)

The existence of a three-day cooling-off period is one of the most widely held misconceptions about the law. There are only very limited instances in which you have three days to change your mind. For example, you have this right if you sign a contract that puts a lien on your home, a contract for time-share property, a health spa contract, or most contracts negotiated door-to-door. In other cases, though, once you sign you are bound.

The bottom line is simple. Don't sign anything until you have had time to read it and think about it. And as far as that high-pressure salesperson is concerned, go home and really think about the deal. If it really is a good deal, it will still be there the next day.

How can I get out of a long-term health club contract?
"There is a law."

Dear Mr. Alderman:

Like everyone else, my New Year's resolution was to get back in shape. The first thing I did was rush off to the local health club to sign up. The salesperson told me the club had a special that day and it would only cost $19.99 a month. He told me that to save time I should just sign the forms and he would have them ready when I came back that afternoon. I signed and then picked them up a few hours later. When I got home, I was shocked to see the membership cost $19.99 a month plus an initiation fee of $300. I don't have that kind of money. When I called and told him I wanted to cancel, his manager told me a contract is a contract and I should have read it before I signed. What can I do? Is this just an expensive lesson not to sign anything before you read it?

Although learning not to sign blank forms is a good lesson to learn, it is not all you can do in this case. Texas has a **Health Spa Act** that protects you. Basically, this law protects against false and deceptive acts or misrepresentations, such as what you describe. More importantly, this law has a cooling-off period and requires that health clubs post bonds with the secretary of state.

Under the law, any health spa contract must give you three days to cancel. The law requires that notice of this policy appear in bold print in the contract. The law also requires a bold notice telling consumers not to sign a contract with any blanks.

I suggest you contact the manager again and let her know you know about this law. If she doesn't agree to cancel it, you should file a complaint with the secretary of state. That is the office that enforces this law and keeps the bonds health clubs must file.

What happens if the photographer dies?
"You should get your money back."

Dear Mr. Alderman:

We hired a photographer to take pictures at an event. We gave him a large deposit. Before the event occurred, the photographer died. His office called and said it was going to hire a replacement. We did not want just any photographer and refused the offer. The office now refuses to return our deposit, saying it was nonrefundable. What are our rights?

The first thing you should do is read your agreement with the photographer. If the contract has a provision dealing with this situation, that provision probably controls your rights.

If the contract doesn't say anything about the death of the photographer, you may have the right to have the deposit returned. In most contracts, the person who delivers the goods or performs the service is not important, and you would have to allow substitute performance.

In personal service contracts of this kind, however, the person providing the service does not have the right simply to provide another person. As far as I am concerned, you do not have to accept a substitute photographer, and you are entitled to the return of your deposit.

Can a 15-year-old be liable to a music club?
"Minors generally cannot be forced to pay."

Dear Mr. Alderman:
My 15-year-old son joined a music club. After buying a few CDs, he stopped paying. They now want my husband and me to pay. Do we have to? What is our son's liability?

Basically, you have no liability for contracts entered into by your son. If you did not agree to pay, you do not have any liability to the music club.

Your son also may not have any liability. Under the law, a minor generally cannot enter into enforceable contracts. Some exceptions exist for necessities, such as food, basic furniture, and housing. This exception does not apply in this case.

From an ethical or moral standpoint, you should take care of liabilities incurred by your family members. As far as the law is concerned, however, there may not be a legal obligation on your part, or your son's, to the music company.

CHAPTER FIVE

Credit Cards

IN Chapter One, you saw how important credit is and that there are laws to help you obtain credit at a fair price. But once you have the credit, all sorts of complications can arise while using it.

Have you ever wondered if you could stop payment on a credit card the same way you can on a check? Or who is responsible when your credit card is stolen and the tacky thief enjoys an around-the-world cruise—via your charge cards?

As you will see, credit cards offer more protection than any other payment plan.

Do I have to pay if the plant has mites?
"Luckily, you used a credit card."

Dear Mr. Alderman:

Approximately three weeks ago, I bought a new houseplant. It was quite expensive, and the local florist told me it was in excellent shape and, with good care, would be a real showpiece. Shortly after I got it home, I noticed it had a horrible case of spider mites. The plant was so infested I couldn't even bring it into the house. The next day, I returned it to the florist, who told me the mites must have come from my house, as his plants were "all spotless." I told him the plant was never in my house and it was obvious the mites had been there a long period of time. He said he was sorry, but he wasn't going to do anything, and according to him, I could have the plant back or leave it with him. He then laughed and said, "Remember the old maxim 'Caveat emptor:' Let the buyer beware." At any rate, last week I received my credit card bill with the $80 charge for the plant on it. Can I do anything?

If you had paid for the plant with cash, your only remedies would be to try to get the merchant to refund your money or to go to small claims court. But luckily you used a credit card, and as you will see, this gives you substantial rights. Under federal law, a charge card company is not allowed to recover any amount from you that the merchant would not be allowed to recover. In legal jargon, the card company takes the account subject to all "claims and defenses" the buyer has against the merchant.

What this means is you have a chance to explain to the charge card company why you don't want to pay. For example: If the florist tried to collect the $80 from you, you would be able to refuse, saying the goods were defective and did not live up to the promise of being show quality.

Under the law, the charge card company is treated like the merchant. You can say to the charge card company, "I don't have to pay my bill because the goods I purchased and tried to return are defective." You have this right against the charge card company *until you pay the charge* and if the following three conditions have been met:

1. You have made a good faith effort to settle the matter with the merchant.
2. The goods cost more than $50.
3. The sale took place within your home state or within 100 miles of your home address.

This law protects you whenever you pay for goods or services with a charge card. If you receive your bill and there is a charge for goods or services that you did not receive or that were defective, you should immediately contact the charge card company in writing and tell the company of the dispute.

Do not pay the charge you are disputing!

You must write the credit card company and explain you are disputing the charge. Check the back of your billing statement for the proper address. Sometimes the credit card company will listen to your version of the dispute over the phone. But to fully retain all your rights under the law, follow up any phone call with a letter sent via certified mail, return receipt requested, confirming the call.

The law we are discussing is called the **Fair Credit Billing Act.** To find out how to use this law, read the next letter.

What can I do when a company goes bankrupt? "Next time, use a credit card."

Dear Mr. Alderman:
It seems like every day another business is going bankrupt or just disappearing. I am worried I will buy something from a business

and before it is delivered the company will go bankrupt. Some of my friends are stuck with tickets on bankrupt airlines. How can I protect myself?

As a consumer, you can't prevent a company from going bankrupt, but by using an alternative payment method, the credit card, you can usually protect yourself from having to bear any loss. Under the Fair Credit Billing Act, a credit card company may not collect for goods or services you purchased but never received. The same rule would probably apply if you charged a plane ticket and never have an opportunity to use it because the airline has gone bankrupt, canceling your flight.

The law is easy to use, but you must follow a few simple rules.

First:
    You must send a separate, written billing error notice to the card company. (Your billing insert will give you the address.)
Second:
    Your notice must reach the card company within 60 days after the first bill containing the error was mailed to you.

These steps must be explained in your bill. Usually there will be a statement like the following:

BILLING RIGHTS SUMMARY
(In Case of Errors or Questions About Your Bill)

If you think your bill is wrong or if you need more information about a transaction on your bill, write us (on a separate sheet) at (the address shown on your bill) as soon as possible. We must hear from you no later than 60 days after we sent you the first bill on which the error or problem appeared. You can telephone us, but doing so will not preserve your rights. In your letter, give us the following information:

• Your name and account number.
• The dollar amount of the suspected error.
• A description of the error and explain, if you can, why you believe there is an error. If you need more information, describe the item you are unsure about.

You do not have to pay any amount in question while we are investigating, but you are still obligated to pay the parts of your bill not in question. While we investigate your question, we cannot report you as delinquent or take any action to collect the amount you question.

Special Rule For Credit Card Purchases

If you have a problem with the quality of goods or services that you purchased with a credit card, and you have tried in good faith to correct the problem with the merchant, you may not have to pay the remaining amount due on the goods or services. You have this protection only when the purchase price was more than $50 and the purchase was made in your home state or within 100 miles of your mailing address. (If we own or operate the merchant, or if we mailed you the advertisement for the property or services, all purchases are covered regardless of amount or location of purchase.)

You may use the following form for your letter. Send this letter to your credit card company at the address listed on your monthly statement. Send it via certified mail, return receipt requested:

Date   Your name
                                                              Address

Credit Card Company
Address
RE: Account #_____

I am disputing the charge in my (month) statement in the amount of $(give amount), for the purchase of (item).

State reasons for refusal to pay. For example, the writer of the prior letter would say:

This charge was for the purchase of a plant that the store told me was in great condition, a showpiece. The plant was infected with mites. I have returned the plant and refuse to pay because it is defective. The store now has the plant.

Please remove this charge from my bill. Thank you for your expected cooperation.

_____
Signed

Next time you buy goods or services, think about the advantages of using your credit card. If the goods or services never arrive or the company goes out of business, you will not have to bear a loss because the law allows you to dispute your bill and assert your legal rights against the credit card company.

THE FAIR CREDIT BILLING ACT

The Fair Credit Billing Act (FCBA) protects you in the case of "billing errors." Billing errors are defined by the law and include:

1. Charges not made by you or anyone authorized to use your account.
2. Charges that are incorrectly identified or for which the wrong amount or date is shown.
3. Charges for goods or services that you did not accept or that were not delivered as agreed.
4. Computational or similar errors.
5. Failure to properly reflect payments or other credits, such as returns.
6. Not mailing or delivering bills to your current address (provided you give a change of address at least 20 days before the billing period ends).
7. Charges for which you request an explanation or written proof of purchase.

This law applies to any business you have an account with, including stores, credit card companies, and even bank overdraft checking accounts. If you feel a billing error has occurred, you must send the creditor a billing error notice. This notice must reach the creditor within 60 days after you receive the first bill containing the error. Send the notice to the address provided on your bill. In your letter you should include the following information:

1. Name and account number.
2. A statement that you believe your bill contains an error and that includes the dollar amount involved.
3. A statement describing why you think there is a mistake.

The law requires only that you send this notice, but to protect yourself, send it certified mail, return receipt requested.

What must the creditor do?

The creditor must acknowledge your letter claiming a billing error within 30 days after he receives it, unless of course the problem is resolved within that time period. In any event, within two billing cycles (but not more than 90 days) the creditor must conduct a reasonable investigation and either correct the mistake or explain why he believes the bill to be correct.

What happens while a bill is being disputed?

You may withhold payment of the amount in dispute, including the affected portions of minimum payments and finance charges, until the dispute is resolved. You are still required to pay any part of the bill that is not disputed, including finance and other charges.

While the FCBA dispute settlement procedure is going on, the creditor cannot take any legal or other action to collect the disputed amount. Your account cannot be closed or restricted in any way, except the disputed amount may be applied against your credit limit.

What about your credit rating?

While a bill is being disputed, the creditor cannot threaten to damage your credit rating or report you as delinquent to anyone. The creditor is, however, permitted to report you are disputing your bill.

Another federal law, the **Equal Credit Opportunity Act,** prohibits creditors from discriminating against credit applicants who in good faith exercise their rights under the FCBA. You cannot be denied credit merely because you have disputed a bill.

What if the creditor makes a mistake?

If your bill is found to contain a billing error, the creditor must write to you, explaining the corrections to be made on your account. In addition to crediting your account with the amount not owed, the creditor must remove all finance charges, late fees, and other charges relating to the amount. If the creditor concludes you owe part of the disputed amount, this too must be explained in writing. You also have the right to request copies of documents proving you owe the money.

What if the bill is correct?

If the creditor investigates and still believes the bill to be correct, you must be told promptly in writing how much you owe and why. You may also request copies of relevant documents. At this point, you will owe the disputed amount plus any finance charges accumulated while the amount was being disputed.

What if you still disagree?

Even after the Fair Credit Billing Act dispute settlement procedure has ended, you may still feel the bill is wrong. If this happens, write to the creditor within 10 days after receiving the explanation, stating you refuse to pay the disputed amount. At this point, the creditor may begin collection procedures. If the creditor, however, reports you to a credit bureau as delinquent, he must also state that you do not think you owe the money. You must also be told who receives such reports.

What if the creditor doesn't follow the procedures?

Any creditor who fails to follow strictly the Fair Credit Billing Act dispute settlement procedure is penalized by not being allowed to collect the first $50 of the amount in dispute, even if the bill turns out to be correct. For example: This penalty would apply if a creditor acknowledges your complaint in 45 days (15 days too late) or takes more than two billing cycles to resolve a dispute. It also applies if a creditor threatens to report or improperly reports your billing situation. Thus, if you owed $200 the creditor's delay would mean he can only recover $150.

The bottom line is: Use a credit card whenever you have any doubts about a company or whenever you are buying something to arrive or to be used in the future.

Don't I have to give my consent for someone to get my credit report? "No."

Dear Mr. Alderman:
I recently learned a mortgage company got a copy of my credit report. I was never told the company requested this. I thought anyone who requested a credit check needed my permission. Am I wrong?

Yes. Under the Fair Credit Reporting Act, a company can get a copy of your report if it is using the report to furnish you credit or review your account. Credit reports may also be provided in connection with employment and insurance. Based on what you say in your letter, the mortgage company had a legitimate basis for requesting the report and therefore was entitled to it.

The best way to find out who has requested copies of your report is to contact the credit bureau. It keeps records of who has made inquiries. If you feel a report was requested for unlawful reasons, you should let the credit bureau and the Federal Trade Commission know.

What happens when my card is stolen?
"Good news for you."

Dear Mr. Alderman:

The other day I went into a restaurant and paid for my meal with a credit card. The waiter had me sign the receipt but forgot to return my card. I didn't discover this until several days later, when I went to charge another meal and found the card missing. Of course, I immediately called the restaurant and was told the waiter had been fired. I informed the credit card company my card was stolen and was told to write the credit card company a letter confirming this. Now I am worried about what will happen if my card is used by the waiter.

Don't worry. Federal law protects you when your credit card is lost or stolen. Under the law, your maximum liability for the unauthorized use of your credit card is $50. But that liability may be even less if you quickly notify the credit card company. You have no liability for charges incurred after you have given the company notice that your card was stolen or lost. Notice may be given in any reasonable way, including over the telephone. In your case, you will not have to pay for any charges after the date you phoned the card company, and the most you will have to pay for unauthorized charges made before you gave notice is $50.

If you want to make certain you never have to pay anything if your credit card is lost or stolen, keep the telephone number for the credit card company handy and call as soon as you find your card is missing. A quick phone call could save you $50.

Good advice: Make a photostatic copy of the contents of your wallet so you can quickly report any lost or stolen credit cards.

Someone is charging things to my account. What are my rights?
"You may not have to pay anything."

Dear Mr. Alderman:

I recently received my credit card bill, and there were three charges for things I didn't buy. I disputed the charges as you suggested and was told they were for mail-order items charged to my account and sent to someone else. The store said it was a phone order and it got my account number that way. I didn't make these calls, and I don't feel I should have to pay anything, even the $50.

I agree; I think you are correct. Under the law you don't have to pay for any unauthorized charge. A store that simply accepts a credit card number over the phone and mails the merchandise to a different address runs the risk that the cardholder won't pay. I suggest you make it clear to the credit card company that you did not order the items and you do not intend to pay.

As far as the $50 is concerned, I don't think you should have to pay even that much. As I stated on page 51, if you lose your card or it is stolen, you may be required to pay up to the first $50. This rule doesn't apply when someone fraudulently uses your number but not the card. In other words, the law imposes some obligations on you if you are careless and lose the card or it is stolen. But as long as you have the card, you have no liability for the unauthorized use of your card number.

I lost my bank card—what now?
"All plastic is not equal."

Dear Mr. Alderman:

I recently used a walk-up teller machine to get some cash. I withdrew $50 and left. Apparently I dropped my card, because I can't find it. I have looked everywhere, but it is just missing. I remember reading something about the fact that I am only liable for $50 if I lose my credit card. Am I protected if someone finds my bank card and uses it?

No! The law protecting you in the case of lost credit cards does not apply to cards that electronically transfer money directly out of your account. Unlike a credit card, which extends credit during the period between the time of making the charge and the time you pay the bill, a bank card immediately debits your account.

Remember: The law regarding bank cards such as MPACT or Pulse is very different from the law regarding credit cards. If your bank card is lost or stolen, *your liability depends on how quickly you report the loss.* Your liability is limited to $50 only if you notify the institution within two business days of learning of the loss. If you wait, your liability may be as high as $500. And should you fail to report the loss within 60 days after your statement is mailed to you, you are responsible for all transfers made after 60 days (even they total more than $500). This means you could lose all the money in your account, plus any overdraft protection you may have with the bank.

For example, suppose your automated teller machine card is stolen by some nefarious thief who has also discovered your code number. (*Remember: A good way to protect yourself is to keep your code number a secret.*) The first stop the villain makes is the ATM, where he promptly withdraws $75 from your account. The next day, he returns and withdraws a hefty $200 (he's getting greedy!). A week later you attempt to use your card only to discover it's missing.

If you call the bank within two business days after you discover the card missing, all you lose is $50. But should you wait a week, you will be responsible for the entire $275; if you wait longer you may lose all the money in your account. For instance, many people put their bank statements aside, planning to find a "free moment" later to look it over. Meanwhile, two and one half months go by. The thief decides to hit the ATM again and, with your card and code in hand, wipes out your entire account, which amounts to $1,000. Because you did not report the discrepancy in your statement within 60 days after the bank mailed the statement, the entire loss will fall on your shoulders.

Remember: A delay of two days in reporting the loss of a debit card could cost you $500. Promptly review all bank statements and report any unauthorized transfer of funds.

The law regulating misuse of bank cards is called the **Electronic Fund Transfer Act.** It covers not only your bank cards but also any preauthorized payments you allow the bank to make. For example, many of us use electronic fund transfers to pay some of our monthly bills automatically, such as mortgage payments. Electronic fund transfers are expected to replace checks as the most common way to do business in the future. Soon we will pay for our groceries at the supermarket with a card that automatically deducts the money from our account and transfers it to the supermarket's account.

If you would like more information about electronic fund transfers and your rights, you may send for this free booklet:

"Alice in Debit-Land"
Board of Governors
Federal Reserve System
Washington, DC 20551
(202) 452-3000

When are my payments really due?
"On the stated date."

Dear Mr. Alderman:
I have been paying on an installment loan on my truck for the past year. I always mail my payment by the 15th. For the past two months the company I'm paying has called me on the 16th and demanded payment, asking why I am late. It has even threatened to repossess my car. What can I do to stop these harassments?

You seem to believe that because you mailed your payment on the 15th you are paying your note on time. In fact, in most cases the due date is when the payment must arrive, not when it must be sent.

In your case the payment is due on the 1st of the month. The creditor has given you a 15-day grace period to help you make sure the payment arrives. I suggest you mail the payment on a date that ensures it arrives before the 15th. If you do not, you run the risk of having your truck repossessed.

Can a credit card company change the rules?
"Yes and you can switch."

Dear Mr. Alderman:
I have had a charge card for several years. The company now has started charging me a $20 annual fee. Is this legal?

It is perfectly legal for a credit card company to begin charging you a fee, even if it did not in the past. It is also perfectly legal for you to cancel the card and get one from the many competitors who do not charge fees.

CHAPTER SIX

Debt Collection

EVERYONE will surely agree we all should pay our bills and they should be paid on time. But once in a while things happen, and somehow we just can't. If you are unable to pay all your bills all the time, you should know federal and state laws exist to protect you from unscrupulous debt collectors.

Most consumers pay their debts. Even though less than 2% of all consumer credit obligations ever become delinquent, late or unpaid accounts total several billions of dollars. As one might expect, with this vast sum of money at stake, debt collectors often devote considerable energy to collection of delinquent debts, and some of their efforts are illegal.

Debt collection usually begins with a polite letter from the company informing the late party that the bill is overdue and requesting payment, or at least requesting a payment plan. If nothing can be resolved, additional letters will be sent telling the debtor of more drastic actions to follow.

But if the letters fail to get the needed funds, the account is usually forwarded to a collection agency. The correspondence at this point will become more urgent, and the tone more harsh. The debtor also may receive telephone calls, both at home and at work, pleading for payment. If payment does not result, the next step is to turn the matter over to an attorney, who will file suit. But suing is expensive and only used as a last resort. If possible, the debt collector wants to be paid without going to court, and sometimes this means resorting to more forceful, and often illegal, means.

The ingenuity of debt collectors is unlimited, and unfortunately, their approaches are oftentimes questionable. Tales of the misconduct of debt collectors could fill the pages of many books. Finally, aggressive tactics of some of them became so abusive that Congress found it necessary to pass a law to protect debtors. This law is called the **Fair Debt Collection Practices Act,** and it provides protection to consumers who experience harassing and threatening conditions at the hands of pesty debt collectors. This law, along with the **Texas Debt Collection Act,** should ensure that honest debtors, who are trying to do their best but just get in a little over their heads, are treated fairly and humanely by debt collectors.

Before talking about these laws, however, you should know what legal rights your creditors have if they do sue you. As the next letter shows, Texas law is generous to debtors.

What can the debt collector get?
"Not much."

Dear Mr. Alderman:

I owe a local department store about $1,000. I have been unable to pay in full, and even though I send as much as I can each month, the store has said it will sue me. I have a steady job and a small house with a large mortgage. Every penny I earn goes to pay my bills. If the store sues, what can it get from me?

Every state has a law that "exempts" some of a debtor's property from his creditors. Exempt property is property your creditors can never take. No matter how much money you owe, there is some property the state feels is so important to you that you should be able to keep it. *Texas has about the most favorable exemption statutes in the country.* Under Texas law your creditors cannot take your homestead or a specified amount of personal property, in most cases up to $60,000. Here is what the law says:

PERSONAL PROPERTY EXEMPTION

(a) Personal property, as described in Section 42.002, is exempt from garnishment, attachment, execution, or other seizure if:
  (1) the property is provided for a family and has an aggregate fair market value of not more than $60,000, exclusive of the amount of any liens, security interests, or other charges encumbering the property; or
  (2) the property is owned by a single adult, who is not a member of a family, and has an aggregate fair market value of not more than $30,000, exclusive of the amount of any liens, security interests, or other charges encumbering the property.
(b) The following personal property is exempt from seizure and is not included in the aggregate limitations prescribed by Subsection (a):

(1) current wages for personal services, except for the enforcement of court-ordered child support payments;

(2) professionally prescribed health aids of a debtor or a dependent of a debtor.

(c) This section does not prevent seizure by a secured creditor with a contractual landlord lien or other security in the property to be seized.

(d) Unpaid commissions for personal services not to exceed 25% of the aggregate limitations prescribed by Subsection (a) are exempt from seizure and are included in the aggregate.

Personal Property

(a) The following personal property is exempt under Section 42.001(a):

(1) home furnishings, including family heirlooms;

(2) provisions for consumption;

(3) farming or ranching vehicles and implements;

(4) tools, equipment, books, and apparatus, including boats and motor vehicles used in a trade or profession;

(5) wearing apparel;

(6) jewelry not to exceed 25% of the aggregate limitations prescribed by Section 12.001(a);

(7) two firearms;

(8) athletic and sporting equipment, including bicycles;

(9) a two-wheeled or four-wheeled motor vehicle for each member of family or single adult who holds a driver's license or who does not hold a driver's license but who relies on another person to operate the vehicle for the benefit of the nonlicensed person;

(10) the following animals and forage on hand for their consumption:

(A) two horses, mules, or donkeys and a saddle, blanket, and bridle for each;

(B) 12 head of cattle;

(C) 60 head of other types of livestock; and

(D) 120 fowl;

(11) household pets; and

(12) the present value of any life insurance policy to the extent that a member of the family of the insured or a dependent of

a single insured adult claiming the exemption is beneficiary of the policy.

(b) Personal property, unless precluded from being encumbered by other law, may be encumbered by a security interest under Section 9.203, Business & Commerce Code, or Sections 41 and 42, Certificate of Title Act (Article 6687-1, Vernon's Texas Civil Statutes), or by a lien fixed by other law, and the security interest or lien may not be avoided on the ground that the property is exempt under this chapter.

INTERESTS IN LAND EXEMPT FROM SEIZURE

(a) A homestead and one or more lots used for a place of burial of the dead are exempt from seizure for the claims of creditors except for encumbrances properly fixed on homestead property.

(b) Encumbrances may be properly fixed on homestead property for:
  (1) purchase money;
  (2) taxes on the property; or
  (3) work and material used in constructing improvements on the property if contracted for in writing as provided by Sections 53.059(a), (b), and (c).

(c) The homestead claimant's proceeds of a sale of a homestead are not subject to seizure for a creditor's claim for six months after the date of sale.

Definition of Homestead

(a) If used for the purposes of an urban home or as a place to exercise a calling or business in the same urban area, the homestead of a family or a single, adult person, not otherwise entitled to a homestead, shall consist of not more than one acre of land which may be in one or more lots, together with any improvements thereon.

(b) If used for the purposes of a rural home, the homestead shall consist of:
  (1) for a family, not more than 200 acres, which may be in one or more parcels, with the improvements thereon; or
  (2) for a single, adult person, not otherwise entitled to a homestead, not more than 100 acres, which may be in one or more parcels, with the improvements thereon.

(c) A homestead is considered to be rural if, at the time the designation is made, the property is not served by municipal utilities and fire and police protection.

(d) The definition of a homestead as provided in this section applies to all homesteads in this state whenever created.

So what does all this mean to you? In summary, it means you can keep your home, free from all your creditors except the one that loaned you the money to buy the house and any that are owed money for improving it. If you don't pay these debts or if you don't pay your taxes, you may be forced to sell your house to pay your debts. You also can keep personal property, up to $60,000 for a family, so long as the property is included in the list and you didn't voluntarily give your creditor a lien. For example, if you own a car, your creditors cannot take it to satisfy your debt. But the dealer who sold you the car can repossess it if he took a lien when he sold it to you. On the other hand, if you own a boat, an item not included in the list, your creditors could sue you and have the sheriff or constable take the boat and sell it to pay off the debt.

As you can see, most of what the average person owns is exempt. This means even if you are sued, you do not have to worry about losing your property. Of course the person who extended credit to you to buy the item will usually have a lien allowing him to take the goods back if you don't pay.

And remember, your creditors know the law also. They know they can't force you to pay and therefore would probably like to talk with you about finding a way to work things out.

Can they take my wages?
"Probably not . . ."

Dear Mr. Alderman:

I owe lots of people money, but my family comes first. I buy groceries and clothing, and everything else I earn goes to pay my bills. I am worried that if I don't pay my bills soon, the creditors will take part of my wages. I couldn't even afford the basics if this happened. Can they do this?

The Texas Constitution guarantees that a person's wages are protected from his or her creditors. Under the law there are only two groups of debts you must be concerned with: child support and taxes. If you owe money for either of these, your wages may be attached to pay the debt. *In all other cases, your creditors may not take any of your wages.*

Remember, this is a Texas law. In nearly every other state a portion of your wages may be taken by any creditor to satisfy the debt. For example, if you work part-time in Texas and part-time in Oklahoma, your Oklahoma wages may be subject to your creditors.

Best advice: As you can tell from this letter and the one right before it, creditors in Texas have few legal remedies when it comes to enforcing debts. Because of this they are usually more than willing to work with you to arrange a fair payment plan. *If you are having trouble with your creditors and just need some time to rearrange your debts, contact your creditors and see what you can work out. It is in everyone's best interest to reach a compromise.*

Can my creditors take my IRA?
"Not anymore!"

Dear Mr. Alderman:
I recently lost my job and have fallen behind in paying my bills. I am trying to keep up, but some of my creditors want to be paid in full and have threatened to sue me. I heard you say they can't take my wages, but I am concerned we will lose our savings if they take our IRA. Is there any way I can protect my retirement money?

Before to September 1, 1987, a creditor that sued you and won in court could probably take your IRA funds to satisfy the judgment. This was an unfortunate situation because, as the previous letters show, most other property is exempt from your creditors. The legislature has changed this, however, by passing a law that exempts most retirement plans and IRAs from your creditors.

Under this law a qualified IRA may not be taken by your creditors, even if they go to court, sue, and win. This money is considered so important for your retirement that the state has decided to allow you to keep it. In other words, the answer to your question about protecting your money . . . keep it in the IRA. Of course, as I pointed out before, other savings, such as a simple savings account, may be taken by your creditors once they sue and win.

Is an IRA in another state exempt?
"It probably depends on the law of the other state."

Dear Mr. Alderman:
I read that in Texas an IRA is exempt from creditors. I live in Texas, but I have an IRA with a California bank. Can my creditors take it, or is it still exempt?

Good question. If the account was in a Texas bank, and a creditor attempted to enforce a judgment in Texas, Texas law would govern. Under Texas law, the creditor could not take the money in the account.

If, however, a creditor tried to collect the judgment in California, California law may apply. There has been some litigation in this area, and the courts are not uniform in their decisions. The best thing to do may be to transfer the money into a local bank account to ensure the protection of Texas law.

Can my creditors take my wife's property?
"Maybe not."

Dear Mr. Alderman:
I have a judgment rendered against me in Harris County by a California credit card company. I have not heard from the company about trying to enforce the judgment. I have no assets or funds that would be available to the company if it tried to enforce the judgment. I am now concerned because my wife may inherit a large sum of money. She is not named in the judgment. Can the company try to collect against her if she inherits the money?

As I discuss on pages 204–205, Texas is a "community property state." This means most of the property owned by a husband and wife is "community." Community property may be viewed as being jointly owned. Community property, therefore, generally is subject to the debts of either of the spouses.

On the other hand, "separate property" is property that belongs to just one spouse and is not subject to the debts of the other. Separate property includes property owned before the marriage, as well as property inherited. In your case, your wife's inheritance probably would be considered separate property and would not be subject to your debt. She should be careful not to commingle the property or do anything to ratify your debt. If she does, the inheritance could become subject to the debt.

Can I stop harassing phone calls?
"They must stop."

Dear Mr. Alderman:
My creditors won't leave me alone. I know I should pay my bills, and I will as soon as I can, but I am even going to lose my job if I don't get some sleep. The most annoying thing they do is call me in the middle of the night and say things like, "I don't know how a deadbeat like you can sleep. Don't you feel guilty about not paying your bills?" I have started pulling my phone cord out at night, but as soon as I plug it in, the calls begin. How can I stop this? Do I report it to the telephone company? I have even tried changing my phone number.

As the introduction to this chapter points out, two laws protect you from harassment by debt collectors, the **Texas Debt Collection Act,** and the federal **Fair Debt Collection Practices Act.** Both laws prohibit debt collectors from harassing you over the phone.

The federal law makes it illegal for debt collectors to engage in any conduct designed to harass, oppress, or abuse you in connection with the collection of a debt. It is specifically made illegal to cause a phone to ring repeatedly with intent to annoy, abuse, or harass; to call without giving the caller's identity; or to call after 9 p.m. or before 8 a.m. The federal law also states that once you notify the debt collector in writing that you want him to stop communication with you, *the debt collector must stop all communication except advising you of his next step.*

Under the Fair Debt Collection Practices Act, you can stop the debt collector from calling you, and he may have already violated the law by his conduct so far. *But the Fair Debt Collection Practices Act applies only to a "debt collector," that is, someone in the business of collecting debts for another.* It doesn't apply to a creditor collecting his own debts. If the calls have been from a collection agency, the federal law applies. If the calls are directly from the store, the federal law does not apply; but the Texas law does.

Unlike the federal law, the Texas Debt Collection Act applies to anyone trying to collect a debt. This includes the store that sold you the goods and any agency it hires to collect the debt. Although the Texas law is not as broad as the federal law, you still can use it to prevent any further harassment. Under the Texas law, it is illegal to oppress, harass, or abuse any person in connection with the collection of a debt. The law specifically provides that a debt collector may not place phone calls without disclosing the name of the person calling, may not call with the intent to annoy or harass, and may not cause the phone to ring repeatedly or continuously with the intent to harass.

If you feel you are being harassed, immediately contact the creditor and the debt collector (if they are not the same person), and tell them you expect them to cease all further harassment. Do it in writing and mail it certified, return receipt requested. You also should contact the appropriate state and federal agencies that enforce these laws. The federal law is enforced by the Federal Trade Commission, and the state law is enforced by the attorney general's office. Additionally, both these laws let you collect substantial civil damages if you have been injured as a result of unlawful collection. If you have suffered injury, see a private attorney about filing a lawsuit. I should remind you that, if you are successful, you are entitled to recover your attorney's fees as well.

Can they tell my boss?
"You may be protected."

Dear Mr. Alderman:

I owe several stores money. I just got a new job, and I am paying them back as fast as I can. Most of the creditors have been nice and have allowed me to pay as best I can, but one debt collector told me that if I don't pay everything I owe, he will call my boss and tell him he has a deadbeat working for him. I know I will be fired if he does that. The only way I can pay this particular store is to not pay anyone else. Is there any way to protect myself? Can the debt collector tell people that I owe money?

If it really is a debt collector calling you, as opposed to the store itself, then it is illegal for him to call your boss. The federal law governing debt collection, which applies only to someone trying to collect a debt owed to someone else, says debt collectors may only communicate with other people to try to locate you. *The law expressly makes it illegal for them to call your employer and try to force him to make you pay.*

I suggest you contact the debt collector in writing and demand he stop all communication with third parties. *The federal law also provides that if you write debt collectors to stop collection efforts, they must cease all communication except to tell you they are stopping and what they intend to do next.* If they continue, contact the Federal Trade Commission. If their action has harmed you, you may also consider seeing an attorney to bring a private lawsuit. Under the law you may be entitled to punitive damages, as well as your actual loss.

Be aware that this law does not apply to people collecting their own debts. They are governed by the Texas law, which probably lets them contact your employer, unless it is done in a harassing or abusive manner.

My check bounced. What can they do?
"It may be a crime."

Dear Mr. Alderman:
The new dress at the department store was irresistible. The only problem was that the check I used didn't have any money to back it up. After the check bounced I told the store manager that as soon as I got paid I would pay off the check, but the manager insisted I pay right away. The manager said it is criminal to pay for something with a check that bounces and unless I paid soon, the store would turn it over to the district attorney. Can the store do this? I didn't steal the dress—I plan to pay for it.

What you have done is probably criminal under Texas law, and the store has the right to turn the matter over to the district attorney, who could prosecute. *I strongly recommend you immediately pay the store the money you owe it.*

Under Texas law the issuance of a "bad check" is a Class C misdemeanor, and you could receive a fine or even be put in jail. This law states it is illegal to give someone a check knowing you do not have enough money in the bank to cover it. As a practical matter, if you quickly pay the check, you probably will not be prosecuted; but based on what you say in your letter, you have violated the law.

You should be aware, however, of the difference between passing a bad check and stopping payment for a reason. It is not illegal to stop payment on a check when you have enough money in your account to pay it. For example, suppose when you got the dress home, you discovered it was damaged, so you took it back to the store. The store refused to give you back your money, even though it had a sign saying it would give a refund if the goods were returned within 24 hours. If you stopped payment on the check, the store could not have you prosecuted under this law. If the store wanted to try to collect the money, it would have to pursue its civil remedies.

But be careful if you are thinking about stopping payment on a check to a mechanic. Read the next letter before you do.

My check bounced. Can they repossess my car?
"They can if the check was for repairs."

Dear Mr. Alderman:
The other day I had the brakes fixed on my car. I paid the bill of $79.95 with a check. I thought I had more than enough money in the bank, but apparently I didn't. The check bounced, and a few days later I found my car missing. When I called the police to report it stolen, they said it had been repossessed. I called the repo man and was told I had to pay the $79.95 plus $350 in repossession costs to get it back. I paid, and now I am mad. What are my rights?

You have probably heard me say that in most cases if someone isn't paid for what he sells you, he can't just come and take it back. He has to go to court and sue you. Well, unfortunately for you there is one big exception to this.

A mechanic has a lien on your car whenever he repairs it. Until you pay he does not have to give it back. And if you pay with a check that is dishonored or if you stop payment, the mechanic has the right to repossess your car. The mechanic cannot forcefully take your car, but he can have a repo man come out in the middle of the night and remove it. So it looks like the mechanic does have the right to take your car back.

The harder question is what are your rights with respect to the repo man who charged you $350 for taking the car and held it until you paid. As of the writing of this book it looks like the repo man has the right to keep the car until you pay, but he will be responsible if he acts unreasonably, for example, by charging an unfair price. The repo man, like anyone else who performs a service, warrants that he will perform in a good and workmanlike manner, and under the Deceptive Trade Practices Act he would be responsible if he charged a grossly excessive price. If you find that the ordinary reasonable charge for this type of service is, for example, $100, I would consider filing a claim in small claims court for a violation of the DTPA. (See Chapter Ten.)

How long is a judgment good for?
"A judgment can be good forever."

Dear Mr. Alderman:

In 1986 my house was foreclosed on, and I was sued. The bank got a judgment against me. How long will this appear on my credit report? How long is the judgment good for? I was told the judgment is only good for 10 years. Is there some period of time after which I will no longer be obligated to pay?

As discussed on page 4, a judgment stays on your credit report for seven years. After that time it becomes obsolete and generally cannot be reported by a credit bureau. This does not mean, however, that you don't still owe the money. As long as there is a valid judgment against you, steps can be taken to collect. A judgment is enforceable for 10 years. It can be renewed for another ten years, however, if the creditor takes certain action. As long as the creditor continues to take steps to enforce the judgment, it can be enforced indefinitely.

The buyer of my house didn't make his payments;
how can I owe the money?
"That is how an assumption works."

Dear Mr. Alderman:

I sold my house to a buyer who assumed my existing mortgage. I have now discovered the buyer has not paid the mortgage and has moved out of the house. The mortgage company has asked me to pay the full amount owed and to continue making payments. I don't mind picking up the future installments, but it doesn't seem fair that I have to pay the past due amounts.

It may not seem fair, but legally you are obligated for these payments. When a house is sold and a buyer assumes the mortgage, the buyer is simply agreeing to pay the money the seller owes on the mortgage. The seller, however, is still obligated on the note and is responsible if the buyer doesn't make the payments. If the buyer defaults, the seller is responsible for all payments the buyer may have missed, as well as any future payments.

So what will happen if you do not make these payments? The mortgage company will probably foreclose on the house and sell it to pay off the note. As the next letter indicates, that may not be the end of your problems. When a buyer assumes a seller's mortgage, the seller remains legally obligated on the note. To eliminate this problem, the seller can require that the buyer arrange his own financing and pay off the seller's note.

My house was foreclosed. How can I still owe money? "Foreclosure does not extinguish a debt."

Dear Mr. Alderman:
Several years ago we had financial problems, and our house was foreclosed. Since that time, we have been able to get back on our feet and are paying all our bills on time. Now we have received a letter saying we owe $23,000 on our house note. How is this possible? Do we have to pay this? What are our alternatives?

Unfortunately, your letter is not the only one I have received about this problem. Many other people find themselves in the same situation. And from a legal standpoint, you owe the money.

When property is foreclosed upon, it is sold, and the proceeds are applied to the debt. If the sale price is more than what you owe, you will get money back. If the sale price is less, as was the case with your house, you still owe the difference between the sale price and the debt. You also will owe the costs of the foreclosure proceeding. In other words, you are legally responsible for the money. As a practical matter, however, you should first see if the creditor will work with you. Perhaps you can come up with a payment plan you can live with.

Because of the large amount involved, you also should consider bankruptcy. I realize many people think of bankruptcy as a radical alternative, but it may be the best way to really get a fresh start on your finances. Many attorneys handle consumer bankruptcy, and specialists are listed in the yellow pages.

My car was repossessed. How do I still owe money? "Repossession doesn't extinguish a debt."

Dear Mr. Alderman:
I bought a new car and could not keep up the payments. After receiving several letters I let the lender repossess the car. I have now

received a letter saying I owe $6,000. How is this possible? I don't even have the car anymore.

Many people do not understand how a repossession works. When you buy a car, you sign two documents. The first is a note promising to pay back a certain sum of money. The second is an agreement giving the lender the right to take the car back if you do not pay and to apply the proceeds to your note. The repossession, however, doesn't extinguish the note. If the money obtained from the sale of the car is not sufficient to pay off the note, you owe the difference.

For example, suppose you buy a new car and finance $13,000. After paying $1,000, you default, and the car is repossessed. The car will then be sold. Assume the costs of the repossession are $500. The balance remaining on your debt is $12,500. If the car is sold for $10,000, the proceeds will be applied to what you owe. You would still owe a balance of $2,500.

In your case the car was apparently sold for substantially less than what you owed on the note. I suggest you ask the lender for a full explanation of your situation and then try to work out a settlement. Under the law, you are entitled to be notified how and why your car will be sold and to be given an accounting of how much was obtained. If the lender did not act reasonably, you may not owe anything.

How do I collect from a defunct corporation?
"You cannot."

Dear Mr. Alderman:

I recently successfully sued a business in small claims court. When I tried to collect, I discovered the company had gone out of business. What can I do? Can I collect from the man who ran the company?

Unfortunately, based on what you say in your letter, you may be out of luck. This is because the business you sued was a corporation. Under the law, a corporation is a separate legal entity. When it ceases to do business, the officers of shareholders of the corporation generally have no personal liability, and you cannot collect from them. Unless the business still has some assets to pay you, such as cash in the bank or inventory, there is little you can do.

Do I have to pay my sister's debts?
"Probably not."

Dear Mr. Alderman:

My sister was in a nursing home before she died. The nursing home is now sending me the bills for the last two months she was in there. Am I responsible?

Generally, a person is not responsible for the debts of another unless she agreed in advance to pay them. When a person dies, her estate is responsible for her bills, and if there is no money in the estate, the bills do not get paid. If you did not agree to pay your sister's nursing home bills, I do not know any reason you would be responsible.

On the other hand, you should check with the home and see if you, in fact, did agree to be responsible for your sister's bills. You may have signed such a statement when she was admitted and not remembered. I suggest you contact the home and ask why it feels you are responsible for your sister's debt.

Can my sister go to jail if she doesn't pay her debts?
"No."

Dear Mr. Alderman:

My sister has gotten over her head in debt. Now one of the credit card companies is threatening her. In the past, our family has always helped her out. Now we cannot, and we are afraid of what may happen. Can she go to jail if she doesn't pay?

No. There is no longer debtor's prison in this country. Although a creditor has the right to try to collect its debt, the law prohibits it from threatening a person. I suggest your sister write the creditor and insist it stop threatening her. If it does not, it will be violating the law.

If a creditor is not paid, it always has the right to try to collect by suing. In most cases, however, once a creditor knows you really are making a good faith effort to pay, it usually will work with you to come up with a payment plan you can live with. Hopefully this will happen to your sister.

C H A P T E R   S E V E N

Divorce & Child Custody

FEW things in a person's life are as traumatic as family law problems—for example, divorce. No matter who wants it or how agreeable the parties are, divorce is always difficult to deal with. And when children are involved, divorce becomes even more complicated, both psychologically and legally.

In most cases, the parties to a divorce will be represented by attorneys, and their legal questions will be answered by those people. But knowing a little bit of law before you see an attorney can help you understand the process that is about to so seriously affect you, for example, how long it should take, what will happen, and what factors can simplify or complicate the process.

Finally, as with any other legal service that usually requires the assistance of an attorney, I strongly urge you to shop around before you hire one. Not too long ago I did a report for TV on attorneys' fees. We called nearly 30 attorneys at random from the phone book and asked them all what they would charge for the same basic legal service. The prices ranged from $45 to $700. The moral is simple for standardized legal services, such as a simple divorce: Shop around and compare prices. You may be surprised how much money you can save.

How long do we have to live together
to have a common law marriage?
"One second."

Dear Mr. Alderman:
My "friend" and I have been living together for nearly six years. We are very much in love but just don't want to be married. Last week, one of my friends told me that if we lived together for seven years we would have a common law marriage, whether we wanted it or not. This has us concerned. Should we live apart for a while? Does it matter if we put it in writing that we are not married? What can we do?

You may not have to do anything. Just living together, for any length of time, is not enough to form a common law marriage. To have a common law marriage in Texas you must do three things: You must agree to be married, hold yourself out as married, and live together. Simply living together is not enough. Once you agree you want to be married and hold yourselves out as married (for example, by using the titles Mr. and Mrs.), the moment you live together you are husband and wife under Texas law. On the other hand, if you keep your separate names and let people know you are not married, you can live together forever and probably not have a common law marriage. If you do not want to be considered married, make sure you take all possible steps to maintain your separate identities, and let people know you are not husband and wife. If you decide to marry, I recommend you have a civil or church ceremony just to end any doubts about your relationship.

Is there such a thing as common law divorce?
"Not really."

Dear Mr. Alderman:

I lived with a man for five years. During that time, we probably were a common law husband and wife. We split up about six years ago, and I assumed I was single and free to marry again. Now I am concerned. I thought I heard you say there is no such thing as a common law divorce. Do I have to go to court and get divorced before I remarry?

As I said above, a common law marriage is no different from any other form of marriage. You are married. This means you will have to get a divorce to end the marriage.

There is, however, one new provision in the law that may help some people end their common law marriages. Under the law, if a marriage is not asserted within two years of the date when the parties stopped living together, there is a presumption that there was no marriage. This means the party who wants to assert the marriage after that time has the burden to prove it existed. This change in the law does not appear to help in your case.

If you wish to legally remarry, I suggest you file for divorce.

Can I receive alimony?
"Texas now has limited alimony."

Dear Mr. Alderman:
I have been married more than 15 years. I have just discovered my husband has been seeing another woman. I am pretty sure he is going to ask me for a divorce. I have no interest in continuing this relationship; however, I am afraid of living on my own. I have not worked since we got married, and it will take me some time to find a job. I heard Texas now allows alimony. Is this true? Will I be entitled to it?

Until recently, Texas law did not permit any form of alimony. At the time of a divorce, community property would be divided, and child support could be awarded; however, the court could not order continuing support for an ex-spouse. In 1995 the legislature changed this by enacting a law allowing for post-divorce "maintenance payments."

The new law designates who is eligible for maintenance payments. Rather than try and paraphrase this law, here is what it says:

In a suit for divorce, annulment, to declare a marriage void, or in a proceeding for maintenance in a court with personal jurisdiction over both former spouses following the dissolution of their marriage by a court that lacked personal jurisdiction over an absent spouse, the court may order maintenance for either spouse only if:

(1) the spouse from whom maintenance is sought was convicted of, or received deferred adjudication for, a criminal offense that also constitutes an act of family violence under Section 71.01, Family Code, and the offense occurred:
   (a) within two years before the date on which a suit for dissolution of the marriage was filed; or
   (b) during the pendency of the suit; or
(2) the duration of the marriage was 10 years or longer, the spouse seeking maintenance lacks sufficient property, including property distributed to the spouse under this code, to provide for the spouse's minimum reasonable needs, as limited by Section 3.9605, and the spouse seeking maintenance:
   (a) is unable to support himself or herself through appropriate employment because of an incapacitating physical or mental disability;

(b) is the custodian of a child who requires substantial care and personal supervision because a physical or mental disability makes it necessary, taking into consideration the needs of the child, that the spouse not be employed outside the home; or

(c) cleary lacks earning ability in the labor market adequate to provide support for the spouse's minimum reasonable needs, as limited by Sec. 3.9605.

Once a court determines a person is eligible for maintenance, it must determine the amount and duration of the payments. The court is directed to consider all relevant factors, including:

(1) the financial resources of the spouse seeking maintenance, including the community and separate property and liabilities apportioned to that spouse in the dissolution proceeding, and that spouse's ability to meet his or her needs independently;

(2) the education and employment skills of the spouses and the time necessary to acquire sufficient education or training to enable the spouse seeking maintenance to find appropriate employment, that availability of the education or training, and the feasibility of that education or training;

(3) the duration of the marriage;

(4) the age, employment history, earning ability, and physical and emotional condition of the spouse seeking maintenance;

(5) the ability of the spouse from whom maintenance is sought to meet that spouse's personal needs and to provide periodic child support payments, if applicable, while meeting the personal needs of the spouse seeking maintenance;

(6) acts by either spouse resulting in excessive or abnormal expenditures or destruction, concealment, or fraudulent disposition of community property, joint tenancy, or other property held in common;

(7) the comparative financial resources of the spouses, including medical, retirement, insurance, or other benefits, and the separate property of each spouse;

(8) the contribution by one spouse to the education, training, or increased earning power of the other spouse;

(9) the property brought to the marriage by either spouse;

(10) the contribution of a spouse as homemaker;

(11) any marital misconduct of the spouse seeking maintenance; and

(12) the efforts of the spouse seeking maintenance to pursue available employment counseling as provided by Chapter 304, Labor Code.

Maintenance probably will not be awarded if the person asking for it has not exercised due diligence in seeking employment or developing the skills necessary to become self-sufficient. An exception to this requirement is made for an individual who is physically or mentally incapacitated.

Once maintenance is awarded, it generally may not continue for more than three years. The law directs the court to limit payments to the shortest period of time reasonably necessary for the person seeking maintenance to obtain the necessary employment or training skills. Payments may, however, continue for more than three years if the spouse receiving payment is incapacitated because of physical or mental disability.

Finally, a court may not issue a maintenance order for more than the lesser of $2,500 a month or 20% of the person's average monthly gross income.

Based on what you say in your letter, you should be eligible to receive an award of maintenance. The attorney you hire to assist you with your divorce, however, will be better able to analyze your situation.

My ex-husband was supposed to pay the debts. Now creditors are coming after me. Can they do this? "A divorce decree is just between you and your spouse."

Dear Mr. Alderman:

My husband and I were divorced about a year ago. In our settlement he agreed to pay all the debts, including a mortgage on the house. He paid some of them but has not paid the mortgage. I should also point out that he was given the house and lives there. Now the mortgage company has contacted me and wants me to pay. I sent the company a copy of the divorce decree, but the creditor said it didn't matter. How can this be? I thought my husband was legally obligated to pay? Can the mortgage company really sue me if I don't pay?

Unfortunately, the answer is probably yes. Even though your divorce decree says your husband agrees to pay the mortgage, if he does not, you are still obligated. This would be true of any debt you incurred while you were married.

The reason is that when you incurred the debt, you and your husband entered into a contract with the creditor in which you promised to pay. When you were divorced, you entered into an agreement between you and your husband determining who would pay what. That agreement is not between you and the creditor. In effect, your husband has agreed to pay what you owe the creditor. If he does not, the creditor comes after you, and then you have to go after your ex.

The bottom line is a divorce decree only affects the relationship between the parties to the marriage. It does not release either party from existing obligations. To protect yourself against this, make sure debts are paid in full before the divorce becomes final or get the creditor to agree in writing. If you trust your ex-spouse to pay and he or she does not, you may end up footing the bill.

Is a house owned before marriage community property?
"Probably not in your case."

Dear Mr. Alderman:
Four years before we married, my wife bought a home. A few years after we married, I used $50,000 of my money to pay off the mortgage. We are now divorcing. Is the home community property? Do I have any rights?

The home is not community property. You have a right of reimbursement, however, for the money you paid. In other words, you should be entitled to an additional $50,000 as part of the divorce settlement. For more information about community and separate property, see page 204.

How much child support should I get?
"There is no set amount."

Dear Mr. Alderman:
I have been married seven years. Last month my husband left me. I have decided to file for divorce, and I was wondering how much money I could get my husband to pay for the children. He has a good job and left me with little. I asked him how much he would pay, and he told me, "As little as I can. I will have a new family soon, and I need my money." This doesn't seem fair. I think my children should get paid before his new family. What does the law say?

Until recently no set guidelines for how much money a spouse should pay in child support existed. The judge looked at all the facts of the case and did what he or she thought was fair. In 1989, however, the legislature enacted a law providing guidelines for awarding child support. Although the guidelines are not binding on the court, they are generally followed and should give you a good idea of how much you are entitled to.

What follows is the relevant part of this law. Section numbers refer to the Texas Family Code.

COURT-ORDERED CHILD SUPPORT

Sec. 154.001. SUPPORT OF CHILD. The court may order either or both parents to support a child in the manner specified by the order:

   (1) until the child is 18 years of age or until graduation from high school, whichever occurs later;
   (2) until the child is emancipated through marriage, through removal of the disabilities of minority by court order, or by other operation of law;
   (3) until the death of the child; or
   (4) if the child is disabled as defined in this chapter, for an indefinite period.

Sec. 154.002. CHILD SUPPORT THROUGH HIGH SCHOOL GRADUATION.

   (a) If the child is fully enrolled in an accredited secondary school in a program leading toward a high school diploma, the court may render an original support order or modify an existing order providing child support past the 18th birthday of the child.
   (b) The request for a support order through high school graduation may be filed before or after the child's 18th birthday.
   (c) The order for periodic support may provide that payments continue through the end of the month in which the child graduates.

Sec. 154.010. NO DISCRIMINATION BASED ON MARITAL STATUS OF PARENTS OR SEX. The amount of support ordered for the benefit of a child shall be determined without regard to:

   (1) the sex of the obligor, obligee, or child; or
   (2) the marital status of the parents of the child.

SUBCHAPTER B. COMPUTING NET RESOURCES AVAILABLE
FOR PAYMENT OF CHILD SUPPORT

Sec. 154.061. COMPUTING NET MONTHLY INCOME.

(a) Whenever feasible, gross income should first be computed on an annual basis and then should be recalculated to determine average monthly gross income.

(b) The Title IV-D agency shall annually promulgate tax charts to compute net monthly income, subtracting from gross income social security taxes and federal income tax withholding for a single person claiming one personal exemption and the standard deduction.

Sec. 154.062. NET RESOURCES.

(a) The court shall calculate net resources for the purpose of determining child support liability as provided by this section.

(b) Resources include:

(1) 100% of all wage and salary income and other compensation for personal services (including commissions, overtime pay, tips, and bonuses);

(2) interest, dividends, and royalty income;

(3) self-employment income;

(4) net rental income (defined as rent after deducting operating expenses and mortgage payments, but not including noncash items such as depreciation); and

(5) all other income actually being received, including severance pay, retirement benefits, pensions, trust income, annuities, capital gains, social security benefits, unemployment benefits, disability and workers' compensation benefits, interest income from notes regardless of the source, gifts and prizes, spousal maintenance, and alimony.

(c) Resources do not include:

(1) return of principal or capital;

(2) accounts receivable; or

(3) benefits paid in accordance with aid for families with dependent children.

(d) The court shall deduct the following items from resources to determine the net resources available for child support:

(1) social security taxes;

(2) federal income tax based on the tax rate for a single person claiming one personal exemption and the standard deduction;

(3) union dues; and

(4) expenses for health insurance coverage for the obligor's child.

Sec. 154.063. PARTY TO FURNISH INFORMATION. The court shall require a party to:

(1) furnish information sufficient to accurately identify that party's net resources and ability to pay child support; and

(2) produce copies of income tax returns for the past two years, a financial statement, and current pay stubs.

Sec. 154.064. HEALTH INSURANCE FOR CHILD PRESUMPTIVELY PROVIDED BY OBLIGOR. The guidelines for support of a child are based on the assumption that the court will order the obligor to provide health insurance coverage for the child in addition to the amount of child support calculated in accordance with those guidelines.

Sec. 154.065. SELF-EMPLOYMENT INCOME.

(a) Income from self-employment, whether positive or negative, includes benefits allocated to an individual from a business or undertaking in the form of a proprietorship, partnership, joint venture, close corporation, agency, or independent contractor, less ordinary and necessary expenses required to produce that income.

(b) In its discretion, the court may exclude from self-employment income amounts allowable under federal income tax law as depreciation, tax credits, or any other business expenses shown by the evidence to be inappropriate in making the determination of income available for the purpose of calculating child support.

Sec. 154.066. INTENTIONAL UNEMPLOYMENT OR UNDEREMPLOYMENT. If the actual income of the obligor is significantly less than what the obligor could earn because of intentional unemployment or underemployment, the court may apply the support guidelines to the earning potential of the obligor.

Sec. 154.067. DEEMED INCOME.

(a) When appropriate, in order to determine the net resources available for child support, the court may assign a reasonable amount of deemed income attributable to assets that do not currently produce income. The court shall also consider whether certain property that is not producing income can be liquidated without an unreasonable financial sacrifice because of cyclical or other market conditions. If there is no effective market for the property, the carrying costs of such an investment, including property taxes and note payments, shall be offset against the income attributed to the property.

(b) The court may assign a reasonable amount of deemed income to income-producing assets that a party has voluntarily transferred or on which earnings have intentionally been reduced.

Sec. 154.068. WAGE AND SALARY PRESUMPTION. In the absence of evidence of the wage and salary income of a party, the court shall presume that the party has wages or salary equal to the federal minimum wage for a 40-hour week.

Sec. 154.069. NET RESOURCES OF SPOUSE.

(a) The court may not add any portion of the net resources of a spouse to the net resources of an obligor or obligee in order to calculate the amount of child support to be ordered.

(b) The court may not subtract the needs of a spouse, or of a dependent of a spouse, from the net resources of the obligor or obligee.

SUBCHAPTER C. CHILD SUPPORT GUIDELINES

Sec. 154.121. GUIDELINES FOR THE SUPPORT OF A CHILD. The child support guidelines in this subchapter are intended to guide the court in determining an equitable amount of child support.

Sec. 154.122. APPLICATION OF GUIDELINES REBUTTABLY PRESUMED IN BEST INTEREST OF CHILD.

(a) The amount of a periodic child support payment established by the child support guidelines in effect in this state at the time of the hearing is presumed to be reasonable, and an order of support conforming to the guidelines is presumed to be in the best interest of the child.

(b) A court may determine that the application of the guidelines would be unjust or inappropriate under the circumstances.

Sec. 154.123. ADDITIONAL FACTORS FOR COURT TO CONSIDER.

(a) The court may order periodic child support payments in an amount other than that established by the guidelines if the evidence rebuts the presumption that application of the guidelines is in the best interest of the child and justifies a variance from the guidelines.

(b) In determining whether application of the guidelines would be unjust or inappropriate under the circumstances, the court shall consider evidence of all relevant factors, including:

(1) the age and needs of the child;

(2) the ability of the parents to contribute to the support of the child;

(3) any financial resources available for the support of the child;

(4) the amount of time of possession of and access to a child;

(5) the amount of the obligee's net resources, including the earning potential of the obligee if the actual income of the obligee is significantly less than what the obligee could earn because the obligee is intentionally unemployed or underemployed and including an increase or decrease in the income of the obligee or income that may be attributed to the property and assets of the obligee;

(6) child care expenses incurred by either party in order to maintain gainful employment;

(7) whether either party has the managing conservatorship or actual physical custody of another child;

(8) the amount of alimony or spousal maintenance actually and currently being paid or received by a party;

(9) the expenses for a son or daughter for education beyond secondary school;

(10) whether the obligor or obligee has an automobile, housing, or other benefits furnished by his or her employer, another person, or a business entity;

(11) the amount of other deductions from the wage or salary income and from other compensation for personal services of the parties;

(12) provision for health care insurance and payment of uninsured medical expenses;

(13) special or extraordinary educational, health care, or other expenses of the parties or of the child;

(14) the cost of travel in order to exercise possession of and access to a child;

(15) positive or negative cash flow from any real and personal property and assets, including a business and investments;

(16) debts or debt service assumed by either party; and

(17) any other reason consistent with the best interest of the child, taking into consideration the circumstances of the parents.

Sec. 154.125. APPLICATION OF GUIDELINES TO NET RESOURCES OF $6,000 OR LESS.

(a) The guidelines for the support of a child in this section are specifically designed to apply to situations in which the obligor's monthly net resources are $6,000 or less.

(b) If the obligor's monthly net resources are $6,000 or less, the court shall presumptively apply the following schedule in rendering the child support order:

CHILD SUPPORT GUIDELINES
BASED ON THE MONTHLY NET RESOURCES OF THE OBLIGOR

1 child	20% of obligor's net resources
2 children	25% of obligor's net resources
3 children	30% of obligor's net resources
4 children	35% of obligor's net resources
5 children	40% of obligor's net resources
6+ children	Not less than the amount for 5 children

Sec. 154.126. APPLICATION OF GUIDELINES TO NET RESOURCES OF MORE THAN $6,000 MONTHLY.

(a) If the obligor's net resources exceed $6,000 per month, the court shall presumptively apply the percentage guidelines to the first $6,000 of the obligor's net resources. Without further reference to the percentage recommended by these guidelines, the court may order additional amounts of child support as appropriate, depending on the income of the parties and the proven needs of the child.

(b) The proper calculation of a child support order that exceeds the presumptive amount established for the first $6,000 of the obligor's net resources requires that the entire amount of the presumptive award be subtracted from the proven total needs of the child. After the presumptive award is subtracted, the court shall allocate between the parties the responsibility to meet the additional needs of the child according to the circumstances of the parties. However, in no event may the obligor be required to pay more child support than the greater of the presumptive amount or the amount equal to 100% of the proven needs of the child.

Sec. 154.127. PARTIAL TERMINATION OF SUPPORT OBLIGATION. A child support order for more than one child shall provide that, on the termination of support for a child, the level of support for the remaining child or children is in accordance with the child support guidelines.

Sec. 154.183. HEALTH INSURANCE ADDITIONAL SUPPORT DUTY OF OBLIGOR.

(a) An amount that an obligor is required to pay for health insurance for the child:

(1) is in addition to the amount that the obligor is required to pay for child support under the guidelines for child support;

(2) is a child support obligation; and

(3) may be enforced as a child support obligation.

(b) If the court finds and states in the child support order that the obligee will maintain health insurance coverage for the child at the obligee's expense, the court may increase the amount of child support to be paid by the obligor in an amount not exceeding the total expense to the obligee for maintaining health insurance coverage.

(c) As additional child support, the court shall allocate between the parties, according to their circumstances, the reasonable and necessary health care expenses of a child that are not reimbursed by health insurance.

Do I need an attorney to file for divorce?
"No, but it sure can make life simpler."

Dear Mr. Alderman:

My wife and I have decided brief attempt at marriage isn't going to work. We know Texas is a "no-fault" divorce state, so there wouldn't be any trouble getting a divorce, but we don't have a lot of extra money and can't afford to spend a fortune on attorneys' fees. We have no children and agree on how everything should be split. Is it legal to do your own divorce, and do you think we could handle it ourselves?

Anyone can represent themselves in court. Whether you should do it is another question. Even though a simple divorce is not complicated, any attempt at practicing law by a layperson can be difficult, and there are many traps for the amateur to fall into. There are, however, several books on the market that will take you step-by-step through the divorce. You may want to look at them and see if you think you could do it.

As far as I am concerned, a better approach is to shop around and find an attorney who will handle your divorce inexpensively. Many competent attorneys will do a simple divorce for a few hundred dollars in attorneys' fees. I realize this is still more than it will cost to just buy the book and do it yourself, but with an attorney you are assured it will be done properly, and you may save enough time to make it worth your while. Again, the important thing is to shop around and get prices from several lawyers before you make a selection.

Do I have to live in Texas to get divorced there?
"Yes!"

Dear Mr. Alderman:
I am in the process of relocating to Texas. I am coming without my wife. We have decided to get a divorce, but neither of us has seen a lawyer or filed any papers. I will not live in Texas until two months from now, but I would like to get things going on the divorce. Can I file in Texas now?

No. To file for divorce, the court you file with has to have what is called "jurisdiction." This is a legal term meaning the court has the power to hear the case and make a decision. In the case of a divorce, a court only has jurisdiction if you have been a domiciliary of this state for the preceding six months and a resident of the county where you file for the preceding 90 days. In other words, if you want to get a divorce in Texas you will have to wait until you have made Texas your permanent home for six months. Then you can file where you have lived for the past 90 days. If you want a divorce sooner than that, you will probably have to file in the state where you presently live.

How can I get my husband to pay child support?
"He may be thrown in jail."

Dear Mr. Alderman:
I have been divorced for five years. I have two children, ages 7 and 9. My ex-husband is supposed to pay child support each month, but for the last three months he has not paid. He says he has too many other bills and can't afford it. I know he has other obligations, but I need the money to support the kids. What can I do?

Unlike most debts, child support obligations are very enforceable in Texas. If a person doesn't pay as ordered, his wages can be garnisheed (taken by the court), or in some cases, he can even be thrown in jail until he pays. All this, however, will have to be done through the courts, usually with the assistance of an attorney.

You may want to talk with the attorney who handled your divorce and ask him or her for assistance. Another alternative is to contact the Child Support Enforcement Division of the Texas Attorney General's Office, 1-800-252-8011. This division exists to assist in the enforcement of child support obligations. Usually, once your ex-husband understands the consequences of not paying, he will begin to do so.

What must I show to get a divorce?
"Just that you don't get along."

Dear Mr. Alderman:

My husband and I have had problems for several years. We seem to do nothing but fight. Finally, we decided we just are not right for each other and that we should get a divorce. No one in my family has ever been divorced, and we don't know much about it. Our first question is, what do we have to prove to end our marriage? Do I have to say he committed adultery or beat me?

Not any more. It used to be that to get a divorce it was necessary to show cruelty, adultery, abandonment, or that you had lived apart for three years. This is no longer necessary. The law now allows the court to grant a divorce if you show:

> that the marriage has become insupportable because of discord or conflict of personalities that destroys the legitimate ends of the marriage relationship and prevents any reasonable expectations of reconciliation.

What this legalese means is that Texas is now a no-fault divorce state. You can get a divorce simply by showing that you no longer get along. It is not necessary to prove either party did anything wrong or to explain why you can't remain married. In fact, if one party doesn't want to be married and the other does, this difference alone would be enough for the court to grant the divorce.

I just got divorced. When can I remarry?
"In 30 days."

Dear Mr. Alderman:

My divorce was finalized last year. My ex-husband and I have been living apart for more than two years, and I have been seeing another man for almost a year. He wants to marry me but says we have to wait a year after the divorce. I want to get married right now. Do I have to wait a year?

No. Under Texas law you may remarry 30 days after the day your divorce is decreed. In fact, in some cases you can marry even sooner. For example, if you wanted to remarry your ex-husband there is no waiting period. Also, in special circumstances a court may waive the 30 days prohibition if requested. In other words, if he really wants to marry you, the most you should have to wait is 30 days.

How do I find my adopted child?
"There may be help available if he wants to be found."

Dear Mr. Alderman:
Many years ago I placed my son for adoption. I have no regrets and still believe it was the right thing to do. Now, however, I am curious to know how things turned out and what kind of person he is. Is there any way for me to find out who adopted my son?

Although it is generally difficult to find out who adopted your child, it may be possible if the child also wants to contact you. The Texas Department of Protective and Regulatory Services maintains a Voluntary Adoption Registry. This is a system that allows adopted children, birth parents, and biological siblings to locate each other if they wish. To get more information about the registry, contact:

Central Adoption Registry
Texas Department of Protective and Regulatory Services
701 W. 51st St.
Austin, Texas 78714-9030
(512) 834-4484

What name can I use after the divorce?
"This must be determined at the time of the divorce."

Dear Mr. Alderman:
I was divorced more than a year ago, and now I have decided I want to start using my maiden name again. Can I just do it?

Nike's instructions notwithstanding, you cannot just do it. Under the law in Texas, a woman must legally change her name if she wishes to use her maiden name after a divorce. This is usually done as part of the divorce proceedings. In your case, however, it will be necessary to file a separate pleading to legally change your name.

I suggest you either contact some attorneys to see what they will charge for a name change or file the petition yourself. If you want to do it yourself, check with your local bookstore or law library to see if you can find the proper forms. If you use an attorney, shop around for the best price. This routine legal service should not be expensive. A few phone calls may save you a lot of money.

How can I collect child support?
"You can take a driver's license away."

Dear Mr. Alderman:
Is it true I can have my ex-husband's driver's license taken away if he does not pay child support?

Yes. Under a new law, a person who doesn't pay child support may lose a professional license, such as a license to practice law or medicine, or a driver's license. I should point out that wage garnishment also may be used to enforce a child support obligation.

CHAPTER EIGHT

Door-to-Door Sales

TRADITIONALLY, few salespeople are as persuasive as those who travel door-to-door. We have all heard stories of the person who bought the high-priced vacuum cleaner or the set of encyclopedias from the smooth-talking, fast-moving traveling salesman only to discover later that the price was too high or the goods unnecessary.

But door-to-door selling does provide a good alternative for people who are unable to go out and shop or who, because of their obligations at home, must remain at home during the day. It is convenient and practical for many of us to shop at home.

So how do we balance the problems of high-pressure selling with the convenience of home sales? The answer reached by both Congress and the Texas Legislature is the same: Pass a law that requires that door-to-door salespeople give you a chance to change your mind. In Texas this law is called the **Home Solicitation Sales Act.**

**The books seemed like a good idea,
but now I don't want them . . . Help!
"Door-to-door sales give you time to change your mind."**

Dear Mr. Alderman:
The other day I was sitting at home when the doorbell rang. A nice-looking man, well dressed, asked if he could come in and talk to me about a program that could help my kids in school. I said OK, and after about an hour I agreed to buy the complete set of books. He promised it would help my kids in school and that it was approved by the school board. Right after he left I talked with my neighbor and found out what he said was true, but the school library would loan the books to my kids for free. I really don't want the books. What can I do? He was so nice and persuasive that I couldn't say no. I guess I learned a lesson: Don't talk to door-to-door salesmen.

You may not have learned the lesson you think. The lesson you should have learned is *under the law you have three days to change your mind and get out of a contract entered into in your home.* Both Texas and federal law provides that a door-to-door merchant must give you a three-day cooling-off period to change your mind. Based on what you say in your letter, I believe the salesman has violated the law; you should be able to cancel the sale and not have to pay.

So what should you do? If you paid cash you may have a problem. Try to get in touch with the company and demand your money back. If you don't get it back, you can go to small claims court. If you paid by check, go to the bank at once and stop payment. If the check has already been cashed, you are in the same position as if you paid cash. If you used a credit card, contact the credit card company, tell them you are not paying the bill, and explain why. The credit card company stands in the shoes of the merchant and can't collect because the merchant has violated the law.

If you don't get your money back, contact the district attorney's office and the attorney general's office and report the company and the salesperson. You can also take steps to recover your money, and if you are successful in court you can recover under the Deceptive Trade Practices Act, because any violation of the Home Solicitation Sales Act is automatically a violation of the Deceptive Trade Practices Act. Look over Chapter Ten, and you will see how to get substantial damages.

Be careful when dealing with door-to-door salesmen, and don't pay cash or with a check unless you are absolutely sure you want the goods. And remember, under the law all door-to-door contracts must have the following printed on them:

NOTICE OF CANCELLATION

<u>(enter date of transaction)</u>

You may cancel this transaction without any penalty or obligation within three business days from the above date.

If you cancel, any property traded in, any payments made by you under the contract or sale, and any negotiable instrument executed by you will be returned within 10 business days after receipt by the merchant of your cancellation notice, and any security interest arising out of the transaction will be canceled.

(notice continued on next page)

(notice continued from previous page)

If you cancel, you must make available to the merchant at your residence, in substantially as good condition as when received, any goods delivered to you under this contract or sale; or you may if you wish, comply with the instructions of the merchant regarding the return shipment of the goods at the merchant's expense and risk.

If you do not agree to return the goods to the merchant or if the merchant does not pick them up within 20 days of the date of your notice of cancellation, you may retain or dispose of the goods without any further obligation.

To cancel this transaction, mail or deliver a signed and dated copy of this cancellation notice or any other written notice, or send a telegram to (<u>Name of merchant</u>) at (<u>Address of merchant's place of business</u>) not later than midnight of (<u>Date</u>).

I hereby cancel this transaction.

(<u>Date</u>)

(<u>Buyer's signature</u>)

CHAPTER NINE

Employment

FOR most of us nothing is more important to our economic well-being than keeping a job. Those of you who have lost jobs know how devastating it is, and those who have not can imagine what it would be like. Unfortunately, times have been hard in Texas lately, and more and more people have begun to write with questions about their jobs, such as "When and how can I be fired?" and "What are my rights if I am fired?" Unfortunately, as you will see, Texas is not an employee state.

I don't have a contract. When can I be fired?
"Probably whenever the boss wants."

Dear Mr. Alderman:

I have worked at the same job for nearly two years. I have never had a contract and really didn't think I needed one. It is a small company, and everyone has always trusted everyone else to be fair. Recently, one of my friends came into work and was told, "Go home. You're fired." As far as I know he was doing a good job, and there was no reason to fire him. I think the boss just decided the company could get along without him. Now I am afraid I am next. What are my rights? Am I safe as long as I do my job well and don't violate any company rules?

Not necessarily. Texas is basically an "employment-at-will" state. This means you can be fired at will and you can quit at will. Unless you have a contract or a union agreement, the company can fire you with no notice, for no reason at all. The other side of that coin is you can quit the same way. Although many states have changed this doctrine, the employment-at-will doctrine governs in Texas, at least for now. I should point out, though, this rule is not absolute. The Texas Supreme Court has found at least one exception (you can't be fired for failing to perform an illegal act), and it may be willing to find others. Also, a contract may be found many ways, and you may have an implied or oral contract with the company that would prohibit it from firing you without cause. Generally, however, you can be fired just because the company doesn't want you there.

One final point must be mentioned. In all cases, laws can change, and it is important that you make sure the advice I give you is up to date. In the case of employment law, though, it is even more important you do so because this is a rapidly changing area of law. If a problem arises, you may want to contact an attorney to make sure there hasn't been a recent development in this area.

I think I was fired because of my age. Isn't there a law?
"The law prohibits certain discrimination."

Dear Mr. Alderman:

I am 62 years old, and while I don't think that is very old, my boss does. She is only 34 and thinks I am too old to be dealing with customers. She recently told me to work in the stock room or quit. I do my job well, and the only reason she wants me in the back is because of her image of the store. Is this legal? I have worked hard all my life, and it doesn't seem fair.

It doesn't seem fair, and it doesn't seem legal. Under federal law it is illegal to discriminate on the basis of age against anyone past the age of 39. The major exception to this is when the employer can establish that for the particular task age is a legitimate qualification. For you, it doesn't sound like that is the case.

If you feel you are being discriminated against because of your age, contact the Equal Employment Opportunity Commission, (800) 669-3362.

Can I be forced to take a drug test?
"Probably."

Dear Mr. Alderman:

I work at a small company that manufactures parts used in engines. My job is to box the finished product, and in the six years I have worked here I have never had any problems performing my job well. I know this may not sound too good, but the job is so simple, I could do it in my sleep or drunk (which I may have been on occasion). Last week the company said everyone had to take a drug test. If we refused we would be fired. Is this legal? I don't use drugs, but it doesn't seem fair. Don't I have some kind of constitutional right not to have to take this test?

As of right now, a private employer in Texas probably has the right to force employees to take a drug test and to fire them if they don't. This is the result of the employment-at-will doctrine discussed in the first letter. Since you can be fired without a reason, it follows that you can also be fired for nearly any reason—including your refusal to take the test. This issue is in the courts, however, and Congress is also looking at preventing this kind of drug testing. But as of right now, you may want to take the test or risk losing your job.

The same rule would not apply, however, if you were employed by a public employer, such as the post office or state motor vehicle department. In the case of a public or governmental employer, the constitutional right of privacy protects you. Drug testing can usually only be done under certain limited circumstances. Without getting too detailed, governmental entities may only drug test if they can justify who is going to be tested (e.g., someone who will endanger himself or others if impaired), when the testing is done (e.g., there was a reasonable suspicion the person may have been using drugs), how the tests were performed (e.g., the most accurate test was used), and what was done with the result (e.g., testing will be authorized more readily if the person is rehabilitated, not fired).

Can I be forced to take a lie detector test?
"Probably not."

Dear Mr. Alderman:

I recently applied for a job and was asked to take a lie detector test. I refused and was told to look elsewhere. I don't have anything to hide, but I just don't trust those things. Is this a common practice? Do I have any legal rights?

What happened to you is probably illegal. Under a recent federal law, it is basically illegal for an employer to ask an employee or prospective employee to take a lie detector test. It is also illegal to refuse to hire or fire someone because he or she refused to take the test. The law provides both criminal and civil penalties for an employer who violates the law.

There is, however, a limited exception to this law. An employee may be asked to submit to a lie detector test if it is part of an ongoing investigation regarding economic loss or theft to the employer. If the employer has a reasonable suspicion that an employee was involved, a lie detector test may be given. The only other exception is with respect to government entities. They are not subject to this law.

This law is enforced by the secretary of labor and can be used by individuals in private lawsuits. I suggest you either file a complaint with the secretary of labor's office or consider a private lawsuit if you feel you have been harmed as a result of what may be an illegal practice.

**The union negotiates my contract, but I am not a member.
Isn't Texas a right-to-work state?
"It is, but the union still negotiates your contract."**

Dear Mr. Alderman:

I work for a medium-size company in West Texas. About two years ago, there was a vote in the company about joining a union. I voted no and did not join. Most of the employees voted yes. I was told that because Texas is a right-to-work state, I would not have to join the union and would not have to pay dues.

Last week, the union, which I did not join, voted to reduce the number of overtime hours employees are allowed to work. The company has agreed. Now, I am losing money. How can this happen? How can a union I don't even belong to make contracts for me? What happened to my right to work?

In a right-to-work state, an employee does not have to join a union or pay union dues as a condition of employment. "Right-to-work" means the right to work without joining a union. Nevertheless, if a majority of the employees vote to be represented by a union, then the union is the exclusive bargaining representative of all the employees, even those employees who are not members or who voted against union representation. Likewise, the union has a duty to represent, in contract negotiations and grievances, the interests of all employees. This is sometimes referred to as "majority rule with minority rights." The bottom line is the union negotiates for you even though you are not a member.

I work with chemicals. Do I have a right to know what they are?
"Probably yes."

Dear Mr. Alderman:

I work for a small company that cleans ships. In the course of my employment I use a chemical supplied to me in an unmarked drum. I have been told to always wear gloves and to be careful not to spill it on myself.

I never really thought about what was in the drum until I went to the doctor and he asked if I had been working with any dangerous chemicals. I told him I didn't know, and he said, "Find out." When I asked my boss what was in the drum he said, "Don't worry. Just wear gloves and be careful." I tried to push for an answer, but he got mad. How can I find out what is in the drum? I am afraid I will be fired if I insist on knowing.

Under the **Occupational Safety Health Act (OSHA)** an employer has a duty to disclose to employees if they are working with hazardous chemicals. This law, enforced by the Department of Labor, has a list of dangerous chemicals, and if you are working with any of these chemicals, you must be told. On the other hand, if the substance you are working with is not on the list, your employer has no duty to tell you.

Your employer's actions in not telling you indicate one of two things. Either the chemical you are working with is not on the list and is probably not dangerous, or he is violating the law. If you are still concerned, I suggest you contact the Department of Labor and ask for an investigation. You also should know that the law protects you if you are fired for trying to find out. An employer can't just fire employees who insist on their legal rights.

I just quit. Can my former boss stop me from going into
business for myself?
"Perhaps."

Dear Mr. Alderman:

For the past five years, I have been in the sales business. I am no longer satisfied working for a large company and want to work for a smaller one, where I have more of a future. Because my background

*is basically in one field, the companies I am interested in are all in
competition with my present employer.*

*I have been told that if I leave, I will not be able to work for any
competing company in the southwestern states. My employer told me
my contract has a covenant-not-to-compete clause that prevents me
from working for someone else. Can this be true? I thought I had the
right to work for whomever I wanted. Can I be prevented from
earning a living?*

I cannot give you a specific answer to your question because it will
depend on what your contract says and all the facts surrounding your
employment. I can tell you there are such things as covenants not to compete, and they are enforceable.

Under Texas law, an employer has the right to enter into an agreement
with an employee that prevents the employee from competing with the
employer after the employee terminates employment. Because of the
harshness of such clauses, they are only enforceable if they are reasonable. This means the geographical area and scope of the limitation must
not be overbroad. The test is a balance between the employer's right to
be protected against unreasonable competition from a former employee
and the employee's right to work. Based on what you say in your letter,
the clause may be unreasonable because it prohibits you from working
within a very broad geographic area. Usually, the limited area is much
smaller. For the clause to be enforceable, your employer would also have
to show that, due to the nature of the business and the knowledge you
obtained while working for the employer, the restriction is reasonable. If
a lawsuit were to develop, the court would have the right to limit the
clause to a reasonable geographic area.

Generally, the courts do not favor covenants not to compete. They do,
however, serve a legitimate purpose when applied to situations in which
employees receive special training and knowledge that could be used in a
competitive way against the employer. In these cases, the law enforces
such agreements as long as they are reasonable.

Am I entitled to a leave if I have a child?
"You may be."

Dear Mr. Alderman:
*I am three months pregnant. I recently told my employer I would
need some time off when the child was born. He told me I could have*

a few weeks maximum. I thought it was the law that I had to be given three months of leave?

Effective August 5, 1993, the **Family and Medical Leave Act** generally provides that eligible employees may take family or medical leave for up to 12 weeks during any 12-month period. Unpaid leave may be taken for any of the following reasons: (1) birth of a child; (2) adoption of a child or placement of a foster child; (3) to care for a child, spouse, or parent with a serious health condition; or (4) the employee's own serious health condition. Upon termination of the leave, you must be reinstated to the same or an equivalent position. Your employer must also maintain health coverage during the leave period, just as though you had continued working.

To be eligible to take a leave, you must satisfy two requirements. First, you must have been employed for at least one year. Second, you must have worked at least 1,250 hours during the previous 12-month period. In other words, even some part-time employees are protected by this law.

This law, however, does not apply to all employers. Because of the burden this law could place on small employers, it is limited to larger employers. The law applies only to employers with 50 or more employees for each working day during 20 or more workweeks in the current or preceding calendar year. Both part-time and full-time employees count for purposes of meeting this requirement.

If you think you are protected by this law, you should speak with your employer. If you still cannot resolve the problem, you can either consult a private attorney about a civil lawsuit or complain to the secretary of labor. This is the government office that enforces the Family and Medical Leave Act.

Can my company require a see-through purse?
"Probably."

Dear Mr. Alderman:
My employer requires that employees carry plastic see-through bags as purses. Is this legal? I do not like everyone knowing what I have in my purse.

Under the law, employers generally may impose whatever restrictions they want on employees. I do not see anything illegal about see-through purses. While you and I may not agree with the methodology, your employer appears concerned with employee theft. Although the law may give your employer the right to require see-through purses, your right as an employee is to find employment elsewhere.

Do I have to wear a funny uniform?
"You have to if you want to keep your job."

Dear Mr. Alderman:
I work for a company that requires me to wear a funny-looking uniform. I know it is important for workers to be neat and tidy, but can I be forced to wear a silly uniform?

Unfortunately for you, the answer is yes. A company has the right to require employees to wear whatever uniforms it wants. You, of course, also have the right to quit and go to work for whomever you want.

Can my company tell me when to take my vacation?
"Yes."

Dear Mr. Alderman:
I work for a company that forces all of its employees to take vacations when the company wants, not when we want. Can it do this?

The company can do this unless you have a contract saying it cannot. Under the law, a company does not have to give employees vacation time. Once the company decides to do so, it will be governed by whatever agreement it has with the employees. If when you were hired you were told vacations could be taken anytime or if the employee handbook states so, you would have this right under your contract with the company. On the other hand, if this has been the policy from the time you were hired, there probably is nothing you can do.

Do I have free speech rights at work?
"Yes, but you still may be fired."

Dear Mr. Alderman:

I was recently fired for simply speaking my mind at work. How can this happen in this country? Whatever happened to the right of free speech? Can I sue my employer?

Unfortunately for you, the right of speech does not give you the right to say whatever you want at work. The Constitution's right of free speech applies to the government's attempt to restrict an individual's speech. It does not have anything to do with a private employer's right to fire an employee.

For example, if the government tried to pass a law that said you could not express your opinion on the war in Bosnia, it would be an unconstitutional restriction on free speech. On the other hand, a private employer can have a policy that employees will not discuss the war in the office. If you were to violate this policy, you could be fired.

Can my employer deduct from my check?
"Probably not."

Dear Mr. Alderman:

My employer recently deducted $10 from my paycheck because I didn't follow one of his rules. I know I should follow rules, but I don't think it is fair to take money from my paycheck without warning. Is this legal?

No. Under the law, employers generally do not have the right to deduct money from your paycheck. An employer may deduct from an employee's wages only if the employer

is ordered to do so by a court;

is authorized to do so by law; or

has written authorization from the employee.

Based on what you say in your letter, none of these three events occurred. This means your employer had no right to penalize you in this manner. I suggest you speak with your employer about paying you the wages you are owed. You also may want to speak with the Texas Employment Commission, the agency that enforces the **Texas Payday Law.** You can contact the commission at (800) TEC-WAGE. For more information about the Texas Payday Law ask for "An Employer's Survival Guide to the Texas Payday Law."

Finally, I should point out that even if an employer has the right under state law to deduct from a paycheck, he may not do so if it reduces an employee's pay below minimum wage.

Can I be required to take a blood test?
"Probably not."

Dear Mr. Alderman:
Can my employer require me to take an HIV blood test?

Generally, no. Texas employers usually cannot require the test. If, however, the employer can show that knowledge of the employee's HIV status is related to the employee's job performance, the employer may be able to require the test. The employer must show, however, there is a reasonable basis for believing that no HIV-positive person could perform the job with safety or efficiency.

CHAPTER TEN

False & Deceptive Acts

TEXAS has a law that every consumer should know by name, **The Texas Deceptive Trade Practices Act.** This is one of the most powerful consumer protection laws in the country. But as you will see, it covers a lot more than you might think. Nearly every transaction you make, from buying a house to selling a toaster at a garage sale, falls within the scope of this law.

The Deceptive Trade Practices Act lists 25 things considered false, misleading, or deceptive. And unlawful. Basically, anything someone does that has the potential to deceive is prohibited by the law; and more importantly, the law is a no-fault statute.

No-fault means that in most cases you don't have to intend to violate the law—or even know you are violating the law—to be held responsible. For example, someone thinks a car is in excellent shape and, without any intent to hurt you, says, "This car is in excellent condition." If it turns out the car was in poor condition, the seller is liable under this law. It doesn't matter that the seller had no idea there was anything wrong with the car.

What is the Deceptive Trade Practices Act?
"The consumer's best friend."

Dear Mr. Alderman:
I have watched you on television, and you always talk about some great law that helps consumers. I think it is a deceptive practices law. Could you please tell me about this law and what it covers?

The Texas Deceptive Trade Practices Act is one of the most powerful consumer protection laws in the country. *Anyone who violates the Deceptive Trade Practices Act may be liable for up to three times your damages plus all your court costs and attorneys' fees.* The following list identifies all the things made unlawful under this law. The list may sound a bit technical, but that is merely because I have used the same language the law uses.

1. Passing of goods or services as those of another;
2. Causing confusion or misunderstanding as to the source, sponsorship, approval, or certification of goods or services;
3. Causing confusion or misunderstanding as to affiliation, connection or association with, or certification by another;
4. Using deceptive representations or designations of geographic origin in connection with goods or services;
5. Representing that goods or services have sponsorship, approval, characteristics, ingredients, uses, benefits, or quantities that they do not have, or that a person has a sponsorship, approval, status, affiliation, or connection that he does not;
6. Representing that goods are original or new if they are deteriorated, reconditioned, reclaimed, used, or second-hand;
7. Representing that goods or services are of a particular standard, quality, or grade, or that goods are of a particular style or model, if they are of another;
8. Disparaging the goods, services, or business of another by false or misleading representation of facts;
9. Advertising goods or services with intent not to sell them as advertised;
10. Advertising goods or services with intent not to supply a reasonable, expectable public demand, unless the advertisements disclosed a limitation of quantity;
11. Making false or misleading statements of fact concerning the reasons for, existence of, or amount of price reductions;
12. Representing that an agreement confers or involves rights, remedies, or obligations that it does not have or involve, or that are prohibited by law;
13. Knowingly making false or misleading statements of fact concerning the need for parts, replacement, or repair service;
14. Misrepresenting the authority of a salesman, representative, or agent to negotiate the final terms of a consumer transaction;
15. Basing a charge for the repair of any item, in whole or in part, on a guaranty or warranty instead of on the value of the actual repairs made, or work to be performed on the item, without stating, separately, the charges for the work and the charge for the warranty or guaranty, if any;

16. Disconnecting, turning back, or resetting the odometer of any motor vehicle so as to reduce the number of miles indicated on the odometer gauge;

17. Advertising any sale by fraudulently representing that a person is going out of business;

18. Using or employing a chain-referral sales plan in connection with the sale or offer to sell of goods, merchandise, or anything of value which uses the sale's technique, plan, arrangement, or agreement in which the buyer or prospective buyer is offered the opportunity to purchase merchandise or goods and, in connection with the purchase, receives the seller's promise or representation that the buyer shall have the right to receive compensation or consideration, in any form, for furnishing to the seller the names of other prospective buyers, if receipt of the compensation or consideration is contingent upon the occurrence of an event subsequent to the time the buyer purchases the merchandise or goods;

19. Representing that a guaranty or warranty confers or involves rights or remedies, which it does not have or involve, provided, however, that nothing in this subchapter shall be construed to expand the implied warranty of merchantability, as defined in Sections 2.314 through 2.318 of the Business & Commerce Code to involve obligations in excess of those which are appropriate to the goods;

20. Promoting a pyramid scheme;

21. Representing that work or services have been performed on, or parts replaced in, goods when the work or services were not performed or the parts not replaced;

22. Filing suit, founded upon a written contractual obligation of and signed by the defendant, to pay money arising out of or based on a consumer transaction for goods, services, loans, or extensions of credit intended primarily for personal, family, household, or agricultural use in any county other than in the county in which the defendant resides at the time of the commencement of the action or in the county in which the defendant in fact signed the contract; provided, however, that a violation of this subsection shall not occur where it is shown by the person filing such suit he neither knew nor had reason to know that the county in which such suit was filed was neither the county in which the defendant resides at the commencement of the suit, nor the county in which the defendant in fact signed the contract;

23. The failure to disclose information concerning goods or services that was known at the time of the transaction if such failure to disclose such information was intended to induce the consumer into a transaction into which the consumer would not have entered had the information been disclosed;

24. Using the terms "incorporation," "incorporated," or an abbreviation of either of these terms in the name of a business entity that is not incorporated under the [laws of a state];

25. Taking advantage of a disaster declared by the governor, by: (a) selling or leasing fuel, food, medicine, or another necessity at an exorbitant or excessive price; or (b) demanding an exorbitant or excessive price in connection with the sale or lease of fuel, food, medicine, or another necessity.

As stated before—anyone who does any of these 25 things has violated the law, and you may have the right to recover substantial damages. But don't count on having to sue everyone. Once they know you know about this law, you will be amazed how cooperative some folks can become— and how quickly you can settle your dispute.

To find out who the law applies to and how to use it, read on.

Who can use the Deceptive Trade Practices Act? "Nearly everyone."

Dear Mr. Alderman:

I own a small business called Bob's Repair Shop. I run the business part time out of my garage, repairing lawnmower motors and other small engines. The other day I bought some replacement parts from a dealer who told me the parts were as good as the ones I usually buy. They weren't . . . and as a result, three engines I fixed needed extensive repairs. I believe what the salesman told me wasn't true— the parts were nowhere near good as new. I want to know: Can I use the Deceptive Trade Practices Act to sue?

You surely can! The act applies to any "consumer," and the term is defined to include any individual, partnership, corporation, or governmental entity. The only exception is a business consumer with more than $25 million in assets. I assume from your letter that you are running your business as a sole proprietorship, and therefore, you would sue as an individual. If it is a partnership or corporation, you can still use this law, but you will have to sue in the name of your business.

The other requirement of the law is you must have purchased (or tried to purchase) goods or services. This obviously applies to you—as you bought parts from the dealer. About the only time the law doesn't apply is when someone makes representations in connection with free gifts. For example: If the local burger restaurant had a promotion and promised you could win a new car, free, and that car was, in fact, not new, you could not sue under this law because you did not try to purchase the car—it was a gift.

Depending on how much money is involved, you may not need a lawyer. You can represent yourself in small claims court if your damages are less than $5,000. To find out the procedures you should use to sue under the Deceptive Trade Practices Act, read the next few letters. As you will see, the act is easy to use.

To whom does this act apply?
"Nearly everyone."

Dear Mr. Alderman:

I just bought a stereo for $150 from someone at a garage sale. When I looked at it, the girl told me it was less than a year old and in good condition. It turns out it is three years old and needs a lot of work. Does the Texas law about false statements apply here, and can I get three times my damages?

Under the Texas Deceptive Trade Practices Act, you can sue anyone, including an individual not in business, if he or she violates the law. In your case, making a false representation about the stereo violates the law. If you can prove the statement was made knowingly and was false, you will be entitled to three times your damages. In this case, your damages are the difference between the value of a 1-year-old stereo and a 3-year-old stereo.

The law protects consumers, and this means whenever you sell anything, you must be careful. You may not think about it, but whenever you have a garage sale or place an ad in the paper, you are governed by this law. Unless you are willing to stand by your word, be careful when you say something is in excellent condition or good as new.

Advice: If you are selling something, make sure the buyer knows you are just giving your opinion, unless you are willing to stand by your word.

As the seller in the next letter discovers, you may be in trouble—even if you are acting innocently and in good faith.

What if I didn't know it wasn't true?
"Tough luck!"

Dear Mr. Alderman:

I am a geologist. I have never been in the business of selling boats, and I have never sold one before. About one month ago, I decided to sell my small outboard motorboat. I took it to my mechanic, who said he would put the engine in excellent shape. I paid him $500, and he told me it was "good as new." I put the boat, with the engine, in my front yard with a For Sale sign. Someone I didn't know stopped and asked me about it. I told him the motor was in "excellent condition," "perfect condition," and "just like new." As far as I knew, these statements were true. What I didn't know was my mechanic did not do the work. The buyer has now written me a letter telling me he wants $450 (the cost of having the engine repaired). He says unless I pay he is going to sue me under the Deceptive Trade Practices Act and may recover three times the $450. What should I do? Does this law apply to me?

The law applies to anyone who sells goods or services. This includes you—even though you are not in business. The Texas Deceptive Trade Practices Act is very broad. It protects consumers regardless of who deceives them.

The law is clear that you do not have to intend to deceive or trick someone. Your honesty or good faith does not matter. The law simply states it is unlawful to misrepresent the nature of goods. You stated that the boat engine was in excellent condition, and it wasn't. That violates the act. The buyer will be entitled to three times his damages, however, only if he shows you made the misrepresentation knowingly.

The best advice I can give you is try to settle this with the buyer. Then contact the mechanic and tell him you expect a reimbursement. If he refuses, you have a claim against him under the Deceptive Trade Practices Act. Next time, be careful.

Remember: Whenever you sell anything, you are responsible for whatever you say. If you are not sure, don't say it, or make it clear that it is just your opinion.

Is there a law regarding construction defects?
"Yes, and it preempts the Deceptive Trade Practices Act."

Dear Mr. Alderman:
I am a small independent contractor. I recently heard that the legis-
lature passed a law that protects us when we are sued under the
Deceptive Trade Practices Act. Is there such a law, and if there is,
what does it say?

You are right. There is a law that offers contractors additional protection when they are sued based on construction defects. This law is important to both consumers and contractors because the consumer who does not comply with the provisions of this law will collect substantially less in damages.

The law applies to any action to collect money from a contractor based on a construction defect, unless it is a personal injury action. Under the law, you must give written notice by certified mail to the contractor at least 60 days before filing suit, specifying in reasonable detail the defects that are the subject of the complaint. For 35 days after receiving this notice, the contractor has the right to inspect the defective property. Within 45 days after receiving notice, the contractor may make a written offer of settlement to the consumer. The offer may include an agreement to repair the defects or have them repaired. The repairs must be made within 45 days, if the offer is accepted.

The most important aspect of this law arises when the consumer fails to accept the contractor's offer of settlement. If the consumer unreasonably rejects the settlement offer, he may not recover an amount in excess of the reasonable costs of the repairs and may only recover attorneys' fees incurred up to the time the offer was rejected. In other words, before filing a claim under the Deceptive Trade Practices Act or any other law, you must give a contractor an opportunity to repair the defects, and if it does or offers to do so, you proceed with a lawsuit at your peril.

Here is a quick example of how the law works: Suppose Tom hires a builder to repair his garage. After the work is completed and paid for, Tom discovers the siding was not of the quality represented by the contractor. Tom wants to file suit under the Deceptive Trade Practices Act for misrepresentation. Tom must first give the contractor 60 days notice of his complaint. He must then allow the contractor to come and look at the problem. If the contractor subsequently writes to Tom that it will change the siding at no cost, Tom must accept the offer, or else if he sues, his damages will be limited to what it will cost to make the change. He also will not recover his attorneys' fees for the lawsuit.

What can I do about a "free" prize that wasn't really free? "The Deceptive Trade Practices Act may help."

Dear Mr. Alderman:
I recently won a contest from a radio station. The prize was jewelry stated to be worth $10,800. I had the jewelry appraised at $5,400. A second appraisal said $2,700 was more like it. The station sent a Form 1099 to the IRS for $10,800, and my taxes on this free prize came to more than it was actually worth. Do any laws prohibit such false advertising by a radio station?

First, as you found out, whenever you win a prize you must pay income taxes on the value of the prize. The question is, then, what is the value? I should point out that the value indicated on the Form 1099 is not necessarily the value you have to use for taxes. The IRS requires that you pay taxes on the fair market value. This is generally what a willing buyer would pay a willing seller.

In your case, your estimates are as good an indication of this amount as is the 1099. You may want to protest the 1099 from the station and insist it reissue one with a corrected amount. Additionally, if you sell the item you won, the IRS will usually use that amount as the value on which you are required to pay taxes.

The question you ask, however, is a good one. Are there laws regulating false advertising of contests? The simple answer is yes. False, misleading, or deceptive advertising is unlawful under the Texas Deceptive Trade Practices Act. The attorney general enforces this law and could bring an action against any radio station that advertised falsely. The real issue under this law would be whether you as an individual would be entitled to damages.

To recover under this law, you must be a consumer. This basically means you must be looking to purchase something. The free prize would not qualify unless you were required to do something to win. For example, if you had to purchase a product, count songs, send in an entry, or allow the station to use you for publicity purposes, then, in my opinion, the prize had strings attached and was not free. On the other hand, if you just called in and were given the prize, you probably do not have an individual claim under this law.

The seller didn't say anything. Am I out of luck?
"There is a duty to speak."

Dear Mr. Alderman:
I must have bought a junker. It is a 1986 Oldsmobile, and I paid more than $1,000 for it. As soon as I got it home, I found out the transmission was so bad that the car would not run for more than a few miles. I took it to the repair shop and learned it would cost nearly $800 to fix. The shop couldn't imagine how the seller wouldn't have known it. When I went back to the used car dealer, he admitted he knew the car needed a new transmission, but he said, "You didn't ask about the transmission, and I didn't tell you about it. . . . What you saw is what you bought." Is this true? The car isn't worth more than a few hundred dollars in this condition. It seems to me the law should require someone to tell you when there is something wrong.

The law is just what you assume it should be. Under the Texas Deceptive Trade Practices Act it is unlawful for a person to fail to disclose known defects if "such failure to disclose such information was intended to induce the consumer into a transaction which the consumer would not have entered into had the information been disclosed."

In your case, if you can show that the dealer didn't disclose the information because he knew you wouldn't pay the same price if you knew the car didn't work, the dealer would be violating the law. It doesn't matter that you didn't ask any questions. Your failure to inquire is not a defense to this law.

If the seller has violated the Deceptive Trade Practices Act, you could be entitled to up to three times your damages. In your case your damages would be how much it will cost you to get the car into the condition it should have been in when you bought it: $800. If you prevail in court, you will also be entitled to any court costs or attorneys' fees you incur.

The best advice I can give you is to contact the dealer, certified mail, return receipt requested, and tell him you want your car fixed or money damages. Let him know you know your rights under the Deceptive Trade Practices Act, and unless you can settle things, you will pursue your legal rights.

The contract said "as is." Am I out of luck?
"Not necessarily, under the Deceptive Trade Practices Act."

Dear Mr. Alderman:

I recently bought a used car. It was advertised in the paper as being in "excellent condition." When I looked at the car, the owner (he was not a dealer) assured me the car ran well and was in great shape mechanically. I bought it, and before I got it home it broke down. The mechanic says the car is a piece of junk and is in terrible mechanical condition. When I asked for my money back, the seller told me to read the contract we had. I did, and it says the car is sold "as is." Am I out of luck? I guess it was my own fault for not carefully reading the contract.

Good news! The Deceptive Trade Practices Act generally may not be waived, even in a written contract. If a seller makes a statement of fact about a product, and it is false, and you in fact rely on the misrepresentation and purchase the product, the seller is liable under the Deceptive Trade Practices Act. Saying something is sold "as is" does have the legal effect of eliminating many warranties, but it does not necessarily change the Deceptive Trade Practices Act.

I suggest you talk to the seller and let him know you know the law. As you probably already know, the Deceptive Trade Practices Act applies to any seller, even one not in business, and you could be entitled to three times your damages if you sue. I also should point out that the Texas Supreme Court has said the good faith, intent, or knowledge of the seller who made the statement is irrelevant. If a misrepresentation is made, the Deceptive Trade Practices Act has usually been violated. The owner assured you the car was in excellent condition, and it was not. Small print in a contract usually doesn't change the effect of the Deceptive Trade Practices Act.

What can I do about something I paid for but never received?
"That may be unconscionable and unlawful."

Dear Mr. Alderman:

I made arrangements with an auto repair shop to rebuild my car's motor. I made payments until I had paid $750 in advance. The deal *was that after I paid the $750, the mechanic would do the work. So far he has done nothing. I have tried numerous times to get him to make the repairs or give me my money back, and he won't. I don't know anything about cars, and every time I ask a question, I get the runaround.*

Fortunately for you, the Deceptive Trade Practices Act protects you against someone taking unfair advantage of you. Under the law, it is unconscionable for someone to "take advantage of the lack of knowledge, ability, experience, or capacity" to a grossly unfair degree. In my opinion, the merchant is taking advantage of your lack of knowledge and ability, and this would violate the Deceptive Trade Practices Act.

I suggest you let the mechanic know you know about this law and that you promptly want your money back or your car repaired.

The real estate agent didn't tell me the former owner of the house died of AIDS. Doesn't this have to be disclosed? "Not under the law."

Dear Mr. Alderman:

I just bought a new house. Right after I moved in I found out the former owner of the house had died of AIDS in the house. I don't want to sound like a crazy person, but I am afraid of getting the disease. I probably would not have bought the house if I had known about this. I thought the Texas Deceptive Trade Practices Act required that sellers disclose things like this. Do I have any legal rights?

First, from everything I have heard or read, there is no possibility of you contracting AIDS from living in a house where someone with the disease died. Hopefully, you will be able to enjoy the house and not worry about its prior occupants.

As far as your legal rights, you probably have none in this situation. You are right that the Deceptive Trade Practices Act, as well as the new real estate disclosure law discussed in the next letter, requires a seller to disclose material facts to you if he knows these facts would matter. Under the law, a seller would probably have an obligation to tell you about the prior occupant's death. But the legislature has passed a law that preempts the DTPA and allows people to remain silent with respect to

AIDS. This law is consistent with federal laws that prohibit discrimination against persons with AIDS. The bottom line is that under present law there probably is no liability for the failure to disclose information regarding AIDS or related complexes to a prospective home buyer.

No one told me the appliances didn't work. Do I have any rights? "Yes! There is a new disclosure law."

Dear Mr. Alderman:
I recently bought a new house—actually a new used house. Everything appeared in good condition. The seller never told me everything worked, but I assumed it did. Shortly after we moved in, we discovered serious problems with the air conditioning unit. We didn't think to ask about this because it was winter when we bought the house. Are we just out of luck?

Luckily for you, you bought your house after January 1, 1994. Even though you may have rights under the Deceptive Trade Practices Act before this date, after it you are entitled to a full disclosure by the seller. Under the new law, a seller of residential real estate must give you written notice that contains certain required information. Although the notice does not have to be in any specific form, what follows is a copy of the form suggested by the legislature. If you did not receive such disclosures, you have the right to terminate the contract. You also may have a claim under the Deceptive Trade Practices Act. As a practical matter, however, my guess is once the seller finds out about this, he will promptly negotiate a fair settlement with you.

(text continued on page 116)

Example of the type of real estate disclosure statement now required by law.

SELLER'S DISCLOSURE NOTICE

CONCERNING THE PROPERTY AT _____
(Street Address and City)

THIS NOTICE IS A DISCLOSURE OF SELLER'S KNOWL-
EDGE OF THE CONDITION OF THE PROPERTY AS OF
THE DATE SIGNED BY SELLER AND IS NOT A SUBSTI-
TUTE FOR ANY INSPECTIONS OR WARRANTIES THE
PURCHASER MAY WISH TO OBTAIN. IT IS NOT A WAR-
RANTY OF ANY KIND BY SELLER OR SELLER'S
AGENTS.

Seller ___ is ___ is not occupying the property.

If unoccupied, how long since Seller has occupied the Property?___
_____

1. The Property has the items checked below:

Write Yes (Y), No (N), or Unknown (U).

___ Range	___ Oven	___ Microwave
___ Dishwasher	___ Trash Compactor	___ Disposal
___ Washer/Dryer Hookups	___ Window Screens	___ Rain Gutters
___ Security System	___ Fire Detection Equipment	___ Intercom System
___ TV Antenna	___ Cable TV Wiring	___ Satellite Dish
___ Ceiling Fan(s)	___ Attic Fan(s)	___ Exhaust Fan(s)
___ Central A/C	___ Central Heating	___ Wall/Window Air Conditioning
___ Plumbing System	___ Septic System	___ Public Sewer System
___ Patio/Decking	___ Outdoor Grill	___ Fences
___ Pool	___ Sauna	___ Spa
___ Hot Tub	___ Pool Equipment	___ Pool Heater

(continued on next page)

(continued from previous page)

___ Automatic Lawn
    Sprinkler System
___ Fireplace(s) &   ___ Fireplace(s) &
    Chimney   Chimney (Mock)
    (Woodburning)
___ Gas Lines   ___ Gas Fixtures
    (Nat./LP)

Garage:
___ Attached   ___ Not Attached   ___ Carport

Garage Door Opener(s):
___ Electronic   ___ Control(s)

Water Heater:
___ Gas   ___ Electric

Water Supply:
___ City   ___ Well   ___ MUD
___ Co-Op

Roof Type:_____

Age: ____(approx.)

2. Are you (Seller) aware of any of the above items that are not in working condition, that have known defects, or that are in need of repair?

    ____ Yes ___No ___Unknown

    If yes, then describe. (Attach additional sheets if necessary):

    _____
    _____
    _____

3. Are you (Seller) aware of any known defects/malfunctions in any of the following? Write Yes (Y) if you are, write No (N) if you are not aware.

___ Interior Walls   ___ Ceilings   ___ Floors
___ Exterior Walls   ___ Doors   ___ Windows
___ Roof   ___ Foundation/   ___ Basement
                             Slab(s)

(continued on next page)

(continued from previous page)

___ Walls/Fences   ___ Driveways   ___ Sidewalks
___ Plumbing/   ___ Electrical   ___ Lighting
    Sewers/Septics   Systems   Fixtures

Other Structural Components (Describe):

_____

_____

_____

If the answer to any of the above is yes, explain. (Attach additional sheets if necessary):

_____

_____

_____

4. Are you (Seller) aware of any of the following conditions?
___ Active Termites   ___ Previous Structural or Roof Repair
    (includes wood-destroying insects)
___ Termite or Wood Rot Damage
___ Hazardous or Toxic Waste
Needing Repair:
___ Asbestos Components
___ Previous Termite Damage
___ Urea Formaldehyde Insulation
___ Previous Termite Treatment
___ Radon Gas   ___ Lead-Based Paint   ___ Previous Flooding
___ Aluminum Wiring ___ Improper Drainage ___ Previous Fires
___ Water Penetration ___ Located in 100-Year Floodplain
___ Unplatted Easements
___ Present Flood Insurance Coverage
___ Landfill, Settling, Soil
___ Subsurface Structure or Pits
___ Movement, Fault Lines

If the answer to any of the above is yes, explain. (Attach additional sheets if necessary):

_____

_____

(continued on next page)

(continued from previous page)

5. Are you (Seller) aware of any item, equipment, or system in or on the property that is in need of repair? _____ Yes (if you are aware) _____ No (if you are not aware). If yes, explain (attach additional sheets if necessary):

_____

6. Are you (Seller) aware of any of the following?

Write Yes (Y) if you are aware, write No (N) if you are not aware.

___ Room additions, structural modifications, or other alterations or repairs made without necessary permits or not in compliance with building codes in effect at that time.

___ Homeowners' Association or maintenance fees or assessments.

___ Any "common area" (facilities such as pools, tennis courts, walk-ways, or other areas) co-owned in undivided interest with others.

___ Any notices of violations of deed restrictions or governmental ordinances affecting the condition or use of the Property.

___ Any lawsuits directly or indirectly affecting the Property.

___ Any condition on the Property that materially affects the physical health or safety of an individual.

If the answer to any of the above is yes, explain. (Attach additional sheets if necessary):

_____
_____
_____
_____

_____   _____
Date   Signature of Seller

The undersigned purchaser hereby acknowledges receipt of the foregoing notice.

_____   _____
Date   Signature of Purchaser

(text continued from page 111)

What are treble damages?
"Good news for you."

Dear Mr. Alderman:
I have heard you speak about the Deceptive Trade Practices Act and the fact that it allows you to recover "treble damages." Just what does this mean?

The Deceptive Trade Practices Act is designed to do two things: first, to compensate consumers for their losses and, second, to deter people from engaging in false or deceptive practices. To deter wrongdoers, the law enables you to collect what may be viewed as punitive damages, damages designed to punish the wrongdoer, not just to compensate you for your loss.

Under the law, you may recover up to three times your damages—"treble damages." To recover treble damages, you must show that the person you sued acted "knowingly." This means he knew or should have known what he did was false, misleading or deceptive, or breached a warranty.

For example, suppose someone sells you a car and says it is in excellent condition when it is not. Because the statement is false, you have a claim under the Deceptive Trade Practices Act. You would only be entitled to treble damages, however, if you could show the seller knew the car was not in excellent condition when he said it was. In other words, an innocent misrepresentation does not result in treble damages.

The possibility of treble damages is what lends teeth to the Deceptive Trade Practices Act. *Once a person knows he may have to pay a large sum if he loses in court, he is more likely to treat you fairly and try to settle.* Make sure the seller is aware that you know the law and how much his damages may be. My guess is you will quickly be able to work out an agreeable settlement.

How do I use the Deceptive Trade Practices Act?
"It's simple."

Dear Mr. Alderman:
I have heard about the consumer protection law in Texas called the Deceptive Trade Practices Act. From what I have been told, this could be just the law to help me with a problem I'm having with my

mechanic. I was just wondering—is there anything special I have to do to utilize this law? Can I go to small claims court? I only want the $75 he took from me.

The Deceptive Trade Practices Act allows a consumer to recover up to three times his or her damages plus court costs and attorneys' fees, if any. But if you are going to use this law there are a few steps you must follow.

First, remember you cannot go to small claims court if you are asking for more than $5,000. If the amount you are seeking is more than $5,000, you probably will need an attorney to file suit in county or district court.

Next, once you decide to use this law, you must give written notice of your problem at least 60 days before you file your claim in court. The notice must give the specific nature of the claim in reasonable detail and the amount of actual damages, including attorneys' fees if any. The following letter could be used as a model:

Mr. C. Consumer
435 Central Dr.
Consumer, TX 77597

Dear Mr. Merchant:

On Wednesday, June 16, I brought my car into your shop to be repaired. I told you to tune it up, and you stated it would cost $49.95. This is the same amount advertised in the paper the day before. When I picked up my car you charged me $124.95. You told me the $49.95 was for imports only. This was not stated in the ad or told to me before.

I feel your conduct in stating one price and charging another is a false and deceptive practice under the Texas Deceptive Trade Practices Act. I have been damaged in the amount of $75.

Under the law I must give you 60 days' notice of my complaint prior to filing a claim. Unless I receive a satisfactory settlement from you within that period, I intend to pursue my claim in court. I should point out that if I am successful I may be entitled to three times my damages.

Thank you for your expected cooperation.

Sincerely yours,
C. Consumer

During the 60 days, the person you notified has the right to inspect any goods that are part of your complaint. The purpose of the notice require- ment is to give the other party a chance to settle the case without costly litigation. Under the law, if the other side offers a settlement and you refuse it, and if then the court awards substantially the same amount, you are not entitled to three times your damages. *If you are offered a settle- ment substantially the same as what you asked for, you should accept.*

If you do not give the proper notice, the other side may be able to delay the proceedings, so make sure to send your notice certified mail, return receipt requested, so you have proof it was sent. And be sure to include a description of what you think the person has done that violates the law and exactly how much your damages are.

One final comment: Should you see an attorney? The simple answer is: It is up to you. If the amount is less than $5,000, small claims court is simple to use and quick. But an attorney may increase your potential for recovery and may know of damages you are entitled to that you over- looked. But litigation with an attorney takes a longer time and costs mon- ey. You must balance all these factors and make the decision yourself. You may want to talk with an attorney before going to small claims court, just to get an idea of how he or she could help.

Does a car lease include extra taxes?
"You probably owe personal property taxes."

Dear Mr. Alderman:
My son leased a car and was unpleasantly surprised to receive a personal property tax bill for more than $400. The tax makes the lease much more expensive than he thought. Does he have to pay the bill? If this had been explained up front, he would not have leased.

Personal property taxes are assessed against the owner of the car, in this case the company that leased it to your son. As you point out, however, the small print in the lease makes your son responsible. Personal property taxes can greatly increase the cost of a lease in Texas. You should always inquire about this before you lease. Always carefully read your agreement.

In your case, your son is responsible for these payments unless he can show that the dealer violated the Deceptive Trade Practices Act by either misrepresenting the amount the car would cost or failing to disclose the payments in an effort to get your son to lease the car.

I suggest your son contact the dealer and try to work out a settlement. He should let the dealer know he knows about the Deceptive Trade Practices Act. If, however, your son had the opportunity to read the lease when he signed, and there were no fraudulent inducements, he probably owes the money.

CHAPTER ELEVEN

Immigration*

FEW areas of law have sparked as much public interest and contro-versy as immigration law. Immigration law determines who has the right to live and work in the United States. As you might imagine, this area of law is of great concern to many people.

The most common questions that arise concerning immigration law involve the rights of "undocumented aliens" to live and work in the United States legally. Recent changes in the law, brought about by the **Immigration Reform and Control Act of 1986** (IRCA) allow more people to legally remain in this country, but the changes also have caused much concern. The following questions and answers may help resolve some of this uncertainty.

What should I do to see if I can legally stay in the U.S.?
"First, contact an INS-designated counseling center."

Dear Mr. Alderman:
I have come to Texas illegally from Honduras and now want to stay here. However, I have been told that if I am discovered I will be deported. I have been here almost 10 years and have a good job, and my wife is here legally. I am thinking of quitting my job because I am afraid of being caught. Is there anything I can do to stay here legally? Is there any organization that can help me?

Several laws may provide you with an opportunity to remain in the U.S. For example, depending on how your wife is here legally, you may be entitled to remain here. The first thing you should do is see an immi-gration counselor at one of the INS-designated counseling centers in Texas. Here is a list of some of the centers:

---

* I must give special thanks to Professor Michael Olivas of the University of Houston Law Center for assisting me with the preparation of this chapter.

Amarillo
- Catholic Family Services, 200 S. Tyler, (806) 376-4571.

Austin
- Austin-Travis County Refugee Services, 5555 N. Lamar, Suite K-100, (512) 467-9816 and 467-9817.
- Catholic Family Services, Caritas of Austin, 308 E. Seventh St., (512) 472-3185 and 320-0270.
- Child and Family Services, 2001 Chicon St., (512) 478-1648.
- Cristo Vive for Immigrants, 5800 Manor Rd., (512) 929-9100.
- Immigration Counseling and Outreach Services (ICOS), Diocese of Austin, 1600 N. Congress, (512) 476-1009.
- Jewish Federation, 11713 Jollyville Rd., (512) 331-7059.
- Political Asylum Project of Austin, 1715 E. Sixth St., Suite 206, (512) 478-0546.
- Catholic Charities, Diocese of Beaumont, 1297 Calder Ave., (409) 832-7994 and 983-4586.
- East Texas Legal Services, 527 Forsythe St., (409) 835-4971.

Brownsville
- South Texas Immigration Council, 845 E. 13th St., (210) 542-1991.

Bryan
- Chaplain Outreach Service, 717 S. Main St., (409) 775-8980 and 775-8981.

Carrollton
- First Baptist Church Carrollton, 2400 N. Josey Ln., (214) 242-6464.

Cleveland
- Motivation, Education, and Training (MET), 307 N. College, (281) 592-6483.

Corpus Christi
- Catholic Social Services, Immigration Assistance Program, 1322 Comanche, (512) 884-0651 and 884-6913.
- Jewish Community Council, 750 Everhart Rd., (512) 855-6239.

Dallas
- Casita Maria Inc., Servicios Migratorios, 227 W. 10th St., (214) 946-7167.
- Catholic Charities, Immigration Counseling Service, 325 W. 12th St., Suite 200, (214) 946-4889.
- Centro Social Hispano, 610 N. Bishop (Davis St.), (214) 946-8661.
- International Rescue Committee, 2515 Inwood Rd., Suite 217, (214) 351-6864.
- Proyecto Adelante, 3100 Crossman, (214) 741-2151.
- Refugee Services of North Texas, 4113 Junius St., (214) 821-4883.

• St. Matthew's Episcopal Church, 5100 Ross Ave., (214) 824-2942.
Del Rio
• Texas Rural Legal Aid, 309 Cantu St., (210) 775-1535.
Edinburg
• Texas Rural Legal Aid, 316 S. Clofner, (210) 383-5673, 383-5674, and (800) 369-0437.
El Paso
• Border Rights Coalition, 109 N. Oregon, Room 404-D, (915) 577-0724.
• Catholic Diocese of El Paso, Migration and Refugee Services, 1117 N. Stanton St., (915) 532-3975.
• Centro del Obrero Fronterizo Inc., 2021 Texas Ave., (915) 533-9710.
• Jewish Federation of El Paso, 405 Wallenberg Dr., (915) 584-4438 and 584-4437.
• Las Americas Refugee and Asylum Project, 715 Myrtle Ave., (915) 544-5126 and 544-5127.
• United States Catholic Conference, Catholic Legal Immigration Network Inc. (CLINIC), 1205 N. Oregon St., (915) 533-3971.
Fort Worth
• Catholic Charities, Immigration Counseling Program, 1216 W. Magnolia Ave., (817) 338-0774.
• Jewish Federation of Fort Worth, 6801 Dan Danciger Rd., (817) 292-3081.
• Lutheran Social Services, 100 E. 15th St., Suite 203, (817) 332-2820 and (800) 291-4006.
• San Juan Episcopal Church, 3725 S. Adams St., (817) 927-5135.
• World Relief, 5000 James Ave., (817) 924-0748.
Harlingen
• Agape Missions, 809 E. Jackson St., (210) 428-2854.
• Law Offices of Refugio del Rio Grande, 402 E. Harrison, 2nd Floor, (210) 421-3226.
• Proyecto Libertad, 113 N. First St., (210) 425-9552.
• South Texas Immigration Council, 107 N. Third St., (210) 425-6987.
• South Texas PRO-BAR Asylum, Representation Project, 301 E. Madison Ave., (210) 425-9231.
Houston
• American Red Cross, 2700 Southwest Frwy., (713) 526-8300.
• Association for the Advancement of Mexican Americans Inc., Bldg. B-3, Suite 165, 6001 Gulf Frwy., (713) 926-4756.
• Catholic Charities, Refugee Resettlement Office, 3520 Montrose Blvd., (713) 526-4611 and 526-5812.

- Central American Refugee Center (CARECEN), 6006 Bellaire, Suite 100, (713) 665-1284.
- Chaplain Services Inc., 6223 Richmond, Rm. 209, (713) 974-4791.
- Episcopal Migration Ministries, 3217 Montrose Blvd., (713) 522-3955.
- Gulf Coast Legal Foundation, 1415 Fannin St., 3rd Floor, (713) 660-0077.
- Houston Community Services, 5115 Harrisburg, (713) 926-8771.
- Immigration Counseling Center, 5959 Westheimer, Suite 207, (713) 953-0047.
- Interfaith Ministries for Greater Houston, IM Refugee Services, 3217 Montrose Blvd., (713) 522-3955.
- International Community Services, 3131 W. Alabama, Suite 100, (713) 521-9083.
- International Program Services, 6315 Gulfton, Suite 100, (713) 995-4005.
- Jewish Family Services, 4131 S. Braeswood Blvd., (713) 667-9336.
- Jewish Family Services, Refugee Resettlement Office, 10101 Fondren Rd., Room 244, (713) 777-2030.
- Lutheran Social Services of Texas, 3101 Richmond Ave., Suite 150, (713) 521-0110.
- National Association of Latino Elected and Appointed Officials (NALEO), 4920 Irvington Blvd., Suite B, (713) 697-6400.
- Refugee Service Alliance, 6315 Gulfton, Suite 200, (713) 776-4700.
- Texas Center for Immigrant Legal Assistance, Catholic Charities, 3520 Montrose Blvd., (713) 520-9382 and 228-5200.
- Texas Citizenship Educational Project, 3333 Fannin, Suite 112, (713) 528-6722.
- YMCA International Services, 6315 Gulfton, Suite 100, (713) 995-4005 and 659-5566.

Irving
- SER-Jobs for Progress National Inc., 100 Decker Dr., Suite 200, (214) 541-0616.

Laredo
- Asociacion Pro Servicios Sociales Inc., Centro Aztlan, 406 Scott St., (210) 724-6244.
- Catholic Social Services, 402 Corpus Christi St., (210) 724-3604.
- Texas Rural Legal Aid Inc., 1719 Matamoros, (210) 727-5191.

Lubbock
- Catholic Family Services, 102 Avenue J, (806) 765-8475 and 741-0409.

McAllen

- Border Association for Refugees from Central America (BARCA), 1701 N. Eighth St., Suite B-28, (210) 631-7447.
- South Texas Immigration Council, 1201 Erie St., (210) 682-5397.

Mount Pleasant

- St. Michael's Catholic Church, 1403 E. First St., (903) 572-5227.

Nacogdoches

- Nacogdoches Adult Learning Center Inc., Bldg. B, 2400 South St., (409) 564-8789.

Plainview

- Texas Rural Legal Aid Inc., 114 E. Seventh St., 2nd Floor, (806) 293-2625.

Plano

- Organization for Latin Americans (OLA), 1100 W. 15th St., Suite 539, (214) 422-2252.

San Antonio

- Bexar County Legal Aid Association, 434 S. Main St., Suite 300, (210) 227-0111.
- Catholic Charities, 2903 W. Salinas, (210) 433-3256 and 432-6091.
- Center for Legal and Social Justice, Immigration and Human Rights Clinic, 2507 N.W. 36th St., (210) 431-2596 and (800) 267-4848.
- Chaplain Services Inc., 1595 Bandera Rd., (210) 435-9711.
- Episcopal Diocese of West Texas, 111 Torcido, (210) 824-5387.
- Jewish Family Service, 1931 N.W. Military, Suite 202, (210) 349-5481.
- Refugee Aid Project, 1305 N. Flores, (210) 226-7722.
- San Antonio Literacy Council, 4650 Eldridge Ave., (210) 433-9300.

San Juan

- Catholic Social Services, Diocese of Brownsville, 400 N. Nebraska St., (210) 702-4088.

One final note: Your local Bar Association may have some volunteer agencies or lawyers it can recommend. You may also want to contact the Mexican American Legal Defense and Education fund in San Antonio, (210) 224-5476. It does not counsel individual clients, but it does initiate suits for groups of Hispanics who are discriminated against and can recommend Spanish-speaking lawyers.

Who can get amnesty?
"The law has expired."

Dear Mr. Alderman:
I have heard and read a lot about the new amnesty law, but I am afraid to contact anyone official until I know if I am covered. It would be a big help if you could just briefly explain who is eligible for amnesty and what could happen to me if I went to apply and wasn't eligible. Can I be deported? Do I have to give my address?

Under the Immigration Reform and Control Act of 1986, commonly referred to as IRCA, the following persons were eligible for amnesty:

A. *In general.* The alien must establish that he or she entered the United States before January 1, 1982, and that he or she has resided continuously in the United States in an unlawful status since such date and through the date the application is filed.

B. *Nonimmigrants.* In the case of an alien who entered the United States as a nonimmigrant before January 1, 1982, the alien must establish that the alien's period of authorized stay as a nonimmigrant expired before such date through the passage of time or the alien's unlawful status was known to the government as of such date.

C. *Exchange visitors.* If the alien was at any time a nonimmigrant exchange alien, he or she must establish that he or she was not subject to the two-year foreign residence requirement, or has fulfilled that requirement or received a waiver.

I say "were" because the law expired on May 5, 1988. The amnesty law was a one-shot chance for people to legally stay in this country. Now that it has expired you must qualify under another law if you want to remain here legally. To find out if there is a provision in the law that may help you, I suggest you contact one of the agencies listed on pages 121–124.

What does someone from another country need to visit this country?
"A visa."

Dear Mr. Alderman:
I have a friend in another country who wants to visit me for awhile. I have heard all the complaints about illegal aliens, and I want to know what she has to do to comply with the law while she lives with me.

Basically, to enter the United States from another country you must have the permission of the United States. This permission is called a "visa." Your friend can obtain a visa from the American consul. Because she is only coming to visit you temporarily, she can obtain a nonimmigration visa. These are issued to people who plan on staying in the United States temporarily. For example, a nonimmigrant visa can be used by a businessperson who is coming only to work for his company, a student who will be attending school, or a tourist, such as your friend.

I should point out that a tourist visa authorizes your friend to stay here but not to work here. She also must return after the visa expires, unless she has it extended or changes her status to an immigrant visa.

What is a green card?
"The right to stay in the United States."

Dear Mr. Alderman:
I am an American citizen and have never paid much attention to immigration laws. Now that I own a small business, I have been told I shouldn't hire any aliens unless they have green cards. Just what is a green card?

As I said in the letter right before this one, someone from another country can be in this country legally only if he or she has permission. The law prohibits you from hiring an alien who is not properly documented. For example, a worker with a worker's visa would be properly documented and could be hired to work for you. A visa is the document given to aliens who are here temporarily.

If an alien wants to reside in this country permanently and wants the right to come in and go out of the United States, he or she must obtain an Alien Registration Receipt Card. Although this card is no longer green, its common name is still "green card." Not everyone, however, can get green cards. To receive one, you basically must show you have family here, you are a worker entitled to special treatment, or you are a businessperson making a large investment in this country.

The most common way of obtaining a green card is by having a family relationship with someone in this country. For example, if you are a spouse, child, parent, brother, or sister of an American citizen or are engaged to an American citizen, you can become a permanent resident. To do this, the person you have the relationship with must file an application with the INS or the American Embassy of the country where the alien lives. You also can obtain a green card if you are the spouse or child of a person with a green card. In this case, the relative who is a permanent resident of the United States must file the application. Although it is less common, permanent resident status can also be obtained if you have a job that this country considers a priority. For example, scientists, professors, or high-level business executives may be eligible to remain in this country as permanent residents.

Finally, the **Immigration Act of 1994** allows 55,000 immigrants from certain countries to come to the United States as permanent residents without the need to meet the above requirements. The countries are those that have sent the fewest immigrants to this country in the past. The INS can give you the list of countries whose citizens are considered "diversity immigrants."

What is a notary?
"Not a lawyer or a notario."

Dear Mr. Alderman:

I am from Mexico, and I wanted legal advice in Dallas, where I live. I went to a notary public, where the notary said for $500 he would help me with my problem. What is a notary public? Is it a "notario" (lawyer)?

In Mexico and other Spanish-speaking countries, a "notario" performs many of the same functions as an attorney. In the United States, a notary public is not an attorney and cannot hold himself out as a lawyer to represent you in court or in other legal proceedings. Basically, all a notary public does is attest to signatures or certify that you signed a document and perform some other clerking services. Nearly anyone can become a notary public just by paying a small fee.

If you need legal services, see an attorney ("abogado" or "licenciado"). If you think the notary public misrepresented himself or engaged in unauthorized legal work, you should report him to the district attorney's office, the attorney general, or the State Bar of Texas, (800) 932-1900. The unauthorized practice of law is a crime.

And by the way, notaries usually charge very little for their services. Beware of anyone charging a high fee for performing his or her duties as a notary public.

I am afraid to go home. What can I do?
"You may be entitled to asylum."

Dear Mr. Alderman:
I am from El Salvador and fled to the United States because my brother was killed by government soldiers and I heard they were looking for me, too. Is there any way I can stay in the United States, at least until things get better in my country and it is safe for me to return?

You should seek assistance from an immigration attorney or the counseling agencies listed on pages 121–124. If you have reason to believe you may be harmed, you may be eligible for asylum "because of persecution on account of race, religion, nationality, membership in a particular social group, or political opinion." These are highly technical terms, but an attorney or qualified immigration counselor could help you apply for asylum if you qualify. You are entitled to a series of legal rights and hearings and may even be eligible to work in the United States. Even more than other persons, however, you should be careful not to commit a crime or break a law, because any immigration hearings will include a record of your time and behavior while in the United States.

I am a U.S. citizen, but I am still asked for ID.
Is this legal?
"All people must show they are eligible to work."

Dear Mr. Alderman:
I am a citizen, but I notice my union won't hire anybody without ID or a green card. Is this legal? I am a third-generation American, and I resent having to prove I am legal.

Employers must screen all new employees (those hired since November 6, 1986) to determine if they are eligible to work. However, they must ask the same questions and require the same papers of everyone, not just people who may look Mexican or who speak with accents. There are no sanctions for employers who hired undocumented employees before November 6, 1986, but there may be penalties for people hired after that date. All employees must be treated equally in the hiring process.

Does my child have to have a social security number
to stay in school?
"No!"

Dear Mr. Alderman:

My daughter brought home a letter from school that said all school children must have social security numbers and that we should fill out forms to get a social security number. I'm afraid not to get one because they might not let my daughter stay in school. What can I do?

No child has to have a social security number to enroll in school. Even undocumented children can attend public schools if their parents reside in the school district. Last year's tax law makes changes in who may be eligible for a tax deduction, but you are not required to take any action that exposes you or your children to possible deportation. As with any such case involving immigration, you should consult an attorney or reputable immigration counseling center. (See pages 121–124.)

I am a small employer;
must I comply with the immigration law?
"Probably yes."

Dear Mr. Alderman:

I have a small business, delivering documents for local firms. I employ 5–10 people. The other day someone told me I could get in trouble if I didn't comply with the immigration law. I don't have anyone working for me who is not a permanent resident or U.S. citizen; do I still have to bother with this law?

Yes. The law applies to nearly everyone who employs someone to perform work, labor, or services in return for wages. Under the law you must complete what is called a Form I-9 for:

- *Persons hired after May 31, 1987.* For these employees, you must complete a Form I-9 within three business days of the date of the hire. (If you employ the person for less than three days, you must complete the Form I-9 before the end of the employee's first working day.)
- *Persons hired between November 7, 1986, and May 31, 1987.* For these employees, you must have completed Form I-9 before September 1, 1987.

Note: If you employ people for domestic work in your private home on a regular (such as weekly) basis, these requirements also apply to you.
 You do not need to complete Form I-9 for:

- Persons hired before November 7, 1986.
- Persons hired after November 6, 1986, who left your employment before June 1, 1987.
- Persons you employ for domestic work in a private home on an intermittent or sporadic basis.
- Persons who provide labor to you and who are employed by a contractor providing contract services (e.g., employee leasing).
- Persons who are independent contractors.

Form I-9 is designed to verify that people are eligible to work in the United States. The form is easy to complete, and a free book is available to help you. To get the book, write or contact the U.S. Immigration Service and ask for the *Handbook for Employers: Instructions for Completing Form I-9.*

Note: You can be fined if you do not comply with this law, and don't try to get around it by not hiring anyone you think may be unauthorized to work here. Under the law it is also unlawful for a business with four or more employees to discriminate against any individual because of that person's national origin or citizenship status. In other words, ask for papers from everyone you hire, not just minority workers.

CHAPTER TWELVE

Landlord & Tenant Rights

Landlord-TENANT law is centuries old, and for most of that time, it has been very one-sided. Landlord-tenant law historically has favored the landlord. But recently, there have been some changes, and while you may not have all the rights you would like, you are not without recourse.

Two laws in particular give you rights against the landlord when he doesn't keep up the apartment or when he doesn't return your security deposit.

The most important part of any landlord-tenant relationship is the lease. Read yours carefully before you sign. If you don't like something in the lease, don't sign until the landlord agrees to remove it.

Do I need a lease?
"No, but it can help."

Dear Mr. Alderman:
I just moved to the city. I found an apartment I liked and told the landlord I would take it. He said, "Fine. You can move in on the 1st." When I asked for a lease he told me not to worry—he never uses them. Now I am worried. Is it legal to rent an apartment without a lease? What if he just throws me out?

A landlord-tenant relationship is created by an agreement called a lease. This agreement can be oral or written and can be as informal or formal as the parties want to make it. *There is no requirement that you have a formal lease to rent an apartment.*

If you do not have a written lease, the law implies a lease for at least as long as the period between rent payments. For example, if you agree to pay rent once a month, the law says you have a month-to-month lease. This means neither you nor the landlord may terminate the agreement without giving at least one month's notice to the other. If you were

131

paying rent once a week, your agreement would be weekly, and one week's notice of termination would be required.

In your case, you can have an implied lease with your landlord; however, it is only a month-to-month agreement. This means you can only leave or be evicted after 30 days' notice. If you want a longer guarantee, you may want a written lease. You also may want to have a written lease so all the terms of your agreement are spelled out. This is a good way to avoid later problems that might arise concerning who is obligated to do what, for example, who pays for utilities or repairs.

As far as your question about the landlord just throwing you out, read the next letter.

If I am late with my rent, can my landlord just throw me out? "No. You can be evicted only after a court hearing and only by a constable or sheriff."

Dear Mr. Alderman:
I was recently laid off, and I don't have enough money to pay my bills. I am already one month late in my rent. I just received a notice from my landlord to vacate. It says if I am not out in three days, he will have me evicted. I have a place to move to, but it won't be ready for a week. Does the landlord have the right to throw me out in the street in three days?

No. Under the law a landlord cannot personally evict a tenant. You may only be evicted after (1) the landlord commences a legal proceeding against you; (2) you have an opportunity to appear in court; (3) the judge orders you to leave; and (4) you do not leave. Even then the eviction must be done by a constable or sheriff pursuant to a court order.

If your landlord were to throw you out, he would be responsible for any damages you suffered and may even be liable for criminal and civil penalties. I suggest you talk to your landlord and tell him you are moving out in a few days. It will take the landlord at least that long to have you evicted legally, and he may prefer just to cooperate.

I should emphasize one point. Even though you are moving out, you are still responsible for the rent you owe, including rent for the period remaining on your lease after you move. Your landlord has the right to sue to try to collect this money.

When can I move out?
"Read your lease."

Dear Mr. Alderman:
My company just transferred me to another city. When I gave my landlord a 30-day notice, he told me my lease still had six months left. I told him I was transferred, and there was no way I could stay. He told me if he couldn't rent the apartment to someone else, I would have to pay the six months' rent. This does not seem fair. Don't I have the right to move if I am transferred?

This may not be what you want to hear, but unless your lease says so, you do not have the right to move out if you are transferred, and you may be responsible for rent for the remainder of the lease term. *A lease is a binding legal agreement, and you are controlled by its terms. You may only terminate a lease early for reasons permitted by the lease.* For example, if your lease says you may terminate by giving 30 days' notice if you are transferred, you are all right. But if the lease is silent as to early termination, you may not terminate early just because you have been transferred. If you do terminate early you may be responsible for all the damages the landlord incurs, including rent for the period he cannot lease the apartment to someone else.

If you do not have a lease agreement, the law will imply one for the period of time between rent payments. For example, if you pay rent once a month, the law will create what is called a month-to-month tenancy. This type of arrangement can be terminated by either the tenant or the landlord for any reason by giving one month's notice. A lease protects you by ensuring the landlord does not terminate the lease or raise the rent, but it also protects the landlord by obligating you for the entire period of the lease. *If you think you may have to terminate your lease early, make sure there is a clause permitting you to do so. Otherwise, you may end up owing rent on two apartments.*

What if I don't get my security deposit back?
"There's a law."

Dear Mr. Alderman:
My apartment was a dump. The landlady never fixed it, and as soon as my lease was up, I moved. Now my landlady refuses to return my

security deposit. I have called her and written many times, and she just won't respond. Don't Texas tenants have any rights?

Your landlady may not wrongfully keep your security deposit. If she does, you may be entitled to three times your deposit plus an additional $100 and any court costs or attorneys' fees you may incur.

A law known as the **Texas Security Deposit Law,** which may not be waived or changed by your lease, requires a landlord to return a security deposit within 30 days after the tenant moves out or give the tenant written notice why the deposit is being kept.

Remember you are only entitled to have your deposit returned if you complied with your lease and left the apartment in good condition. For example: If you move before your lease is up, you may not be entitled to the return of the deposit. A landlord can also deduct the costs of cleaning the apartment if you left it damaged. *No damages may be deducted for ordinary wear-and-tear.*

If your landlady has not returned your deposit within 30 days or written you why it was not returned, you should send her a certified letter, return receipt requested, to make certain she has your forwarding address. You should also tell her that should you not get your deposit back soon, you will take advantage of the security deposit law. You can use the following letter as a model.

Landlord Name
Street Address
City, State, Zip

Dear Landlord:

On (<u>fill in date</u>) I moved out of the house/apartment I was renting from you. As our lease agreement provided, I gave proper notice and left the apartment in good condition. I was also current in my rent.

When I moved in, I paid a security deposit of (<u>amount</u>). You have not returned my deposit, as the law requires. Under the law, a landlord must refund a security deposit or send written notice of the reason(s) it is being withheld within 30 days after the tenant vacates the property.

(letter continued on next page)

(letter continued from previous page)

> Unless I receive my security deposit from you within a reasonable time, I intend to go to small claims court. I should tell you that if I do go to court, I may be entitled to three times the amount of my deposit plus $100.
>
> Thank you for your expected cooperation in this matter. If you need to reach me, my present address is: (street address).
>
> Sincerely,
> (sign your name)

(Send this letter certified mail, return receipt requested, 30 days after you move out if your security deposit has not been returned.)

If you still do not receive your deposit or written notice, consider small claims court. Under the law, a landlord who acts in bad faith in not returning your deposit may be liable for three times the deposit plus $100 in additional damages. *If the landlord does not return your money or give you a written explanation, the burden will be on the landlord to prove he did not act in bad faith.* The burden is also on the landlord to prove any deductions, such as money taken out for cleaning, were reasonable.

The Texas Security Deposit Law is one of the few landlord-tenant laws that really helps the tenant. It is my experience that once the landlord knows you know about this law, he quickly returns your deposit. Just sending the form letter should be enough to retrieve your money.

What if my landlord won't fix my apartment?
"Keep paying rent."

Dear Mr. Alderman:
Nothing in my apartment works right. It seems every day something else is breaking, and it always takes the landlord weeks to fix it. Even though the problems are small, it is still an inconvenience. Last week, for example, I had to use a wrench to turn the stove on and off. Right now six things are wrong, and it has been one week since I reported them. What I would like to do is just not pay my rent until everything is fixed. My landlord keeps saying he will fix it but never does. What do you recommend?

The first thing I should point out is, unless your lease says so, your landlord does not have a general obligation to repair the property. Recently, however, a law was passed that requires a landlord to repair conditions that materially affect physical health or safety. This law is discussed in the next letter, and it doesn't seem to apply to your problem. Small inconveniences, such as problems with a door or a drawer in the kitchen, or the knobs on an appliance, are not the responsibility of the landlord unless he has agreed to make these repairs.

So what should you do? First, read your lease. See if the landlord has undertaken to repair your apartment. If he has, you should contact him in writing and request that he make the necessary repairs. If he still refuses, you can make them yourself and recover the amount it costs from him in small claims court. You cannot, however, deduct the amount from your rent unless the landlord agrees.

Even if the lease does not say anything about repairs, your landlord may still be responsible if he has otherwise agreed to make repairs. From what you say, the landlord has repaired the apartment before and seems to understand this is his obligation. Assuming you can show he has agreed to make repairs, then he would be responsible just as if it were in the lease.

The law generally does not impose an obligation on the landlord to repair your apartment, *and in most cases you must continue to pay rent regardless of whether your apartment needs repairs.* But there is an exception to this general rule. As the next letter shows, if the condition is serious enough, the law makes the landlord repair it and lets you move or withhold from your rent if he doesn't.

What can I do if the apartment is in such bad shape
I can't live in it?
"The warranty of habitability applies here."

Dear Mr. Alderman:
I need help! The roof in my apartment leaks, and the landlord won't fix it. The leak keeps getting worse, and now when it rains I have to go somewhere else to sleep. Is there any way I can force the landlord to fix this place? I don't want to move because moving is so expensive.

First of all, do not stop paying rent. Under the law, even if you have a claim against your landlord for not maintaining your apartment, you are not excused from paying rent until you take the necessary steps. *If you stop paying rent, your landlord could have you evicted.* Here is what you have to do to withhold rent or get damages.

In 1979, the Texas Legislature passed a law requiring that a landlord make a reasonable effort to repair or remedy any condition that materially affects the health or safety of an ordinary tenant once the tenant gives the landlord notice of the problem. This law imposes an obligation on the landlord to make sure your apartment is "habitable." If the landlord does not comply with this law, you may be entitled to withhold rent and have the repairs made yourself, to get a rent reduction and a penalty of one month's rent plus $500, or to terminate the lease and move out. Recent amendments to the law allow you to have the condition repaired yourself and the amount deducted from your rent if:

(a) the landlord has failed to remedy the backup or overflow of raw sewage inside the tenant's dwelling or the flooding from broken pipes or natural drainage inside the dwelling.

(b) the landlord has expressly or impliedly agreed in the lease to furnish potable water to the tenant's dwelling, and the water service to the dwelling has totally ceased.

(c) the landlord has expressly or impliedly agreed in the lease to furnish heating or cooling equipment; the equipment is producing inadequate heat or cooled air; and the landlord has been notified in writing by the appropriate local housing, building, or health official or other official having jurisdiction, that the lack of heat or cooling materially affects the health or safety of an ordinary tenant.

(d) the landlord has been notified in writing by the appropriate local housing, building, or health official or other official having jurisdiction that the condition materially affects the health or safety of an ordinary tenant.

Here is how the law works: First, you must give your landlord written notice of the problem with your apartment. I recommend you send this notice via certified mail, return receipt requested. Explain the problem, and tell the landlord it materially affects your health and safety. Next, under the law the landlord has a reasonable time to repair the problem. What is reasonable depends on the facts of the situation, but a leaking roof is serious, and I would say a few days is a reasonable time.

If your apartment is not repaired within a reasonable time, you must give the landlord a second notice that unless the condition is repaired you will terminate the lease, repair the condition yourself, or bring a civil action for damages. If you terminate the lease, you will be entitled to a refund of any rent paid for the period after you move out. If you want to stay there but want damages, you can sue by yourself in small claims court for up to $5,000 in damages, or you can have the repairs done yourself and withhold the cost from your rent.

In summary:

1. Texas law imposes an obligation on landlords to make a diligent effort to repair any condition that materially affects the physical health or safety of a reasonable tenant.
2. You must give the landlord notice of the condition and a reasonable time to repair it.
3. If it is not repaired you must give the landlord a second notice that if it is not repaired you will either terminate the lease, seek damages, or have the repairs made and the cost deducted from your rent.
4. If the landlord doesn't repair the condition, you have the right to move out, have the condition repaired, sue and force a rent reduction, or recover damages of a month's rent plus $500. If you have to hire an attorney, the landlord must pay your attorney's fees if you win.

Here are some form letters you can use to show your landlord you are serious and that you know the law. Send the following letter after your landlord hasn't made the repairs. Send it certified mail, return receipt requested. Be sure to keep a copy.

Landlord
Landlord Street
City, Texas 77000

Dear Landlord:

On (<u>fill in date</u>) I discovered that [state nature of problem] my roof was leaking.

This condition materially affects the health and safety of an ordinary tenant. I have in no way caused or contributed to this condition.

Please repair this condition immediately. If you need more information or would like to arrange for a repair person to enter my

---

(letter continued on next page)

(letter continued from previous page)

---

apartment, I can be reached during the day at (<u>phone number</u>) and in the evening at (<u>phone</u>).

Thank you for your expected cooperation in this matter.

Sincerely yours,
Your Name

If after a reasonable period of time repairs are not made, send the following letter. Send it certified mail, return receipt requested. Be sure to keep a copy.

Landlord
Landlord Street
City, Texas 77000
Dear Landlord:

On (<u>fill in date</u>) I wrote you concerning (state nature of problem) my leaky roof. I have attached a copy of that letter.

It has now been more than a reasonable time to make repairs, and you have not fixed it. As I told you in my earlier letter, this condition materially affects my physical health and safety.

Unless the repairs are made to my apartment immediately, I intend either to terminate the lease, seek damages for your failure to repair, or have the condition repaired and withhold the cost from my rent. I should advise you that, under the law, I may be entitled to a refund of any rent already paid if I terminate or a penalty of one month's rent plus $500 and court costs and attorneys' fees if I seek damages.

I hope it will not be necessary for me to take any further action. Thank you for your expected cooperation.

Sincerely yours,
Your Name

Can we move out early?
"Not without paying rent."

Dear Mr. Alderman:

We left our apartment a half month early. We did not pay rent for the last half of the month because the pool was never usable and we didn't live there. Now the owner is suing us for the rent and for cleaning. How can we owe rent for the time when we didn't live there and when things didn't work?

You owe rent because you signed a lease. Under the terms of the lease you were obligated to pay rent until the lease was terminated. It doesn't matter if you moved out early.

The fact that the pool didn't work probably did not give you the right to move out and terminate the lease. You may have been able to claim damages against the landlord for not providing services as promised. In my opinion, however, the defective pool is not a sufficient basis to terminate the lease early and end your obligation to pay rent.

You may want to assert a counterclaim against your landlord, however, for the difference of what the apartment was worth with the pool and what it was worth without it. That difference is how much you lost by being unable to use it.

My apartment promised security, and there is none.
"It may be responsible if you are injured."

Dear Mr. Alderman:

I recently rented a new apartment. I chose one based on the agent's assurance that there was good security. In fact, there is none. All the complex has is a guard who never leaves his house, at the entrance to the complex. I am concerned for my safety and want to know my rights.

First, I should point out that apartments have no obligation to provide additional security. Basically, all the law requires is locks on doors and windows, lights in common areas, and fences and latches at pools.

A landlord may, however, be required to provide additional security in two instances. First, a landlord is responsible if he acts negligently. Negligence generally means not acting as a reasonable person would. For example, suppose the landlord knows about a security problem, such as strangers walking around the complex, and takes no steps to either eliminate it or report it to the police. The landlord could be found to have acted negligently if he did not do what a reasonable person would have. If a reasonable person in the same position would have investigated, hired security, or reported it to the police, the landlord's failure to act would be negligence.

The landlord may also be responsible under the Deceptive Trade Practices Act if he made any misrepresentations about security. This law, discussed in Chapter Ten, is a powerful consumer protection law that also applies to renting apartments.

As far as I am concerned, if the agent told you there was good security, and there is none, the agent and the landlord have violated the Deceptive Trade Practices Act. This law would allow you to recover economic damages if you were injured or your apartment was robbed as a result of the failure to provide the promised security, and it may also provide you with a basis to terminate your lease.

Your best bet may be to talk with the landlord and let him know you know about this law and expect the security you were promised. Hopefully you can negotiate a settlement you are happy with. You may not get security, but you may get him to let you move out without breaching your lease.

My landlord lied to me. What can I do?
"The Texas Deceptive Trade Practices Act applies."

Dear Mr. Alderman:
I just moved into a new apartment. When I looked at the model, the rental agent told me that when new tenants move in, the apartment is painted, and the rugs are shampooed. I was scheduled to move in on Saturday and went to look at the unit on Wednesday. It had not even been cleaned, let alone painted. The agent again told me not to worry, that it would be painted by the time I moved in on Saturday. On Saturday, I arrived with my furniture, and the unit was clean but not painted. Also, the rugs were not shampooed. The owner had changed his mind and wasn't going to paint anymore. What are my rights?

Any time someone leases anything, including an apartment, the Texas Deceptive Trade Practices Act applies. Under this law (discussed in Chapter Ten), it is unlawful to misrepresent the qualities or characteristics of something. For example, telling a tenant an apartment will be painted when it will not be is a misrepresentation. As far as I am concerned, the landlord has violated the Deceptive Trade Practices Act by not providing an apartment as represented. I should also point out that because the agent is the authorized employee of the owner, the owner is liable for the agent's representations.

I suggest you reread Chapter Ten and then send the proper notice to the landlord demanding that your unit be painted and the rugs shampooed as promised or that you be reasonably compensated. A fair amount would be how much you are going to have to pay someone else to perform these services. If the landlord does not comply and you have to go to court to collect, the law entitles you to up to three times your damages plus any court costs and attorneys' fees involved. As a practical matter, it is unlikely you will end up in court. Usually, these problems are resolved once the other side knows you know your rights.

Can I sublease?
"Not without consent."

Dear Mr. Alderman:

I have a simple question to ask: Do I have the right to sublease my apartment? I have seven months left on my lease, and I am getting married. What I would like to do is sublease to a friend for the remainder of my lease term.

You may not like this answer, but the law is clear: *You may not sublease unless your lease expressly gives you this right.* Under the law, a tenant does not have the right to sublease. This right can only be given to you by your landlord. I suggest you read your lease carefully to see what it says about subleasing. If it is silent, then you do not have the right to sublease.

Even if your lease does not give you the right to sublease, your landlord may still agree to it. You should talk to him and try to get him to agree. You also should remember that even if he does agree, you will be responsible for the rent if your subtenant doesn't pay.

Can my landlord come in my apartment and take my property if I don't pay rent?
"Maybe."

Dear Mr. Alderman:

I admit it; I should pay my rent, and it is my own fault I was late, but does my landlord have the right to come in and take my TV and stereo when I am late? I came home last night, and there was a note telling me as soon as I paid I could have the property back. I plan on paying the rent tomorrow, but I want to know if what my landlord did was legal.

The answer is, it is legal if all the steps of the law have been followed. What your landlord is doing is asserting what is called a "landlord's lien." This allows the landlord to peacefully enter your apartment and take your property until you pay the rent. If you don't pay, he has the right to sell the property. But to assert this lien certain requirements must be met.

First, the right to assert this lien must be underlined or printed in conspicuous bold print in your lease. Read your lease carefully; if the lien does not appear, the landlord has no right to take your property, and doing so would, in effect, be theft, entitling you to substantial damages. Second, a landlord may only take certain property under this lien. Here is a list of what the law says the landlord may not take:

1. wearing apparel;
2. tools, apparatus, and books of a trade or profession;
3. schoolbooks;
4. a family library;
5. family portraits and pictures;
6. one couch, two living room chairs, and a dining table and chairs;
7. beds and bedding;
8. kitchen furniture and utensils;
9. food and foodstuffs;
10. medicine and medical supplies;
11. one automobile and one truck;
12. agricultural implements;
13. children's toys not commonly used by adults;
14. goods the landlord or the landlord's agent knows are owned by a person other than the tenant or an occupant of the residence; and

15. goods the landlord or the landlord's agent knows are subject to a recorded chattel mortgage or financing agreement.

If the landlord has taken any of this property he has violated the law. Finally, the landlord must leave you a note telling you what he took and what you need to do to get it back (the note must also tell you how much you owe in back rent). The bottom line is, although a landlord may have the right to take your property pursuant to a landlord's lien, the requirements of the law are often not met, and the landlord is acting wrongfully. If you feel your landlord has acted wrongfully, speak with him and try to get your property back. If you can't, you should consider small claims court or an attorney. Under the law, a landlord who violates the provision of the lien law is responsible for all the tenant's damages and one month's rent or $500, whichever is greater, plus attorneys' fees.

My landlord has locked me out. Help!
"There is a law."

Dear Mr. Alderman:
I recently lost my job and got behind in my rent. Last night when I got home, my landlord had changed the locks on the door of my apartment and told me to get off the property until I come up with some money. I don't have any way to get the money I owe him, and I just want to get my things and leave. How long can he hold all my property?

Unless your landlord has a landlord's lien and acts according to state law (read the prior letter) he can't hold your property at all. *In fact, it is illegal for a landlord to just lock you out, no matter how much money you owe.* Under the law a landlord has the right to change the locks on your doors, but he must give you notice of where a key is, and he must let you in whenever you want. He also can't stop you from removing your property and moving out. As I said before, only if he has a landlord's lien can he hold your property.

I suggest you talk with the landlord and let him know you know the law. A landlord who illegally locks you out can be liable for substantial damages.

Do I have to live in an apartment complex with children?
"Yes, unless the complex is for persons over age 55."

Dear Mr. Alderman:
I live in a nice apartment complex just outside town. I have lived here for five years, and it has always been for adults only. Recently, several families with children moved into the complex, and the whole mood has changed. The complex is no longer the quiet place it once was. I am awakened on weekend mornings by the sound of motorized toys in the courtyard.
I complained to the manager and he said there is nothing he can do; a new law requires that he rent to people with children. Is this the law? Don't I have the right to live where I want?

Under recent amendments to the federal **Fair Housing Act**, it is illegal to discriminate against families with children with respect to housing. This means a landlord must rent to anyone, regardless of whether he or she is married, single, or has children. The only restrictions that may be placed are those that apply to all. For example, the number of occupants per unit may be limited. It can't be limited, however, to adults.

There is a major exception to this law, however, that may help you. If a complex has 80% or more units occupied by at least one person over age 55, it is not required to take children. If you are over 55 it may be a good idea to look for one of the "seniors only" complexes. Seniors only is now another way of saying no children.

One last point. Just because apartments cannot discriminate against children or families with children does not mean you have to have your peace and quiet disturbed. If the children are getting up very early and making a lot of noise, the manager has the right to insist they be kept quiet. I suggest you speak with the manager and ask him to take steps to ensure the children comply with the same rules and regulations as everyone else.

I was refused an apartment because the landlord said my wheelchair would ruin the carpet. Is this legal?
"No. You can't discriminate against the handicapped."

Dear Mr. Alderman:
I am handicapped, confined to a wheelchair. I recently found the perfect apartment and when I went to sign the lease was told by the

landlord that I would have to look elsewhere. He told me, "Your wheelchair will ruin my carpet." Is this legal? I thought new laws protected the handicapped. I realize my chair may do some damage, but I am willing to pay for it.

You are right. Recent amendments to the Fair Housing Act prohibit discrimination against a handicapped person. "Handicap" is defined to include a physical or mental impairment that substantially limits one or more of such person's major life activities.

Based on what you say, the landlord has acted illegally. Under the law he could be subject to civil penalties of up to $10,000. You can enforce this law privately, with the assistance of an attorney, or you can contact the Department of Housing and Urban Development. At a minimum, I would contact the landlord and let him know what the law is. Hopefully he was just uninformed and will now take steps to comply with the law.

Can my landlord ask for more security deposit?
"If it is a new lease, yes."

Dear Mr. Alderman:
I live in an apartment and have a six-month lease. This is the third such lease I have signed. Every time a lease is up, my landlord asks me to sign a new one. Each time I sign a new lease, however, my landlord raises my security deposit by $20. Is this legal?

Yes. If you have a lease, the terms of your agreement with your landlord are governed by the lease and cannot be changed without your consent. In other words, during the lease period your security deposit could not be raised. When your lease expires, however, both you and the landlord are free to either renew the lease on its present terms, terminate the agreement, or write a new agreement.

For example, at the end of your lease, the rent could be raised or lowered, or the six-month term could be increased or decreased. Similarly, if your landlord wants additional security, he may ask for it. Of course, if you don't want to pay it you have the right to give notice and move. The amount of the security deposit is a matter to be negotiated by you and the landlord.

My landlord turned off my electricity. What can I do?
"You may withhold rent to pay the electric bill yourself or move out."

Dear Mr. Alderman:
My landlord is supposed to provide electricity for my apartment. Recently he stopped paying the bill, and the power company cut it off. What are my legal rights?

Under the law, a tenant has substantial rights when a landlord fails to provide utilities he promised to furnish. If a landlord expressly agrees or implies he agrees in the lease to furnish and pay for water or electric service to the tenant's dwelling, the landlord is liable if the utilities are cut off or if the tenant receives notice that they are about to be cut off. If this happens, the tenant may

1. pay the utilities company and deduct the amounts paid from the rent;
2. give written notice to terminate the lease within 30 days;
3. deduct the security deposit from the rent (if the lease is terminated);
4. recover damages against the landlord, including the costs of moving, utility connection fees, lost wages, etc.; and
5. recover any attorneys' fees.

In other words, you may either move out and recover the damages you incur or pay the utility company yourself and deduct the amount from the rent. I suggest you let the landlord know you know about this law. That may solve your problem.

Can my landlord come into my apartment?
"It depends on your lease."

Dear Mr. Alderman:
My landlord came into my apartment to exterminate without giving me prior notice. When he came in, my dog escaped. I spoke with the landlord and told him I didn't want him in my apartment when I was not home and that I was concerned that the next time my dog got out I wouldn't be able to find her. Well, it happened again, and now my dog is lost. Do I have any rights?

Your landlord's right to enter your apartment depends on the lease you signed. I suggest, as a first step, you carefully read your lease. If your lease doesn't say otherwise, then the landlord probably does not have the right to enter your apartment whenever he wants. He probably may enter, however, at reasonable times to check the condition of the property. A landlord who wrongfully enters an apartment should be responsible for any damage that results.

Finally, I should point out that even if your landlord has the right to enter your apartment, he must act reasonably. In my opinion, letting your dog escape after you warned him of this danger would be negligence. In this case, the landlord would be responsible for the value of the dog and any mental anguish you suffered as a result of the loss.

What are a landlord's rights if a tenant doesn't pay the last month's rent?
"You may be entitled to three times the rent."

Dear Mr. Alderman:
I am a landlord. Is there anything I can do to make my tenants pay the last month's rent? They tell me to just keep the security deposit, but then I have nothing to cover damages.

As I discuss on page 133, a landlord who does not properly return a tenant's security deposit may be liable to the tenant for three times the deposit plus $100.

Conversely, under the law a tenant who tells a landlord to use the security deposit for the last month's rent is liable to the landlord for three times the rent withheld plus attorneys' fees. My guess is if you let your tenants know about the law, they will pay the last month's rent.

How do I get a tenant to leave?
"File eviction papers."

Dear Mr. Alderman:
I rent out a house. The tenants, who are on a month-to-month tenancy, have not paid rent in two months. They will not pay rent or move out. How do I get them to move?

To evict the tenants, you must give them one more written notice to move. Let them know if they do not leave, you will take steps to have them evicted. To evict them, go to the local justice of the peace and file a forcible entry and detainer, commonly called an FED. This is the device you use to evict them. The clerk of the court will probably be able to help you fill out any necessary forms.

CHAPTER THIRTEEN

Lawyers

THIS book was written to provide some basic legal information that can help you resolve everyday disputes. As I said in the introduction, once someone knows you know your legal rights, you usually can settle the matter in an amicable manner.

Unfortunately, however, some disputes cannot be resolved by the involved parties, and small claims court cannot be used. When you find yourself in this position, you have no choice but to hire a lawyer to assist you. Many letters I receive ask questions about how to find a good attorney and what to do if you have a problem with the one you hire. Here are some answers to the more common concerns.

How do I find a lawyer?
"There are lots of ways."

Dear Mr. Alderman:
I never thought I would have any legal problems, but now I need a lawyer. How do I find one I can trust?

As with any professional, there is not a best way to find a lawyer. I suggest you take the same approach you would if you were looking for a doctor, architect, or accountant.

The best way to start may be to talk with friends and family. See if anyone has used an attorney he or she liked. If so, this person may be able to help or refer you to someone else. You also should look at advertisements for lawyers. Treat these ads like those for any other service. Look for an advertisement that gives you useful information in a way you think is consistent with a good, trustworthy lawyer.

You also should consider calling a referral service operated by the State Bar or your local Bar Association. Look in the yellow pages to see if your city or county Bar Association operates a referral service. The State Bar of Texas operates a state-wide referral service, (800) 204-2222.

Once you get some names of attorneys, speak with several before you make a decision. Remember, you may have to work with this person for a long time. Be sure to find someone you can easily communicate with and with whom you feel comfortable.

What does it mean to be Board certified?
"The lawyer demonstrated special competence."

Dear Mr. Alderman:
I noticed that almost all the attorneys who advertise say they are not certified by the Texas Board of Legal Specialization. What does this mean? Why would anyone hire an attorney who was not certified?

Any lawyer who has passed the State Bar Exam is licensed to practice law and may practice in any area. For example, I am a member of the State Bar. I, therefore, may represent a person with any sort of legal problem.

Under Texas law, however, any attorney who advertises must state if he or she is certified by the Texas Board of Legal Specialization. This is a special certification that a lawyer may seek in one of 17 different areas. If the lawyer passes a special test and complies with other requirements, he or she will be certified in a specialty.

Only about 11% of the attorneys in Texas are "Board certified." Many very good attorneys have chosen not to become Board certified. For example, I am not certified in any specialty.

My advice is to consider the fact that someone is Board certified as a plus when you evaluate an attorney. I would not, however, consider it a negative factor if an attorney is not certified. Evaluate any lawyer you talk with based on his or her qualifications and how well he or she relates to you. Board certification is just one of many factors to consider.

I have a problem with my lawyer. What can I do?
"The State Bar wants to know."

Dear Mr. Alderman:
I hired an attorney to help me with a problem. He took my money,
and I can't get him to even talk to me. I am afraid he has spent the
money, and I am out of luck. What can I do?

The answer to your question will depend on whether your lawyer
engaged in professional misconduct or malpractice. The most important
difference is the Bar Association regulates professional misconduct that
violates the rules of professional conduct established by the State Bar of
Texas. On the other hand, the Bar does not regulate malpractice, defined
as not acting as a reasonably competent attorney would when handling a
matter, and you would have to bring a private lawsuit.

Essentially, the rules of professional conduct require that an attorney
act ethically. This means handling the client's case in a professional manner, keeping funds separate, and communicating with the client before
making any important decisions. In your case, it sounds like your attorney has violated this code of ethics.

Fortunately, the State Bar of Texas closely regulates the lawyers it
licenses. If a lawyer violates any rules of professional conduct, the Bar
Association may begin an investigation into the alleged violation and
may discipline the lawyer. The punishments range from a simple repri-
mand to termination of the license to practice law.

How do you decide whether your claim involves professional misconduct? You don't have to. When you file a complaint with the Bar Association, one of the first things it does is determine if the complaint has been
properly filed.

I suggest you contact the Bar Association and get a copy of its free
booklet about attorney complaints, (800) 932-1900.

CHAPTER FOURTEEN

Mail-Order & Telephone Sales

MAIL-ORDER and telephone sales are big business. Today you can buy everything from food and clothing to furniture from catalogs. You can shop in the privacy of your home or office, with no high-pressure salesperson looking over your shoulder. For the busy worker, catalogs and newspaper ads have replaced department stores.

But shopping at home has one big drawback: You don't see what you are buying, and you don't receive it as soon as you pick it out. When you go into a store and buy a pair of jogging shoes, you pick out the style and size you want, try them on, pay for them, and off you go. You are on your way home to use them.

But when you buy the same pair of jogging shoes through the mail, you must first pay and then wait until they arrive. And two bad things can happen: (1) They may never arrive; or (2) They may not be what you thought they were. These are the risks inherent in shopping by mail or over the phone; you must pay first and then wait for the goods—goods you cannot examine until they arrive, if they arrive at all. However, the next few letters will show you shopping by mail or phone does not have to be risky. Laws ensure you can enjoy the convenience of shopping at home, without the risk of never receiving what you paid for.

What can I do if the goods never arrive?
"Next time, use a credit card."

Dear Mr. Alderman:
I saw an ad in a magazine for a Wizard Roach Remover, guaranteed to keep roaches out of my house for two months. I sent the company $19.95 plus postage more than five weeks ago. I still have not received my roach killer, and the company won't answer my letters. It did cash my check, though. What can I do to get my money back? The company is in Iowa.

I have some good news and some bad. The bad news is you may be out of luck unless the company voluntarily sends your money back. *The good news is you can avoid this problem in the future by taking advantage of a federal law, the Fair Credit Billing Act.*

First, as to what you can do now. As the next letter discusses more fully, under the law a mail-order company can only wait 30 days to send your goods. In your case it has already delayed beyond this period. The problem is that to enforce any of your rights against the company you will have to sue, and even if you used small claims court in Texas, you probably could not collect unless the company has assets or an office here. In other words, you are probably out of luck because it will cost you more to enforce your rights than you lost in the deal. You may take steps to prevent this from happening to others by contacting the Better Business Bureau, the Federal Trade Commission, and the attorney general's office and telling them of your problem.

So what can you do to avoid this in the future? *Use a credit card whenever you order by mail.* Under the Fair Credit Billing Act, the credit card company cannot collect for items you ordered but never received. If you had paid for your goods with a credit card, you could simply contact the credit card company and tell the company there is a billing error and that you are not going to pay your bill. Here is what you should do to protect yourself.

When the goods don't arrive:

When many consumers find mistakes on their bills, such as charges for goods that never arrived, they pick up the phone and call the company to correct the problem. You can do this if you wish, but phoning does not trigger the legal safeguards provided under the law. To be protected under the Fair Credit Billing Act, you must send a separate written billing error notice to the credit card company. Your notice must reach the company within 60 days after the first bill containing the error was mailed to you. Send the notice to the address provided on the bill for billing error notices (and not, for example, directly to the store, unless the bill says that's where it should be sent). In your letter, you must include the following information: your name and account number; a statement that you believe the bill contains a billing error; the dollar amount involved; and why you believe there is a mistake—the goods never arrived. It's a good idea to send it by certified mail, return receipt requested. That way you'll have proof of the dates of mailing and receipt.

If you wish, send photocopies of sales slips or other documents, but keep the originals for your records.

What must the credit card company do?

Your letter claiming a billing error must be acknowledged by the credit card company within 30 days after it is received, unless the problem is resolved within that period. In any case, within two billing cycles (but not more than 90 days), the creditor must conduct a reasonable investigation and either correct the mistake or explain why the bill is believed to be correct.

What happens while the credit card company investigates?

You may withhold payment of the amount in dispute, including the affected portions of minimum payments and finance charges, until the dispute is resolved. You are still required to pay any part of the bill not disputed, including finance and other charges on undisputed amounts.

While the Fair Credit Billing Act dispute settlement procedure is going on, the creditor may not take any legal or other action to collect the amount in dispute. Your account may not be closed or restricted in any way, except the disputed amount may be applied against your credit limit.

What happens once the credit card company determines you never received the goods?

If your bill is found to contain a billing error (the goods didn't arrive), the creditor must write you explaining the corrections to be made on your account. In addition to crediting your account with the amount not owed, the creditor must remove all finance charges, late fees, or other charges relating to that amount.

The credit card company must follow these procedures or it will violate federal law. If you feel the credit card company has not complied with the law, you should report it to the nearest Federal Trade Commission regional office or to the Federal Trade Commission, Fair Credit Billing, Washington, DC 20580.

How long do I have to wait?
"Thirty days."

Dear Mr. Alderman:
Three months ago I ordered a new bathing suit. It cost more than
$30. I still have not received the suit, and it is almost fall. The com-
pany keeps telling me it will arrive any day. What can I do? I want
my money back, not a bikini to wear in the winter.

Under federal law a seller must deliver the goods within the time
promised. If no time is stated in your agreement, there is a presumption
that 30 days is reasonable. *If your bathing suit has not arrived within 30*
days, the company must notify you of when it will be delivered and let
you cancel if you change your mind.

Based on your letter, it appears the company has violated the law and
you have the right to cancel and get your money back. I suggest you
write the company once more via certified mail, return receipt requested,
and say you want to cancel your order. If you do not receive your money
back, contact the Federal Trade Commission and say the company has
violated the mail-order rules.

You should also know that the company, by violating the federal law,
may have violated the Texas Deceptive Trade Practices Act as well. This
means the attorney general could take action against the company and
you could file suit in small claims court for three times your damages.
The problem with filing suit is the company is probably far away, and
collecting anything will be difficult.

So what can you do? Read the letter right before this one, and next
time make sure you use a credit card.

What happens when the wrong thing arrives?
"Protect yourself."

Dear Mr. Alderman:
I recently ordered a woman's size 12 jacket from a company in New
York. It arrived three weeks later as a man's size 42. I sent it back to
the company and was told I would be sent a new one. The company

has not sent a new jacket, and it has cashed my check for $50. What can I do? I don't think the company is even in business anymore.

If you read the letter right before this one, you know a federal law requires companies to deliver goods or give you a refund within 30 days. The problem is that even though you are entitled to your jacket or your money back, it will be difficult, if not impossible, for you to collect. Having legal rights is meaningless unless the company you have rights against is solvent and in a location convenient for you to sue in.

So what do you do? First, report the company to the Federal Trade Commission for violating federal mail-order laws. Then, if the company has a local office or owns property in Texas, you can sue in small claims court. From your letter, though, it sounds like the company has disappeared with your money, and now you should be concerned with making sure this never happens again.

In the future, to protect yourself make sure you use a credit card whenever you order by mail. Then if you don't receive what you ordered, the Fair Credit Billing Act lets you withhold payment from the credit card company. To find out just how this law works, read the letter on page 152.

I didn't order this. What can I do?
"Accept the gift."

Dear Mr. Alderman:
The other day I arrived home and found a box on my doorstep. It was from a company in Nebraska I had never heard of. Inside was all sorts of junk: toys, stationery, ashtrays, and trinkets. The letter that came with the stuff said it was sent to me on approval and I could keep it for only $49.95 or send it back. The post office wants $5 to send the junk back, and I don't want to pay it. It doesn't seem right that I get stuck because of this stupid company. Is there anything I can do?

You are in luck. Texas and federal law provides that you may treat unsolicited merchandise as a gift. *If you did not order the goods* (but be careful, because you may have signed something a long time ago agreeing to accept such orders on approval), *you can do whatever you want with them.* I think that to be polite you should write the company a letter, thank it for the gift, and tell it you will be glad to receive other gifts in the future. If you do not want to keep the merchandise, you may want to tell the company if it will send you postage, you will return the merchandise. Of course, if you want, you can simply throw the box away.

The only requirement that must be met before the goods can be treated as a gift is they must not be ordered or solicited by you. To make sure you didn't order them, you may want to write the company via certified mail, return receipt requested, and ask for proof that you ordered the goods. Tell the company that unless it can show you that you did in fact order the goods, you will keep them as you are permitted to do by law.

The Texas law is a short one, so I thought I would let you see what it says:

> Unless otherwise agreed, where unsolicited goods are delivered to a person, he has a right to refuse to accept delivery of the goods and is not bound to return such goods to the sender. Goods received due to a bonafide mistake are to be returned, but the burden of proof of the error shall be upon the sender. If such unsolicited goods are either addressed to or intended for the recipient, they shall be deemed a gift to the recipient, who may use them or dispose of them in any manner without any obligation to the sender. Provided, however, the provisions of this Act shall not apply to goods substituted for goods ordered or solicited by the recipient.

Remember: This law applies only to unsolicited merchandise. If you authorize a company to send you merchandise on approval, such as with a book club, you do not have the right to keep it, and you must bear the cost of returning the item.

CHAPTER FIFTEEN

Neighborly Problems

MOST of us get along well with our neighbors, and if a dispute arises we settle it by talking it out and reaching a fair compromise. But
sometimes you can have a problem with your neighbor that you just can't
settle—and then knowing your legal rights can help you decide what step
to take next.

*The best advice I can ever give is to try to settle your disputes in a
friendly way. The law is designed to help in those situations in which the
parties themselves can't work it out. Remember, you might be neighbors for
a long time. Compromise is the key when dealing with your neighbors.*

My neighbor's tree fell on my car. Who's responsible?
"Why did the tree fall?"

Dear Mr. Alderman:
*Last week there was a severe thunderstorm. The wind blew down my
neighbor's tree, and part of the tree landed on my car. The damage
to my car will cost approximately $1,500 to repair. I have insurance,
but it has a $500 deductible. I talked with my neighbor, but he refuses
to pay and says it wasn't his fault. Do I have any rights? Can I force
him to pay?*

Your neighbor may not have to pay for the damage to your car, even
though it was his tree. *Under the law your neighbor is only responsible
to you if he was negligent in caring for the tree.* In other words, if the tree
was healthy and blew down in an unusually strong wind, your neighbor
would probably not have any liability. But if the tree was diseased and
your neighbor knew it, he could be responsible for the damage if the tree
fell during a regular storm, one that did not blow over healthy trees.

People have a duty to their neighbors to keep their property in a way
that will not injure their neighbors. If your neighbor was negligent in the
care of his property, he is responsible for the damage caused. But your

neighbor is not responsible for an act of God that could not have been prevented, even by the most careful person.

What can I do about my neighbor's tree?
"Trim it carefully."

Dear Mr. Alderman:
My neighbor's tree hangs over my garage and is close to my roof. I am afraid a strong wind will blow the tree onto my property and damage it. Do I have the right to cut the overhanging branches down? Can I force my neighbor to cut it? Who will be responsible if the tree damages my property?

Problems with neighbor's trees can be among the most difficult to resolve, both legally and practically. Because the tree is on your neighbor's property, you do not have the right to cut it down. You may have the right to cut the overhanging branches; however, if you injure the tree, you could be responsible. The best suggestion may be to speak with your neighbor and let him know about the problem. Explain that the branches are a hazard to your property and that you would like him to cut them down. If you are willing to do it, tell him so. If he still refuses to work with you, he could be liable for any damage that occurs. As I said in the previous letter, the owner of a tree is negligent, and therefore responsible, if he does not take reasonable steps to protect you and your property from harm. In my opinion, not cutting overhanging branches after being warned of a danger is negligence.

What happens if the neighbor's kid is hurt playing on my property?
"You are probably not responsible."

Dear Mr. Alderman:
I don't want to sound like someone who doesn't like kids—I do—but the neighbor's children are worrying me. They seem to find my roof an exciting place to play, and just last week, I caught two 9-year-olds on the roof. They climb up from the fence and then wander around wherever they like. What I need to know is whether I am in trouble if they get hurt up there. I have done everything I can do to stop them, but they keep coming back.

If you have done everything a reasonable person would do to keep the children off your roof, you probably will not be responsible if one of the children is injured. *The law only imposes a duty on you to take ordinary care to protect the trespassing children from injury.* This means taking reasonable steps to keep them off your property and not leaving unusually dangerous conditions where the children play.

For example, if the children climb over a fence to get to your property, you probably are not responsible if they fall and injure themselves. But if you were to leave a gun outside, where you knew the children played, you could be responsible if one of them was shot. The test is what a reasonable person would do in a similar situation.

There is one exception to this general rule you should know about. A doctrine known as "attractive nuisance" places a greater duty on a landowner when there is a condition known to be attractive to children. For example, we all know children like swimming pools. If you have a pool in your yard, the law presumes you know children will try to use it and imposes an obligation on you to take extra steps to keep them out. While a person generally does not have a duty to fence his property to keep out trespassers, an owner with a pool may be required to do so.

Do I have to pay for damage caused by my child?
"As a legal matter, no."

Dear Mr. Alderman
Recently my son and some of his friends were playing baseball in the lot near our house. I am not sure exactly what happened, but somehow my son threw a baseball through our neighbor's window. Now my neighbor has insisted I pay for it. I intend to pay to be a good neighbor, but I was wondering what my legal liability would be if I didn't.

As far as the law is concerned, you probably are not liable. Generally, parents are not responsible for wrongs committed by their children. There are, however, a few exceptions.

First, you would be responsible if the accident occurred as a result of your failure to properly supervise your child. For example, if the kids were playing in the backyard, and you did not take reasonable steps to make sure they hit the ball away from windows instead of toward them, you could be liable. Under the law, parents are also responsible for willful and malicious acts committed by a child between the ages of 12 and 18.

If your child intentionally threw the ball at the window, and he was between the ages of 12 and 18, you would be responsible under this law.

The bottom line, however, is that your decision to pay is probably the best one. Sometimes being a good neighbor is more important than exercising your legal rights.

How can I stop my neighbor's barking dog?
"There may be a law."

Dear Mr. Alderman:

Why is it the smallest dogs seem to make the most noise? My neighbor has a small dog that barks all day when she is gone. My neighbor leaves the dog outside, and it stands at my fence and barks. It is driving me crazy. This would be bad enough, but she lets the dog out every morning at 6 a.m. When the dog wants back in, about five minutes later, it just starts barking. I have talked to my neighbor and she says there is nothing she can do—dogs will be dogs. I don't want to get into an argument with her about who is right and who is wrong until I know my rights. Does a neighbor have the right to force someone to stop their dog from barking like this?

I have been surprised by the number of people who have written me about barking dogs—and unfortunately I don't have a simple answer. However, two areas of law may help you.

Under general legal principles, you cannot use your property or maintain it in a manner that is a nuisance to others. If the barking dog is seriously disrupting your enjoyment of your property, you may be able to sue your neighbor to force the dog to stop. The test, however, would be whether a reasonable person would be seriously disturbed by the dog. For example, if the dog barked occasionally during the day, something all dogs do, you probably would not have any basis for objection. On the other hand, if it barked all night, your neighbor would probably be maintaining a nuisance. If the dog is a nuisance you can bring a lawsuit to stop it.

Before you consider a lawsuit, though, you should see if there are any local laws or ordinances directly on point. The first thing I suggest you do is contact your local governing body. Many cities and counties have laws regulating barking dogs, and you could get them to enforce the law. If there are no specific laws or ordinances, you will have to bring a civil action, a costly and often time-consuming thing to do.

The best advice I can give you is to try to talk to your neighbor and work it out. You may be right legally, but it will be difficult to prove and enforce.

The neighbor's dog bit me. Must the neighbor pay? "It depends."

Dear Mr. Alderman:
My neighbor has a large, vicious dog. The dog is always chasing my children and has bitten one of them before. Last week the dog got out of his fence and bit my son, doing severe damage. The doctor bills were expensive, and our insurance didn't cover them. I asked my neighbor to pay the bills and he said no. I told him I would sue and he said, "Go ahead. An owner isn't legally responsible for what a dog does." Is this true? How can a person let his dog bite people and not have to pay the bills?

Based on what you say in your letter, I think your neighbor is wrong. In some states a pet owner is "strictly liable" for injuries caused by a pet. This means if a dog bites someone, the owner must pay for the damages regardless of whether the owner did anything wrong. Unfortunately, Texas has not yet adopted a rule like this, and in Texas you must show that the owner was "negligent." That is, the owner had reason to know the dog would bite and didn't take reasonable steps to protect you. In many cases this means the dog must either have bitten someone previously or be known to have vicious tendencies.

In your case the dog had chased and bitten people before and the owner should have known the dog was vicious. If the owner did not take reasonable steps to protect you, for example, by keeping the dog well penned, I believe the owner should be responsible. If the amount is low enough for you to go to small claims court (see Chapter Sixteen) you can sue without an attorney.

One final point. In many cases, the breed of dog, for example, a pit bull, is known to be vicious. In my opinion, owners of this kind of dog are held to a higher standard and should be responsible when the dog bites, even if the dog never bit before. While the owner of a poodle may not have to take steps to protect you from injury, the law probably imposes a higher duty on the owner of a dog whose breed is known to be vicious.

My neighbor's dog got my dog pregnant.
Is my neighbor responsible?
"Yes. Owners are responsible for the consequences of their dogs' acts."

Dear Mr. Alderman:
I have a strange problem. I recently came home to find my neigh-
bor's dog engaged in intercourse with my dog in my backyard. My
dog is chained up in our fenced backyard. My neighbor's dog had
been running loose and dug under my fence. My dog is pedigreed,
and we want to breed her. To protect our dog, and to not have to
deal with a litter of mutt puppies, we terminated the pregnancy. I
asked my neighbor to help pay the costs, and he refused, saying he
was not responsible for the misdeeds of his dog. Is he?

Don't think your problem is that strange or unusual. These things do
happen. In fact, in a recent case in Florida the owner of a Rottweiler successfully sued the owner of a Chihuahua for impregnating his dog under
similar circumstances.

As far as I am concerned, your neighbor should be responsible if he
did not take proper steps to ensure that his dog did not run wild and
break into your yard. If your city has a leash law that was broken, your
neighbor should be responsible because he did not comply with this law.
If there is no such law, you must show that your neighbor knew his dog
was running wild and that there was a likelihood the dog would take
advantage of other dogs in heat. Generally, owners are responsible for
conduct such as you describe.

I should point out, however, that the neighbor may not be responsible
if he did everything he could to keep the dog locked up, and it was not
his fault the dog got out. For example, if the dog was locked in the backyard and someone else opened the gate and let the dog out, your neighbor
probably would not be responsible.

Finally, as you might guess, it can be very hard to prove the case of the
promiscuous poodle. The best advice may be to speak with your neighbor
again and try to work things out.

My car was vandalized at a restaurant.
Is the restaurant responsible?
"Possibly."

Dear Mr. Alderman:
The other night, I went to dinner with my boyfriend. We parked the car in front of the restaurant, and when we came out we found that the front window had been smashed and the tape deck stolen. We talked to the manager of the restaurant, and he said the restaurant was not responsible. Is that true? It doesn't seem right. It provides the parking lot. Doesn't it have to provide security?

There is no simple answer to your question. Legally, the restaurant is only liable if it has been negligent, that is, if it did not take reasonable care to protect your property. For example, ordinarily a restaurant does not have to provide security. This means if there is an incident of vandalism, the restaurant probably would not be responsible. But once a restaurant— or any other establishment, for that matter—knows there may be problems or that it is located in a high-crime area, its obligations change. Now the restaurant must take reasonable steps to protect its customers. If it does not, it will be responsible. For example, if every restaurant in that neighborhood had lights and security guards in the parking lots and this restaurant did not, it probably would be liable because it was negligent. On the other hand, if it does the same thing as everyone else has done to protect you and vandalism still occurs, it probably is not liable.

Simply because your property is damaged while in a parking lot is not enough to make the owner responsible. To recover, you will have to show that the restaurant did not take reasonable steps to protect your property. What is reasonable will depend on how high the risk of vandalism is, how much knowledge the owner has of the risk, and what others do under similar circumstances. If you feel an owner did not act reasonably to protect you, you should consider a claim for negligence in small claims court.

My stolen property ended up in a pawn shop. Can I get it back?
"Yes!"

Dear Mr. Alderman:
I was robbed. The thief took all my jewelry and electronic equipment. Now I found out the police caught him and know where he

pawned my property. Can I get my property back from the pawn shop? What if it has been sold? It seems like this is my property and I ought to be entitled to it.

You are right. It is your property, and under the law you can get it back from whomever has it. If a thief steals your property, anyone who receives it is subject to your title. This means the pawnbroker, or anyone who purchased it from the pawnbroker, will have to return it to you. Of course, you will have to prove the property is yours. That is why it is a good idea to keep serial numbers and photographs of all your valuables.

The apartment next door has an unfenced pool. What can I do? "There is a new law."

Dear Mr. Alderman:
We live close to a small apartment complex. The apartments have a swimming pool in the middle of the complex. It does not have a fence, and the door to the courtyard is always open. I am afraid my young son will play in the pool and drown. What can I do to get the complex to fence in the pool? I checked with the city and learned the pool is within city building codes.

In 1993 the Texas Legislature enacted a law governing swimming pool enclosures. Under this law, pools owned by an apartment complex or a property owners' association must be properly enclosed. Basically, to comply with this law, a pool must have a fence at least 48 inches high around it. The pool also must have a gate that is self-closing and self-latching.

This law may be privately enforced by a tenant, homeowner, or any other interested party. Many government agencies, including the attorney general's office, the local health department, and the city or county attorney's office, also can bring an action to enforce it. If the apartment has not taken steps to comply with the new law, I suggest you speak with the manager and then contact the appropriate officials to have them require compliance. I should point out that failure to comply could result in civil penalties of up to $5,000.

Do I have the right to take my neighbor's trash?
"It depends on your neighbor's intent."

Dear Mr. Alderman:
I often pick things out of the trash left on the curb in my neighbor-
hood. Recently someone saw me and told me to leave it alone
because it was his property. Is this correct? Who owns the trash left
for the trash collector?

Good question. I think the answer is the person who left the trash probably owns it unless it was his or her intent to abandon it.

Under the law, a person may abandon title to personal property. For
example, if I no longer want something, I can leave it at a junkyard, and
it would no longer be mine. Anyone who came along would have the
right to pick it up and claim ownership of it.

The question is whether people intend this when they leave trash on
the curb for the trash collector to pick up. My guess is in most cases people do intend to abandon the property, and you, therefore, would have the
right to take what you wanted.

On the other hand, a person could intend to leave the garbage only for
the trash collector. In this case it would belong to that person until picked
up. You, therefore, would not have the right to just take the property.

The intent of the person who placed the property on the street controls
ownership. If your neighbor says to leave it alone, you should.

Is it legal for a dog to ride in the back of a pick-up?
"Unfortunately, yes."

Dear Mr. Alderman:
Is it legal for someone to allow a dog to ride in the back of an open
pick-up? It seems so dangerous.

Although many people would agree with you that it is dangerous for a
dog to ride in the back of a pick-up, it is not illegal.

CHAPTER SIXTEEN

Small Claims Court

KNOWING your legal rights is just the beginning. To make this knowledge work for you, you must be able to assert your rights. Small claims court fills this need. It is inexpensive and simple to use and can promptly settle disputes. Small claims court is where you put your knowledge to work.

As I said in the introduction, once you know your legal rights, you usually will not have to pursue a legal claim. The other party will try to settle the problem. But sometimes a dispute cannot be settled, and you must resort to the legal system to resolve it.

The decision of whether to sue must be made by you, based on the amount of money involved, the importance of the issues, and how much time and expense you are willing to spend to pursue your claim. Don't let emotion reign over common sense. You are always better off trying to settle with the other party before you go to court. But if you cannot settle, small claims court gives you a chance to appear before a judge or jury and have an impartial tribunal decide who is correct.

As you will see from the following letters, small claims court is relatively easy to use and very inexpensive. Also, if you are successful you will be awarded the costs of the lawsuit in addition to your other damages.

Many people ask me, "Is small claims court in Texas like *The People's Court* on TV?" The best answer I can give to that question is what a small claims court judge told me when I asked him how his court compared with the TV court. His answer: "We are a lot like *The People's Court*—just much less formal."

How much can I sue for in small claims court?
"Up to $5,000!"

Dear Mr. Alderman:
I heard that there was a change in the law and that I can now sue for more than $1,000 in small claims court.

Good news. Yes! The legislature amended the law, and now the limit in small claims court is $5,000.

How do I sue in small claims court?
"It's easy."

Dear Mr. Alderman:

My laundry man is incompetent! The other day I brought in a brand new shirt that I had only worn once, and he ruined it. It has grease all over it, and even though I had only worn it once, he said it must have been my fault. Having worn it only to the movies, there was no way I could have gotten grease all over it. My friend who was with me saw that the shirt was clean when I left the movies. Now I am mad! I want to sue, but I am afraid the cleaners will have a big-time lawyer, and I will lose. Do I need an attorney? The shirt only cost $25. Is it worth it?

Small claims court is designed for you. Your claim can be quickly decided by the court based on the information you give the judge. You will not need a lawyer. If you can prove the shirt did not have grease stains on it when you brought it to the laundry and that the laundry stained it, you will be entitled to the value of the shirt, plus the amount it costs you to bring the suit.

Suing in small claims court is easy. However, in order to sue in this court, you must be asking for no more than $5,000. In small claims court, you can sue any person who is actually in Texas, has a permanent home in Texas, or is doing business here. To sue a sole proprietorship, the proprietor must be in Texas; to sue a partnership, the partners must be here; and to sue a corporation, it must do business in the state. For more information on what it means to do business in one of these forms, read Chapter Seventeen.

There are many small claims courts, so after you decide to go to small claims court, you must find the proper location for your complaint. Generally, you must sue in the court that covers the area where the person you are suing lives, where the business operates, or where the transaction took place. Small claims courts are part of the justice courts, so look in the phone book for the justice of the peace in that area. If you have any questions about which court to sue in or whom you can sue, call and ask the clerk of the court. The clerk will be able to answer your question.

After you know which court to go to, go there and tell the clerk you want to sue the laundry. *Make sure that you have the correct name and address of the laundry and, if you can find it, the name of a person at the laundry who can be served with the legal papers.* If the laundry is a corporation, you can call the secretary of state in Austin and find out who the laundry's "agent for service" is. An agent for service is the person the company has designated to accept legal papers for the corporation.

When you get to the court, the clerk will give you a petition to fill out. Read it carefully. If you have any questions, ask the clerk. A typical small claims court petition is shown on page 170.

You, the person suing, are called the "plaintiff." You start the lawsuit by filing a petition. After you file the petition and pay your fees (about $55), the court will have the constable or sheriff serve the "defendant," the person or business being sued, with the papers. The defendant will then either answer your claim (that is, state why he thinks he is not responsible) or default (that is, not respond to the petition). If the defendant does not respond to the petition, you will go before the judge and tell him or her your claim. If you have a case, you will win. The judge will award you the amount of your shirt plus what it cost for you to sue. *Make sure you ask for all the costs of bringing the suit in your petition.*

If the defendant answers your claim, he will be present in the courtroom on the date set for the trial. Unless either party asks for a jury, the case will be heard by the judge alone. In most cases, the hearing is very informal. The judge lets both sides tell their stories and listens to any other witnesses who may appear. For example, if your friend knows the shirt was not stained when you brought it in, you may want to bring him with you to court to tell this to the judge. Also, if you have any pictures or other records that support your case, you should bring them with you. The sales receipt showing that the shirt was new may be important. And, of course, bring the shirt to show the judge the damage.

If the other side has a lawyer, don't worry about being intimidated. Most judges will limit what a lawyer may do. Small claims court is a people's court. Most judges will ensure that you are treated fairly and have a chance to tell your side of the story.

After hearing all the evidence, the judge will usually make a prompt ruling and state who wins. Usually that is the end of the matter. If you win, the other side pays you the money. But sometimes it can be difficult to collect your judgment, as the letter on pages 172–173 shows.

Typical small claims court petition.

In the Small Claims Court of   County, Texas

Plaintiff

vs.

Defendant

State of Texas

County of _____

       (Plaintiff), whose post office address is

_____

Street and Number

_____ , _____

     City   County,

Texas, being duly sworn, on his oath deposes and says that (defendant), whose post office address is   _____

_____ , _____

County, Texas, is justly indebted to him in the sum of _____ Dollars and _____ Cents ($ _____), for _____

_____

_____

(here the nature of the claim should be stated in concise form and without technicality, including all pertinent dates), and that there are no counterclaims existing in favor of the defendant and against the plaintiff, except _____

_____

_____

_____

Plaintiff

    Subscribed and sworn to before me this _____ day of _____ ,

19___.

_____

Judge

What happens if I sue for more than $5,000 in small claims court?
"You will be thrown out of court."

Dear Mr. Alderman:

I recently did contracting work for some people. They asked me to do a small job first, and then another, and then another. They now owe me $6,200. I have tried to get them to pay, but it looks like I am going to have to sue. I recently read that you can only sue for $5,000 in small claims court. I would be satisfied to get this much out of them, and I don't want to have to get a lawyer to sue for more. Can I just take the $5,000 and call it even?

No. If you file a suit in small claims court asking for more than $5,000, the court does not have jurisdiction. This means that it does not have legal authority to hear your case and will have to dismiss it. You are not allowed to simply take less to get into small claims court. If you want to sue for more than $5,000, you will have to file in district or county court. This will probably mean hiring an attorney. But there is another alternative for you.

Although you cannot sue for a total of more than $5,000, when there are several contracts you can sue separately for each. For example, you said that you did more than one job. As far as the law is concerned, each job is a separate contract, and you can file a separate suit for each. As long as each job was less than $5,000, the court has jurisdiction to hear the case. This will cost you a little more in filing fees, but you recover these fees if you win.

One final point. Do not try to get into court by reducing your damages. If you are owed $5,800, you cannot just sue for $5,000 to get into small claims court. The amount in controversy is over $5,000, and the court will dismiss the case.

Can I take less to get into small claims court?
"No!"

Dear Mr. Alderman:

I am owed $5,700 on a debt. I know you can only sue for up to $5,000 in small claims court. Can I sue in small claims court if I am willing to accept $5,000 for what I am owed?

Basically the answer is no. As you correctly state, small claims court jurisdiction is $5,000. This means that it cannot hear cases involving disputes in excess of that amount. In your case your dispute involves $5,700. Even though you are willing to accept $5,000, you have no legal basis to sue for anything less than $5,700. This means that small claims court would not have jurisdiction to hear your case. You should consider a suit in either county or district court. You will probably need an attorney to assist you with this claim.

What do I do after I've won?
"Execute your judgment."

Dear Mr. Alderman:

You may remember me: I am the person who wrote to you about a problem with my cleaner. Well, I took your advice and went to small claims court—and I won! Now, what do I do? He won't pay, and I still don't have my money.

If you win in small claims court, the person you sued will usually pay you the money he or she owes you immediately. However, if you have difficulty collecting your judgment, the law can help you.

The first thing you should do is write the defendant and remind him that you have been awarded a judgment against him. Ask him to pay you the money he owes you. If he still refuses to pay, there are some things you can do with the law's help.

There are two legal devices you can use to force payment of your judgment. One is called an "abstract of judgment;" the other is a "writ of execution." An abstract of judgment is a legal paper you can file that will give you a lien on any real estate, except for a homestead, owned by the defendant. To do this, you must go back to the court where you sued. The clerk will help you get the abstract of judgment. Then you must file it in every county where you think the defendant may own real property. There will be a small charge to do this, but you will be entitled to collect this amount from the defendant. Once you file the abstract, you will have a lien against the defendant's non-exempt real property. This means the defendant will probably not be able to sell the property without first paying you. You also will have the right to force him to sell the property to satisfy your judgment. Most people do not like to have liens on their property and will pay you to get the lien released.

The other method to force payment is called a writ of execution. This is also issued by the court where you got your judgment. It is an order to the sheriff or constable directing him or her to go to the defendant and collect the judgment. If the defendant still does not pay, the sheriff or constable has the right to take the defendant's non-exempt personal property and sell it in order to pay you your money. There may be a small cost for the writ and the services of the law officer, but this is recoverable from the defendant.

Remember, if you are having trouble collecting your judgment, go back to the court clerk and ask for help. The clerk will tell you how to enforce your judgment.

There is one last thing you should keep in mind. Texas law is very favorable to debtors. It is difficult to force people to pay their debts if they really do not want to. For an abstract of judgment to be successfully enforced, the defendant must own real estate other than a homestead. To successfully collect your money with a writ of execution, the defendant must own property not exempted from collection by Texas law. The exemption law in Texas allows a person to keep most of his or her property no matter how much he or she owes. *Read the letter beginning on page 56 to see what property is exempt before you try to collect your judgment with a writ of execution.*

Before taking the time to try to collect your judgment, consider whether it will be worth the time and the effort you will have to put in. While you can usually force a business to pay, be aware that it is much more difficult to force individuals to pay a judgment.

What is garnishment?
"Another way to get your money."

Dear Mr. Alderman:
I sued and won in small claims court. Now the person I sued is refusing to pay. A friend told me that if I knew where he banked, I could use garnishment. What is this, and how do I use it?

Garnishment is the name given to the proceeding that allows you to get money that is *owed to* the person you sued. It can be used to get money in a bank account, rent owed to landlords, or debts owed to individuals or businesses.

In some cases, garnishment may be used to get a portion of a person's wages. Wage garnishment is permitted in Texas only for the collection of child support, back taxes, and certain government-backed student loans. For debts other than these, wages are protected, and garnishment cannot be used to get money from someone who pays wages to the person you sued. But money owed to people who are self-employed, such as independent contractors, builders, accountants, or attorneys, is not considered wages. Therefore, you may use garnishment to reach money owed to these individuals.

To use garnishment you should go back to the court and file a "writ of garnishment." To do this, you must have the name and address of the garnishee—the person who is holding the money you want. For example, suppose you know where the person you sued has a bank account. Under the law, the bank technically owes the money to the owner of the account. Therefore, you can use a writ of garnishment to order the bank to pay the money to you to satisfy the debt.

Garnishment is not necessarily a complicated procedure; however, you may want to consult an attorney to help you with it. If you were to make a mistake, it could result in liability to you.

Does a corporation have to have an attorney to go to small claims court?
"No."

Dear Mr. Alderman:
I am the president of a small corporation. We are owed money by several of our customers, and I want to go to small claims court. A friend told me that a corporation can only go to court if it is represented by an attorney. Is this true? It will cost me more to hire an attorney than the amount of the claims.

Generally, your friend is correct. A corporation can only appear in court or file legal papers through an attorney. This is because the law treats a corporation as a separate legal entity, and as a separate entity, it must act through a representative. The only type of representative that can go to court is an attorney. If someone else went to court, he or she would be guilty of practicing law without a license.

But there is one important exception. A corporation may be represented in *small claims court* by any authorized agent. The legislature recognized that much of what goes on in small claims court is too simple to require the additional expense of an attorney. Therefore, you, as president of the corporation, may file the claim on behalf of the corporation.

What determines where I am sued?
"You may be sued in a number of places."

Dear Mr. Alderman:
I am being sued in small claims court in the precinct where the plaintiff lives. The judge is one of his best friends. I thought I had the right to be sued where I live? What can I do?

Generally, you may sue someone either where he lives, where the contract was to be performed, where the problem arose, or where the work was to be done.

If the problem arose where you live, you have the right to be sued there. I suggest you speak with the clerk of the court about a "change of venue" to get the proceeding moved to the proper precinct.

CHAPTER SEVENTEEN

Starting a Business

EACH year, thousands of brave entrepreneurs venture out into the world of business. Some achieve a measure of fame and fortune while most discover the harsh realities of the small business: Few are successful.

When you start a new business you suddenly find yourself on the other side of the law. To protect yourself it is important to know all the laws that govern your business and to make sure you comply with them. But no matter how diligent and conscientious you may be, things can still go wrong, and you may find yourself being sued by one of your customers.

For example, even if you did not know about the leak in your refrigerator, you may still incur substantial liability when someone slips and falls on the wet floor. And even though the product you sold was manufactured by someone else, you may be responsible when it explodes and injures someone.

There are three ways to avoid liability when you operate a business.

First:
Make sure you comply with the law.
Second:
Purchase enough insurance to cover any unexpected liability, such as the patron who slips on a banana peel and falls.
Third:
Consider incorporating. A business may be run as a sole proprietorship, a partnership, or a corporation. As you will see from the next few letters, the legal form your business assumes can determine the extent of *your* liability.

What is a sole proprietorship?
"The same thing as yourself."

Dear Mr. Alderman:

I just opened up a little fix-it shop in my garage. I put up a sign that reads Sam's Fix-It. So far I am not getting rich, but I am making enough extra money to make it worthwhile. The other day someone brought in a toaster that needed to be repaired. I fixed it and returned it. Today the person came back. The toaster had caught on fire. I had apparently crossed two wires that shouldn't be crossed. The owner was pretty nice about it and told me I was lucky his house hadn't burned down. Then I started thinking. . . . What if the house had caught on fire because of my mistake? Who is responsible for things from my shop that go wrong?

The simple answer to your question is: You are. When you run a business as a sole proprietorship, you are the business. Whatever debts or obligations are incurred by the business are actually incurred by you. The business is not a separate entity. Perhaps the best way to look at it is that the business is just another name you are using.

Many people start a business by simply assuming a name and opening shop. While this is legal (of course you must file the assumed name with the county clerk), it may not be the best form for you. For example, if you didn't properly repair the toaster and it caught the house on fire, you may have had a substantial lawsuit to contend with. Even though you were acting as a business when you repaired the toaster, you would have personal liability for the damages caused. This means that you could lose personal *and* business assets to pay the debt.

As you will see from the next few letters, you may want to consider incorporating. A corporation is a separate entity. You are usually not personally liable for the obligation of the corporation. *Of course, no matter what form your business takes, you should make sure you have adequate liability insurance.*

Who is responsible for partnership debts?
"All the partners."

Dear Mr. Alderman:

I have two partners in a small restaurant. One of them has gone crazy. He thinks we're the Ritz and has started buying caviar and all sorts of expensive junk. Most of the food goes bad because no one orders it. The other day, we got the bills for all this stuff, and we were shocked. There is no way we can pay for all the stuff he bought and still stay in business. We are now talking about splitting up and closing the restaurant, but I am worried about what my share of the bills might be. Do I have to pay a third of everything we owe?

I have some bad news for you. You are not liable for one-third of the debts your partners have incurred. *You are responsible for all of the debts if they are not paid by the partnership.* Basically, each partner has full liability for all the partnership debts. Each partner, however, has the right to recover from the others his fair share.

Here is how the law works:

Suppose A, B, and C form the ABC partnership. Each partner contributes $5,000. The business then incurs $21,000 in debts. The partnership assets will first be used to pay the debt. The remaining $6,000 is now owed by the partners. Each is responsible for $2,000, but if one doesn't pay, the others must pay his share. For example, if a creditor sues all the partners, but only A has any money, A will have to pay the entire $6,000. He will be responsible for getting $2,000 each from B and C.

Remember, a partnership is not a separate legal entity when it comes to liability. It is simply a way for more than one person to do business jointly. As far as the law is concerned, each partner is usually liable for whatever the partnership does. This can even include wrongful acts of the other partners, such as an automobile injury that occurs while making a delivery.

If you are concerned with your individual liability for the debts of the business, don't use a partnership. Read the following letters and set up a limited partnership or a corporation. But first, consider the partnership's liability for the personal debts of the partners.

**Can my partner's creditors take partnership property
for his private debts?
"No, partnerships generally are not liable
for personal debts of the partners."**

Dear Mr. Alderman:

I recently set up a partnership with my friend Bob. We have a small business with about $5,000 in parts. Recently, the bank that loaned Bob money to build a pool at his house told us if Bob didn't pay, it would sue and take the property of the partnership. Can the bank do this? The business didn't borrow the money. Bob borrowed it himself. Our business is going along OK, and I wouldn't want to have to end it.

It is tempting here to go into a lot of law about liability and partnerships. But the simple answer is that your partner's creditors cannot force you to sell the partnership or take partnership assets. The partnership is not responsible for the personal debts of the individual partners. Of course, your partner's creditors can take your partner's interest in the business—and receive his share of the profits—to pay off the debt, but this should not affect the running of the business.

Partners are responsible for partnership debts, and personal assets may be taken to pay them off, but the reverse is not true. A creditor of an individual partner may not take partnership property.

What is a limited partnership?
"A cross between a partnership and a corporation."

Dear Mr. Alderman:
I am about to start a business with some friends. We have considered a partnership and a corporation, but recently someone told us there is such a thing as a limited partnership. We were told this is just like a partnership but without the liability. Because we are worried about our individual liability if we start a partnership, this sounds like a good idea. How does it work? Would you suggest we start one?

You are right. A limited partnership is like a partnership but with limited liability. For example, if you start a partnership, you and each of the partners are responsible for all the debts of the partnership. As I said in the letter beginning on page 177, you, as a partner, could end up losing your personal property to pay off the partnership debts.

In a limited partnership, the limited partners are only responsible for an amount equal to their investments in the business. For example, if you were a limited partner with a $5,000 investment, the most you could lose would be the $5,000 you put in. But there are two big drawbacks to a limited partnership: There must be at least one general partner, who has individual liability for all the partnership debts; and as a limited partner, you cannot be directly involved in the day-to-day running of the business. A limited partner is really a silent partner. He invests in the business and then hopes it succeeds so he can share in the profits. From your letter it doesn't sound like a limited partnership is what you are looking for. You seem to want to be actively involved in the business, and a limited partner cannot be.

But just in case you do decide to start a limited partnership, I should tell you that unlike a regular partnership, which can be started with only a handshake, a limited partnership is created by law and needs a formal agreement to be valid. To start a limited partnership you should consult with an attorney and have him or her draw up the papers.

Is there a way to avoid liability?
"Form a corporation."

Dear Mr. Alderman:
I am going to open a small fruit stand/cheese shop. I just read about a restaurant owner who was sued for over $100,000 by someone who slipped on a banana peel in his store. I am worried about this happening to me. I know my insurance will cover most damage claims, but I really don't want to be held responsible for all the obligations of the business. Is there some way the business can be responsible for its own debts?

One way for an individual to avoid liability for debts incurred by his business is to incorporate. Under the law a corporation is a separate legal being. It sues and is sued in its own name. The individuals involved in a corporation can only lose their investments in the business.

For example, suppose you start your business as a sole proprietorship, and a customer is injured slipping on your floor. She sues for $150,000, not an unusually high amount these days. You lose, and your insurance pays $100,000. *You are personally responsible for the remaining $50,000.* The same result would occur if the business were a partnership.

But if you had incorporated, the business—not you—would owe the remaining $50,000. If the business didn't have enough money to pay the debt, the customer could not collect from you. If the business were to stop doing business or file bankruptcy, that would be the end of the matter. *One of the most important benefits of a corporation is that it shields the shareholders and officers from personal liability for business debts.*

If you are worried about liability from your business I strongly recommend that you incorporate or consider a new business form called a "limited liability company." The limited liability company offers many of the same benefits as the corporation. It may be a good idea to talk with an attorney about which form is best for you. Many attorneys are competent to handle either business form. Shop around and get a fair price before you hire one.

I own a gas station. Someone told me I have to pump gas for handicapped drivers at no extra charge. Is this the law?
"Yes."

Dear Mr. Alderman:

I own a small gas station. I sell both full-service and self-service gas. Of course, there is a substantial difference in price. The other day a customer with a handicapped-person license plate drove up to the self-service pump and told me I had to fill her tank for the self-service price. I told her if she wanted full service to pull up to the full-service pump. She said there was a law that required me to fill her tank at the self-service price. I did it this time, but now I want to know—is there really such a law?

Yes. The Texas Legislature passed a law in 1989 that requires a gas station that has both self- and full-service options to pump gas for a handicapped person at the self-serve price. It is important to emphasize that this law only applies when you have both self- and full-service options. A station that sells only self-serve gas does not have to pump for a handicapped person, and a full-service-only station does not have to charge a different price. As you see, you did the right thing and the legal thing by pumping the gas.

Can I tow cars parked in my spaces?
"Not without a proper sign."

Dear Mr. Alderman:

I own a small store in a strip center. The management has given each store three parking spaces that we can limit to our customers. I have put up a small sign saying the parking is for my customers and others may be towed. So far I have not had any problems. I am wondering, however, whether I really have the right to tow them. Do I?

Probably not. Although you have the contractual right to tow them, you have not provided the proper signs required by law. Under a new state law, parking lot owners generally may only tow cars if they have very specific signs. The law provides in part that the signs must be:

1. Conspicuously visible to and facing the driver of a vehicle that enters the lot;

2. Located on the right-hand or left-hand side of each driveway through which a vehicle can enter the lot;
3. Permanently mounted on a pole, post, wall, or barrier;
4. Installed on the lot; and
5. Installed so that the bottom edge of the sign is no lower than five feet and no higher than eight feet above ground level.

The law also provides details about the sign itself. The sign must:

1. Be made of weather-resistant material;
2. Be at least 18 inches wide and 24 inches tall;
3. Contain the international symbol for towing vehicles;
4. Contain a statement describing who may and who may not park;
5. Bear the words Unauthorized Vehicles Will Be Towed at Owner's or Operator's Expense;
6. Contain a statement of the days and hours towing is enforced; and
7. Contain a current telephone number, including the area code, that is answered 24 hours a day to enable the owner of the towed car to locate it.

The bottom line is that it is unlawful to tow any vehicle from your lot unless you have signs as discussed above. Towing without the proper sign could result in a lawsuit.

What is the ADA?
"A law you should know about."

Dear Mr. Alderman:
I operate a small strip-center shopping area. At a recent chamber of commerce meeting, a speaker told us about the ADA. He stressed the importance of this law and told us we should immediately take steps to comply with it. The only specific thing I remember him saying, however, is that we should have ramps for people in wheelchairs to get in and out. I know there must be much more to this law. Exactly what does it cover, and what do I have to do to comply?

The ADA, or **Americans With Disabilities Act,** is generally referred to as the bill of rights for the disabled. Basically, this law prohibits discrimination against an individual with a disability and requires that public transportation and public accommodations, such as a strip shopping center, must be accessible. This is a rather complex law; however, I will give you a brief overview. I strongly suggest you speak with your attorney to get more details.

A person with a disability is defined by the ADA as anyone with a physical or mental handicap that is a substantial impairment of a major life activity. The law also applies to people who do not have such an impairment but are still considered impaired. For example, the law covers people who have hearing or speech impairments and anyone who does not have the physical ability to walk or see. The law also covers a cancer patient who is cured, if that person is considered by others as still being impaired. It is estimated that more than 43 million Americans have disabilities covered by the ADA.

Under the ADA, an employer with 15 or more employees may not discriminate against an otherwise qualified individual because of a disability. A qualified individual is one who, with or without a reasonable accommodation, is able to perform the job. For example, a person in a wheelchair who is able to perform a job would be considered qualified for the purposes of the ADA even if the employer had to build a special desk to accommodate the employee. Employment discrimination claims under the ADA should be filed with the Equal Employment Opportunity Commission.

The ADA also covers most forms of public transportation and requires that new buses, trains, and other vehicles be made accessible. This means they must be equipped with lifts, ramps, and wheelchair spaces or seats. The law also prohibits discrimination based on a disability. For example, a taxi driver may not refuse to pick up a person using a wheelchair.

Finally, the ADA prohibits discrimination against persons with disabilities in their use of public accommodations, such as restaurants, hotels, theaters, doctors' offices, pharmacies, grocery stores, shopping centers, museums, schools, parks, and other similar establishments. Basically, the law requires that existing barriers be removed, provided this can be done without much difficulty or expense, and that new construction be accessible.

Can I just copy cartoon characters?
"Not under our copyright laws."

Dear Mr. Alderman:
I design T-shirts. I sometimes draw freehand images of cartoon characters I have seen. I do not copy them out of a book. I draw them from memory. I have been told this is illegal. Is it?

Copying the image of a cartoon character is probably a violation of our copyright laws whether you do it from memory or directly from a book. Under federal law, the person who creates a work of art, such as a cartoon character, may "copyright" the image. This gives that person the exclusive right to reproduce it. If the characters you are drawing are copyrighted, you are in violation of the law and could be liable for damages.

Can a business ask for a social security number? "Yes, but you don't have to give it."

Dear Mr. Alderman:
It seems like every person I do business with wants my social security number. Can businesses require this information?

Basically, you don't have to give businesses any information you don't want to. And they don't have to deal with you if they don't want to. In my opinion, many businesses ask for information they either don't need or shouldn't be allowed to have. As a legal matter, however, they can ask for it. Because of the importance of a social security number, I suggest you refuse to provide it.

CHAPTER EIGHTEEN

Warranties

WHEN you buy something, you expect to get what you pay for—this is what warranty law is all about. A warranty is any promise by a seller or manufacturer to stand behind its product. To have a warranty, there is no need to use special words such as "warranty," "guarantee," or "promise." Anything said about a product that you rely on when you purchase it is usually sufficient to give rise to a warranty that the product will do what it is supposed to do. An advertisement, the salesman's promises, and even a sample or a model of the product can give rise to a warranty.

Warranty law is governed by two statutes: a state law called the **Uniform Commercial Code** and a federal law called the **Magnuson-Moss Warranty Act.** Both of these laws protect you by making a seller or a manufacturer responsible whenever a product does not live up to your expectations. As you will see from the letters in this chapter, a few formalities must be followed to establish a warranty. Often, a consumer has more than adequate warranty protection, even though nothing was ever said about a warranty.

What is a warranty?
"More than just a tag."

Dear Mr. Alderman:
I have been shopping for a new lawn mower. I found one I liked and was waiting for it to go on sale when my neighbor told me that I shouldn't buy it because it had a bad warranty. I never really thought about warranties before—they have always been just a tag hanging on the product that I never bothered to read. Just what is a warranty? And how important is it?

Your friend is right. One of the most important parts of any purchase is the warranty you receive. In simple terms, the warranty is the obligation, or promise, of the seller of the goods as to their quality.

Warranties can arise by agreement or automatically by operation of law. For example, most products come with written warranties, which give you specific rights, and implied warranties, which the law imposes in most sales. *But the law allows a merchant to contractually change or disclaim his warranty liability, and most written warranties are actually taking away some of the rights you would otherwise have.*

For example, if you buy a lawn mower and nothing is said about warranties, you have an implied warranty that the mower will cut grass, and if it doesn't, the dealer is responsible. (This warranty is discussed further in the letter on pages 188–190.) But a dealer can sell a lawn mower with no warranties at all by contractually disclaiming them, for example, selling it "as is." If this was done you would have no right to return it if you got the mower home and it only ran for one hour. In fact, the dealer doesn't even promise you it will run. When you buy without a warranty, you accept all the risks that the product is defective.

In your case, consider the warranty as part of what you are buying. For instance, let's assume a store has a lawn mower that sells for $150 but has only a limited 30-day warranty covering replacement of parts, but not labor. Another store is selling a similar mower for $175, but this one has a one-year warranty that covers parts and labor. Which is the better deal? Well, the ultimate decision is up to you, but if the mower breaks down during the year and repairs are more than $25, you would be much better off with the "more expensive" mower.

Remember, your legal rights against a seller are based on the warranty you receive. If you have a good remedy, you will be well protected if something goes wrong. You should shop around for warranties, just like you shop for color or price.

**What is the difference between a full
warranty and a limited warranty?
"Read the small print."**

Dear Mr. Alderman:

Whenever I shop around for a good warranty, I notice most of them say they are "limited" warranties. What does this mean? What is limited? If I don't want a limited warranty, what other choice do I have? Is there such a thing as an unlimited warranty?

Recently Congress found so many problems with warranty law that it passed the Magnuson-Moss Warranty Act. This law requires that warranties be written in simple and readily understandable language. It also requires that all warranties be labeled either "full" or "limited." Under the law a warranty can only be called full if it meets these requirements:

1. The warrantor (the person making the warranty) must repair or replace the product, or give the consumer a refund within a reasonable time and at no charge, if the product does not conform with the warranty.
2. The warrantor may not impose any limitation on the duration of any implied warranty (those warranties that arise by operation of law and are discussed on pages 188–190).
3. The warrantor may not exclude or limit consequential damages (those caused by the defective product) unless the exclusion is conspicuously written on the face of the warranty.
4. If the product can't be repaired after a reasonable number of attempts, the consumer must be permitted to elect to receive a refund or a replacement.
5. The warranty is good for anyone who owns the product during the warranty period.

Under the law any warranty that does not live up to all these requirements must be labeled "limited." When you see the word "limited," the company is telling you it has not given you all the protection it could have. *A full warranty is always better than a limited one.* For example, here and on the following pages are two full warranties. Read them and see what rights you have if the product does work:

A full warranty.

MAXELL FULL LIFETIME WARRANTY

Maxell warrants this product to be free from manufacturing defects in materials and workmanship for the lifetime of the original purchaser. *This warranty does not apply to normal wear or to damage resulting from accident, abnormal use, misuse, abuse or neglect.* Any defective product will be replaced at no charge if it is returned to an authorized Maxell dealer or to Maxell. HOWEVER, MAXELL SHALL NOT BE LIABLE FOR ANY COMMERCIAL DAMAGES, WHETHER INCIDENTAL, CONSEQUENTIAL OR OTHERWISE.

As you can see, the company tells you in simple language that if there is anything wrong with the product, you or any other owner can get it replaced at no charge. In capital letters, the first warranty also tells you what damages it is not responsible for: commercial damages. The companies are responsible for all other damages, for example, if the product caused damage to another piece of equipment or if the cooler damaged your food.

On page 189 is a limited warranty. Can you see what the company has not given you? If the company can't fix the product, do you have to keep taking it back? What damages is the company liable for if the goods are defective? Who pays for labor, insurance? Can someone else use the warranty or is it limited to the original purchaser?

The Magnuson-Moss Warranty Act applies to any consumer product costing more than $10. Under the law, warranties must be available before the sale. Take advantage of the law and read the warranty before you buy. You should shop for warranties the same way you shop for price and quality.

What if he didn't say anything about a warranty? Am I out of luck? "No, just the opposite."

Dear Mr. Alderman:
The other day I went into the hardware store to buy a shovel to plant some bushes. The store had six or seven different models of pointed shovels, so I picked out the one that seemed best. After coming home, I went out back to dig a hole to plant a small bush, and after the first shovelful, the shovel bent. I couldn't believe it. The metal part actually bent in half. I went right back to the store clerk and told him I wanted my money back. He said I must have done something wrong with the shovel. He also said, "Tough luck. You bought it; it's your problem." My wife told me I should take the store to small claims court, but I want to know the law first. What do you think? I am worried because I didn't get any warranty, and I always thought that when this happened it was "tough luck, buyer."

If the store still refuses to give you your money back, take it to small claims court. The law is on your side. Under the law, whenever someone sells you something, you automatically get what is called a "warranty of merchantability." This warranty arises automatically; nothing has to be said or done. This warranty is in addition to any other warranties you may be given.

Under the warranty of merchantability, a merchant guarantees that any product he sells you is fit for its "ordinary purposes" and will "pass without objection in the trade." What this means is that whenever you buy something, the merchant promises you it is going to do what you think it will

A limited warranty leaves out some protection. Read it carefully.

COMPACT DISC PLAYER
LIMITED WARRANTY

Toshiba America, Inc. ("TAI") and Toshiba Hawaii, Inc. ("THI") make the following limited warranties. These limited warranties extend to the original consumer purchaser or any person receiving this set as a gift from the original consumer purchaser and to no other purchaser or transferee.

Limited One (1) Year Warranty
TAI and THI warrant this product and its parts against defects in materials of workmanship for a period of one year after the date of original retail purchase. During this period, TAI and THI will repair a defective product or part, without charge to you. You must deliver the entire product to TAI/THI Service Center. You pay for all transportation and insurance charges for the product to and from the Service Center.

Limited One (1) Year Warranty of Parts
TAI and THI further warrant the parts in this product against defects in materials or workmanship for a period of one year after the date of original retail purchase. During this period, TAI and THI will replace a defective part without charge to you, except that if a defective part is replaced after ninety (90) days from the date of the original retail purchase you pay labor charges involved in the replacement. You must deliver the entire product to one of the TAI/THI Service Centers listed below. You pay for all transportation and insurance charges for the product to and from the Service Center.

Owner's Manual and Warranty Registration
You should read the owner's manual thoroughly before operating this product. You should also insure that your name and address are on file as owners of a TAI/THI product by completing and mailing the attached registration card within ten days after you, or the person who has given you this product as a gift, purchased this product. This is one way to enable TAI/THI to establish the date of purchase of the product, as well as to provide you with better customer service and improved products. Failure to return the card will not affect your rights under this warranty so long as you retain other proof of purchase such as a bill of sale.

Your Responsibility
The above warranties are subject to the following conditions:
(1) You must retain your bill of sale or provide other proof of purchase. Completing and mailing in the attached registration card within ten days after the original retail purchase is one way of providing such other proof of purchase.
(2) You must notify one of the TAI/THI Service Centers listed below within thirty (30) days after you discover a defective product or part.
(3) All warranty servicing of this product must be make by TAI/THI Service Center.
(4) These warranties are effective only if the product is purchased and operated in the U.S.A.
(5) Warranties extend only to defects in materials or workmanship as limited above and do not extend to any product or parts which have been lost or discarded by you or to damage to products or parts caused by misuse, accident, improper installation, improper maintenance or repair or use in violation of instructions furnished by us; or to units which have been altered or modified without authorization of TAI/THI or to damage to products or parts thereof which have had the serial number removed, altered, defaced or rendered illegible.

Step-By-Step Procedures—How to Obtain Warranty Service
To obtain warranty servicing, you should:
(1) Contact one of the TAI/THI Service Centers listed below for warranty service or call the TAI toll free number 800-631-3811 within thirty (30) days after you find a defective product or part.
(2) Arrange for the delivery of the product to the TAI/THI Service Center. Products shipped to the Service Center must be insured and safely and securely packed, preferably in the original shipping carton and a letter explaining the defect and also a copy of bill of sale or other proof of purchase must be enclosed. All transportation and insurance charges must be prepaid by you.
(See TOSHIBA SERVICE PROCEDURE for packing suggestions)
(3) If you have any question about service, please contact one of the following TAI/THI Service Centers:

Toshiba America, Inc.
Service Center
82 Totowa Road
Wayne, New Jersey 07470
Phone Number:
(201) 628-8000

Toshiba America, Inc.
Service Center
19500 South Vermont Ave.
Torrance, Cal. 90502
Phone Number:
(213) 538-9960
(213) 770-3300

Toshiba America, Inc.
Service Center
2900 MacArthur Blvd.
Northbrook, Ill. 60062
Phone Number:
(312) 564-1200

Toshiba Hawaii, Inc.
327 Kamakee Street
Honolulu, Hawaii 96814
Phone Number:
(808) 521-5377

ALL WARRANTIES IMPLIED BY STATE LAW, INCLUDING THE IMPLIED WARRANTIES OF MERCHANTABILITY AND FITNESS FOR A PARTICULAR PURPOSE, ARE EXPRESSLY LIMITED TO THE DURATION OF THE LIMITED WARRANTIES SET FORTH ABOVE. Some states do not allow limitations on how long an implied warranty lasts, so the above limitation may not apply to you. WITH THE EXCEPTION OF ANY WARRANTIES IMPLIED BY STATE LAW AS HEREBY LIMITED, THE FOREGOING EXPRESS WARRANTY IS EXCLUSIVE AND IN LIEU OF ALL OTHER WARRANTIES, GUARANTEES, AGREEMENTS AND SIMILAR OBLIGATIONS OF MANUFACTURER OR SELLER WITH RESPECT TO THE REPAIR OR REPLACEMENT OF ANY PRODUCT OR PARTS.
IN NO EVENT SHALL TAI OR THI BE LIABLE FOR CONSEQUENTIAL OR INCIDENTAL DAMAGES. Some states do not allow the exclusion or limitation of incidental or consequential damages so the above limitaion may not apply to you.

No person, agent, distributor, dealer, service station or company is authorized to change, modify or extend the terms of these warranties in any manner whatsoever. The time within which an action must be commenced to enforce any obligation of TAI and THI arising under this warranty or under any statute, or law of the United States or any state thereof, is hereby limited to one year from the date you discover or should have discovered, the defect. This limitation does not apply to implied warranties arising under state law. Some states do not permit limitation of the time within which you may bring an action beyond the limits provided by state law so the above provision may not apply to you. This warranty gives you specific legal rights and you may also have other rights which vary from state to state.

TOSHIBA AMERICA, INC.   TOSHIBA HAWAII, INC.
Keep this card for your record.   Printed in Japan 22957651   **TOSHIBA**
BTV/MHF/RD/RC-80A

Full warranties offer the most protection.

THIS WARRANTY SUPERSEDES ALL OTHER PRODUCT WARRANTIES
INCLUDING ANY WARRANTY WHICH MAY BE FOUND IN THE USE
AND CARE BOOKLET

FULL ONE YEAR WARRANTY

This appliance is warranted against defects in materials or workmanship for a full one year from the date of purchase.

During the warranty period this product will be repaired or replaced, at Hamilton Beach's option, at no cost to you.

In event of a [warranted] product defect, please deliver the product to the nearest authorized service station, listed on the reverse side of this warranty [or look in your local yellow pages for your nearest authorized Hamilton Beach Service Station].

This warranty does not apply in cases of abuse, mishandling, unauthorized repair or commercial use.

In using your new appliance, as directed in the Use and Care Booklet, we are confident it will serve you faithfully. Should you ever feel our products or services do not meet our high standards, please direct your comments to:

PRINTED IN U.S.A.
3-266-223-00-00

Manager, Consumer Relations
P.O. Box 2028
Washington, N. C. 27889

Hamilton Beach Division

Scovill

do. In your case, the merchant automatically made a warranty that the shovel is fit for its ordinary purpose—that is, digging holes. When the shovel bent, the warranty was breached, and you are entitled to damages.

In other words, *when nothing is said about a warranty, the law gives you a substantial one. The law gives you a guarantee that what you bought will do what it is designed to do, the way it is supposed to do it, and for as long as a reasonable person would think it would do it.*

I suggest you go back to the store and try again to settle the problem. Let the store know that you know about warranty law. Also remember that any breach of warranty automatically violates the Deceptive Trade Practices Act. As the next letter shows, this gives you added leverage when dealing with a merchant.

My laundry ruined my shirt. Is there a service warranty?
"There is a service warranty."

Dear Mr. Alderman:

I recently took a new shirt to the laundry to have it cleaned. When I picked it up I noticed there were several small holes in it. I know they were not there when I took it in because it was the first time I had worn it. The manager said, "Tough luck. Sometimes the machines do that. It is not our fault." He agreed to give me a few dollars, but the shirt cost $25. I want to take him to small claims court. Do you think I have a case?

Whenever someone performs a service for you, there is an "implied warranty" that he will do it in a good and workmanlike manner. This means that he will maintain the same standards as others in the business and will perform as a reasonable person would expect. In my opinion, putting holes in a shirt would breach this warranty. It is not good and workmanlike cleaning to ruin the clothes.

You should also know that any time a warranty is breached, this also constitutes a violation of the Deceptive Trade Practices Act. In other words, the cleaners could be responsible for as much as $75 if you took it to small claims court. Reread the material in Chapter Ten to find out how to use this law.

What can I do if the food made me sick?
"There may be a warranty."

Dear Mr. Alderman:

The other night my friends and I went to a restaurant for dinner. After my appetizer I felt a little nauseated. By the time I got home, I was very sick. I went to the hospital and was told it was food poisoning. I was sick for two days and spent nearly $200 on doctor bills. I went back to the restaurant, and management refused to help pay for my expenses. Do I have any legal rights?

Under the law, whenever companies sell you food, they make what is known as a warranty of merchantability. This, basically, is a guarantee that the food is fit for its ordinary purpose: consumption. Selling tainted food would breach this warranty and give you a claim for damages.

I should point out that this is what is known as an implied warranty, and it arises even though nothing is said about the food. Therefore, if you were to eat in a restaurant and get sick because of tainted food, the restaurant would be liable. As the next letter indicates, this could result in substantial damages.

Is it really worth suing for breach of warranty?
"In Texas you may get three times your damages."

Dear Mr. Alderman:

My husband and I recently bought a plant-light lamp. It came with a written guarantee that said it would be suitable for special "plant lightbulbs." The store assured us it was "just right for us." When we got it home we set it up in front of our plants and put in a new bulb. After a few hours we smelled something burning and realized the lamp casing was melting from the heat of the bulb. Luckily there wasn't a fire, but it did burn our favorite plant.

When we went back to the store, we were told it was the manufacturer's fault and the store would not stand by the warranty. The manufacturer is in El Paso, and we are in Dallas. We wrote, but the manufacturer hasn't responded. The light cost $69, and our plant was worth at least $20. My husband says for $89 we should just forget it; no lawyer would take it, and small claims court takes a lot of time. It seems like the person with the little claim is just out of luck. Can't something be done?

Ask your husband if he would go to small claims court if he would get $267 plus court costs, because under the law that is how much you may recover if you are successful. According to Texas law, any breach of warranty automatically violates the Deceptive Trade Practices Act. If you show the person acted knowingly, you are entitled to up to three times your damages plus court costs and attorneys' fees.

Based on what you say in your letter, you clearly have a claim against the manufacturer for breach of an express warranty, and you also probably have a claim against the dealer for breach of the warranty of merchantability and fitness. I suggest you read Chapter Ten and find out how to use the Deceptive Trade Practices Act. My guess is once you contact the store and the manufacturer, and let them know you know your rights, they will quickly settle the matter.

Texas warranty law is very favorable to consumers. Under the law you are always entitled to your attorneys' fees plus court costs and up to three times your damages if you have to sue. Merchants know the law. Let them know you know it, too, and see how quickly problems are resolved.

I just bought a lemon. Can you help?
"Texas lemon-aid."

Dear Mr. Alderman:
I just bought a new car. It stinks! Ever since the day I got it, I have had nothing but problems: first the brakes, then the transmission, now the air conditioning. The car has been in the shop for over two months, and I have only owned it for three. I need help. Is there anything I can do?

Fortunately for you, the law has changed. Until recently when you bought a car, you lived by the old maxim "caveat emptor" (let the buyer beware). Once you took the car off the lot, it was yours, and if it was a lemon, you were just out of luck. But not so today. Now, when you buy a car, the law is "caveat vendor" (let the seller beware). If you buy a lemon, the law places a burden on the seller to promptly take care of the problem, and you have strong remedies if he doesn't.

There are three separate laws a consumer can rely on after buying what turns out to be a lemon.

1. The Texas Deceptive Trade Practices Act
2. The Uniform Commercial Code
3. The Texas Lemon Law

The Texas Deceptive Trade Practices Act, discussed in Chapter Ten, simply states that if the seller deceives you as to the nature of the automobile, or if there is a breach of warranty, you may be entitled to three times your damages, plus your attorneys' fees. You should read over Chapter Ten, but I want to emphasize one thing here: *If you are having a problem getting your car repaired properly, let the dealer know that you know about the Deceptive Trade Practices Act. You may be amazed at how fast the mechanics improve.*

Another law that can help you with a lemon is the **Uniform Commercial Code.** This law can be somewhat complicated, so I will just give a brief summary of what it does. If you think it applies to your problem, you will probably have to get an attorney to help you.

The Uniform Commercial Code lets a person "revoke his acceptance." In simple, nonlegal terms, this means you can change your mind and not keep the car after you have taken it. You are allowed to revoke your acceptance whenever there is a defect in the car that substantially impairs its value to you, and you took the car without knowing about this defect and without having a reasonable opportunity to discover it. After you revoke your acceptance, you can give the car back to the seller, and he must give you back your money. It is as if you never took the car.

For example, if you buy a new car and, as soon as you get it home, you discover it won't go into reverse, you can return the car and revoke your acceptance. In other words, the law gives you a chance to make sure what you bought is what it was supposed to be. If it is not, you don't have to keep it.

If you buy a car that quickly turns out to be a lemon, you may have the right to revoke your acceptance and retrieve your money. But you must show that the defects in the car substantially impair its value to you and that you didn't know about them when you bought the car. *The application of this law can be affected by your contract with the seller. Before thinking you can revoke your acceptance and return your lemon, read your contract and see an attorney!*

The final law that may help you with your lemon is the **Texas Lemon Law.** Basically, this law applies only to new vehicles and provides that if you buy a lemon, the *manufacturer* must either return your money or give you a new car. Before you get your new auto though, two things must happen.

First:
   Your car must meet the statutory definition of a lemon.
Second:
   You must arbitrate your dispute with the Texas Motor Vehicle Commission and give the manufacturer a chance to fix things.

Under the law, a lemon is defined as a car that has a serious defect that has been reported within the warranty term and has not been repaired in a reasonable number of attempts. A dealer or manufacturer has a reasonable number of attempts to fix the car:

1. When you have taken the car to be repaired two times for the same problem within the first 12 months or 12,000 miles, whichever occurs first, and twice more during the 12 months or 12,000 miles after the second repair attempt; or

2. A serious safety defect is subject to repair once during the first 12 months or 12,000 miles, whichever occurs first, and once more during the 12 months or 12,000 miles following the first repair; or

3. The car has been out of service for a total of 30 days or more during the first 24 months or 24,000 miles, whichever occurs first, and there were two repair attempts during the first 12 months or 12,000 miles, and a substantial problem still exists. Any time for which you were provided a free loaner car does not count toward the 30 days.

In other words, if your car has a defect that substantially affects the use or value of the car and that defect is not repaired within the above time limits, it meets the definition of a legal lemon.

To make certain you protect yourself under the lemon law, or for that matter any time you have a lemon, be sure that the dealer documents your problem each time you bring your car in. Also, tell him your problem in general terms. Under the law you must have had the car in to be fixed four times for the same defect. If your engine stalls out, just tell him that, and make sure that is how it is written up on the service order. If you complain about the carburetor and then bring it back saying it is the fuel pump, and then the fuel line, you will have three different problems, not one problem repaired three times. *It is the dealer's job to pinpoint the exact nature of your problem. Describe the problem in general, nonmechanical terms and let the dealer worry about the exact nature of the defect.*

Once you think you have met the test for a lemon, you must contact the Texas Motor Vehicle Commission at (800) 622-8682 and ask to arbitrate the dispute with the manufacturer. The commission will listen to your complaint and has the power to order the manufacturer to refund your money—or give you a new car.

You can write the commission at: Texas Motor Vehicle Commission, P.O. Box 2293, Austin, TX 78768, or call (512) 476-3618 or (800) 622-8682.

Our house leveler won't live up to its warranty. What can I do?
"The Deceptive Trade Practices Act may help."

Dear Mr. Alderman:
Last year we had our house leveled. The company gave us a 15-year guarantee it would fix any problems. This year the house had major settling problems with the foundation. The company won't return our calls and refuses to talk to us. I sent a certified letter and still have not received a reply. I don't want to sue. What can I do?

Unfortunately, you may have to sue to get your problem solved. Knowing a little bit about the law, however, may help solve the matter without litigation.

The Texas Deceptive Trade Practices Act is our state's consumer protection law. One of the things actionable under this law is a breach of warranty. In your case, the refusal to honor the warranty violates this law.

The Deceptive Trade Practices Act allows you to recover your economic damages plus attorneys' fees. Additionally, if you can show the breach was done knowingly, which appears true in your case, you can recover up to three times your damages plus mental anguish.

Because of the amount of money involved, you will probably need an attorney to assist you with your claim under the Deceptive Trade Practices Act. As a first step, however, you should send another certified letter letting the company know that you know about this law and will use it if necessary.

CHAPTER NINETEEN

Wills & Probate

ONE of the most common questions asked is: "Do I need a will?" Well, frankly, no; you don't need a will. It really isn't going to matter to you. But on the other hand, it may be extremely important to your family, because the only way you can ensure they receive your property with a minimum of time and expense is to make out a will.

When you die without a will, you are said to have died "intestate." If you die intestate, the state decides who gets your property. The process of distributing your property and seeing that all your bills are paid is usually closely supervised by the court.

But if you die with a will, you can give your property to whomever you wish, and you can also appoint an "executor" to handle the distribution of the property. Usually the executor can act without the supervision of the court. In other words, *having a will is the most effective way to make certain your property goes where you want—and that your estate is not tied up with the additional time and expense of court supervision.*

What is a living will?
"Death with dignity."

Dear Mr. Alderman:
A friend told me that a law exists in Texas that permits a person to refuse to be kept alive by machines—when he is going to die anyway. Should I ever be diagnosed as terminal, I would not wish my family to pay for expensive treatment simply to allow me to live a little longer. What can I do to make certain I can refuse such treatment? What if I am in a coma? How, then, can I protect my family?

There is a legal device designed to let you make the choice of whether to be left on a life-sustaining machine after you have been found to be terminally ill. The document is called a "directive to physicians." The common name given to this document is "living will."

Generally, if you are being kept alive by a machine, a physician will not disconnect you or turn the machine off without your consent even if your family requests it. This is because of the potential liability to the doctor. Recently, however, the Texas Legislature passed a law that lets you decide in advance whether to be kept alive by a machine. If you execute a directive under this law, the physician can follow your wishes without worrying about liability to your estate or your heirs. Although a doctor is not obligated to comply with a living will, most do.

Under the **Texas Natural Death Act,** you can fill out a written directive at any time, or you may make an oral directive in front of two witnesses and your doctor. Because you may not be competent to make such a decision when you need to, it is a good idea to make out a directive now and keep it in a safe place.

A natural death act directive, or living will, does not have to be in any special form, but the form on pages 230–231 is suggested by the legislature. Even though it is not necessary in Texas to have a directive notarized, you may want to do so just in case you are in a state that requires it.

The directive to physicians gives you the choice to die with dignity and avoid costly medical bills for your family. The choice is up to you. If you want to make that choice, simply fill in the form, have it notarized, and keep it in a safe place where your family can find it.

For more free information about your right to die a natural death, write or call: Choice & Dying, 200 Varick St., 10th Floor, New York, NY 10014, (212) 366-5540.

I am going into the hospital for complicated surgery. Can my son make medical decisions for me if I am not competent to do so? "Yes, through a Durable Power of Attorney for Health Care."

Dear Mr. Alderman:
I am 72 years old and just found out I have a tumor that must be removed. The doctors said it is a very serious operation and I may not recover. I am able to face the possibility of death, but I am concerned about being subjected to unwanted medical treatment. For example, I do not want to be kept alive by a feeding tube when all hope for recovery is gone. I know that a living will gives me the right to have life support systems disconnected if I have a terminal condition, but I would like to have some control over the type and extent

of treatment I receive. I trust my son's judgment and want to know if there is some way to have him make my medical decisions in the event I cannot.

Texas has passed a law that lets you have your wish. The **Durable Power of Attorney for Health Care Law** allows a person to appoint another to make health care decisions for him. First, you must be given a copy of the Durable Power of Attorney Disclosure form. Then, if you complete the proper form, your son could be appointed to make your health care decisions in the event you were not competent to do so. This would give him the right to refuse treatment for you. As long as you trust that your son will execute the judgment you want, this form is the way to ensure he has that right. I should also point out that you can revoke the power of attorney by just telling your doctor.

Is there a difference between a Durable Power of Attorney and a Durable Power of Attorney for Health Care?
"Yes, a big difference."

Dear Mr. Alderman:

I am seriously ill and do not think I will be able to manage my affairs much longer. I want to give my son the authority to make medical decisions for me and to pay all my bills and handle my financial affairs. I filled out a Durable Power of Attorney for Health Care last year. Now I have been told there is another type of power of attorney I must complete. What is it?

As you already know, a Durable Power of Attorney for Health Care allows you to designate someone else to make medical decisions regarding your health care in the event that you are unable to. This document does not, however, grant any other authority.

If you want to authorize someone else to make your financial decisions, you must fill out a Durable Power of Attorney. This document is a very powerful, legally binding form that gives someone else the power to make decisions regarding your property and financial matters in the event you become disabled or otherwise incapable of making decisions. For example, the person designated as your agent may write checks on your account to pay your bills and can withdraw money from any of your accounts as

(text continued on page 204)

Durable Power of Attorney for Health Care form.

DURABLE POWER OF ATTORNEY FOR HEALTH CARE
DESIGNATION OF HEALTH CARE AGENT.

I, _____ (insert your name) appoint:

Name:_____

Address:_____ Phone _____

as my agent to make any and all health care decisions for me, except to the extent I state otherwise in this document. This Durable Power of Attorney for Health Care takes effect if I become unable to make my own health care decisions, and this fact is certified in writing by my physician.

LIMITATIONS ON THE DECISION-MAKING AUTHORITY OF MY AGENT ARE AS FOLLOWS:_____

DESIGNATION OF ALTERNATE AGENT.

(You are not required to designate an alternate agent, but you may do so. An alternate agent may make the same health care decisions as the designated agent if the designated agent is unable or unwilling to act as your agent. If the agent designated is your spouse, the designation is automatically revoked by law if your marriage is dissolved.)

If the person designated as my agent is unable or unwilling to make health care decisions for me, I designate the following persons to serve as my agent to make health care decisions for me as authorized by this document, who serve in the following order:

A. First Alternate Agent
   Name:_____
   Address:_____ Phone _____
B. Second Alternate Agent
   Name:_____
   Address:_____ Phone _____

The original of this document is kept at _____
The following individuals or institutions have signed copies:
   Name:_____
   Address:_____
   Name:_____
   Address:_____

(continued on next page)

(continued from previous page)

DURATION.

I understand that this power of attorney exists indefinitely from the date I execute this document unless I establish a shorter time or revoke the power of attorney. If I am unable to make health care decisions for myself when this power of attorney expires, the authority I have granted my agent continues to exist until the time I become able to make health care decisions for myself.

(IF APPLICABLE) This power of attorney ends on _____

PRIOR DESIGNATIONS REVOKED.

I revoke any prior Durable Power of Attorney for Health Care.

ACKNOWLEDGEMENT OF DISCLOSURE STATEMENT.

I have been provided with a disclosure statement explaining the effect of this document. I have read and understand the information contained in the disclosure statement.

(YOU MUST DATE AND SIGN THIS POWER OF ATTORNEY)

I sign my name to this Durable Power of Attorney for Health Care on

_____ 19 ___,   _____

                                              (City and State)

_____   _____

     (Signature)   (Print Name)

STATEMENT OF WITNESSES.

I declare under penalty of perjury that the principal has identified himself or herself to me, that the principal signed or acknowledged this Durable Power of Attorney in my presence, that I believe the principal to be of sound mind, that the principal has affirmed that the principal is aware of the nature of the document and is signing it voluntarily and free from duress, that the principal requested that I serve as witness to the principal's execution of this document, that I am not the person appointed as agent by this document, and that I am not a provider of health or residential care, an employee of a provider of health or residential care, the operator of a community care facility, or an employee of an operator of a health care facility.

I declare that I am not related to the principal by blood, marriage, or adoption and that to the best of my knowledge I am not entitled

(continued on next page)

202   Know Your Rights!

(continued from previous page)

to any part of the estate of the principal on the death of the principal under a will or by operation of law.

Witness Signature:_____Print Name: _____
Address:_____Date: _____
Witness Signature:_____Print Name: _____
Address:_____Date: _____

**Disclosure statement form
for Durable Power of Attorney for Health Care.**

INFORMATION CONCERNING THE DURABLE POWER OF ATTORNEY FOR HEALTH CARE

THIS IS AN IMPORTANT LEGAL DOCUMENT. BEFORE SIGNING THIS DOCUMENT, YOU SHOULD KNOW THESE IMPORTANT FACTS:

Except to the extent you state otherwise, this document gives the person you name as your agent the authority to make any and all health care decisions for you in accordance with your wishes, including your religious and moral beliefs, when you are no longer capable of making them yourself. Because "health care" means any treatment, service, or procedure to maintain, diagnose, or treat your physical or mental condition, your agent has the power to make a broad range of health care decisions for you. Your agent may consent, refuse to consent, or withdraw consent to medical treatment and may make decisions about withdrawing or withholding life-sustaining treatment. Your agent may not consent to voluntary inpatient mental health services, convulsive treatment, psychosurgery, or abortion. A physician must comply with your agent's instructions or allow you to be transferred to another physician.

Your agent's authority begins when your doctor certifies that you lack the capacity to make health care decisions.

Your agent is obligated to follow your instructions when making decisions on your behalf. Unless you state otherwise, your agent has the same authority to make decisions about your health care as you would have had.

It is important that you discuss this document with your physician or other health care provider before you sign it to make sure that you understand the nature and range of decisions that may be made on your behalf. If you do not have a physician, you should talk with

(continued on next page)

(continued from previous page)

someone else who is knowledgeable about these issues and can answer your questions. You do not need a lawyer's assistance to complete this document, but if there is anything in this document that you do not understand, you should ask a lawyer to explain it to you.

The person you appoint as agent should be someone you know and trust. The person must be 18 years of age or older or a person under 18 years of age who has had the disabilities of minority removed. If you appoint your health or residential care provider (e.g., your physician or an employee of a home health agency, hospital, nursing home, or residential care home, other than a relative), that person has to choose between acting as your agent or as your health or residential care provider; the law does not permit a person to do both at the same time.

You should inform the person you appoint that you want the person to be your health care agent. You should discuss this document with your agent and your physician and give each a signed copy. You should indicate on the document itself the people and institutions who have signed copies. Your agent is not liable for health care decisions made in good faith on your behalf.

Even after you have signed this document, you have the right to make health care decisions for yourself as long as you are able to do so, and treatment cannot be given to you or stopped over your objection. You have the right to revoke the authority granted to your agent by informing your agent of your health or residential care provider orally or in writing, or by your execution of a subsequent Durable Power of Attorney for Health Care. Unless you state otherwise, your appointment of a spouse dissolves on divorce.

This document may not be changed or modified. If you want to make changes in the document, you must make an entirely new one.

You may wish to designate an alternate agent in the event that your agent is unwilling, unable, or ineligible to act as your agent. Any alternate agent you designate has the same authority to make health care decisions for you.

THIS POWER OF ATTORNEY IS NOT VALID UNLESS IT IS SIGNED IN THE PRESENCE OF TWO OR MORE QUALIFIED WITNESSES. THE FOLLOWING PERSONS MAY NOT ACT AS WITNESSES:

(1) the person you have designated as your agent;
(2) your health or residential care provider or an employee of your health or residential care provider;
(3) your spouse;
(4) your lawful heirs or beneficiaries named in your will or a deed; or
(5) creditors or persons who have a claim against you.

(text continued from page 199)

needed. This power, however, is very broad. Money can be withdrawn to pay your bills, or it could just be taken and used for a trip to Hawaii.

Before you sign a Durable Power of Attorney and designate someone as your agent, you must give very serious consideration to what you are doing. You also may want to contact an attorney to make sure you grant only as much power as you have to.

I have attached a Statutory Durable Power of Attorney form on page 232. This is the form suggested by the legislature. Any document in substantially the same form is effective. As you can tell, the law lets you determine the extent of the powers you grant to your agent. Once you sign the document, however, anyone who in good faith relies on it is protected, even if your agent doesn't do what you wanted.

What is community property?
"Part yours . . . part your spouse's."

Dear Mr. Alderman:
Recently I have married, and my friends tell me that, henceforth, all my property is considered "community property" and that I should keep track of the property I owned prior to the marriage. What does it matter?

When people get married, all their property is either community or separate. This distinction is important because it determines who gets what upon death or divorce. Basically, community property is everything people acquire after they get married. Separate property is everything you owned before you were married and gifts or inheritances acquired after you are married. *Community property is considered to be owned in part by each spouse. Separate property belongs solely to the spouse who owned or acquired it.* Why is this important? Because when the marriage ends, either by death or divorce, community property is split between the parties or the heirs, while separate property goes to just one spouse or his or her heirs. Let me give you an example.

Suppose you are about to get married. You own a car, some clothes, and furniture, and you have about $5,000 in the bank. Your wife-to-be has about the same property. You marry and both open bank accounts in your own names. After a few years you buy a house with money you saved after you were married, and you also buy a car. During the marriage your rich aunt dies and leaves you $25,000. If, at this point, one of you should die, or if you divorce, the house and car would be community property. This means if you were to divorce you would split them (or the money obtained from their sale), and if one of you died, his or her heirs would acquire an interest in the house and car. On the other hand, the money you put in the bank saved from your pre-marriage earnings and the money received from your aunt are separate property. This means that upon divorce it would be exclusively yours, and if you died, all of it would go to your heirs. You should be aware, though, that the interest earned on your separate property is community property, and your spouse is entitled to one-half that amount.

In Texas, people usually do not pay alimony upon divorce. Property is split according to community property laws, and that is the end of it. Remember, once you get married nearly everything you acquire will be considered community property and will be owned by both spouses.

If you are concerned about the community property law—for example, you are an older person getting married for a second time, and you want to make sure your first family is taken care of—you can enter into a contract to change the community property laws. Recently Texas amended its laws to allow people to decide how their property will be designated. If you think this is something you may be interested in, you should consult an attorney.

What if I don't have a will?
"The state writes one for you."

Dear Mr. Alderman:
I recently remarried. My wife and I both have children from our prior marriages and now want to have children together. My friends have told me it is important to have a will if I want to ensure that the children of my first marriage are taken care of. I am going to have a will prepared, but I am curious: What happens if I die without a will?

If you die without a will, the state, in effect, writes one for you. There are very specific laws that determine to whom your property passes after your death. This determination is based on the type of property, whether it is separate or community, and who survives you—for example, is your spouse living, and are your children living? If you are interested in a general idea of what happens in a specific case, you should first read the previous letter to find out what property is separate and what property is community, and then look at the charts on pages 206–208. As you can see, the process can get very complicated, and the best advice I can give you is to prepare a will. *Remember: If you have a will, your property is divided as you direct.*

If you want your property to go to someone other than the person(s) it would go to according to the charts, you must have a will. Your case is a good example of how complicated it can get without a will (see page 207). If you died without a will, the house you bought with your second wife would go half to your second wife and half to the children of your first marriage. This probably is not what you would choose to do in a

(text continued on page 209)

Married Man or Woman With No Child or Children (Father and Mother Surviving)

A. SEPARATE PROPERTY

Real Estate   All Other Property

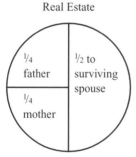 

If only one parent survives, he of she takes $1/_4$ of the real estate in the separate property, and $1/_4$ is equally divided between brothers and sisters of the deceased and their descendants. If there are no surviving brothers and sisters, then the surviving parent takes $1/_2$ of real estate. If neither parent survives, then $1/_2$ of real estate is equally taken by brothers and sisters of the deceased and their descendants. If no parents, no brothers or sisters, or their descendants survive the deceased—then all the real estate is taken by the surviving husband or wife.

B. COMMUNITY PROPERTY

All community property—real or personal—is taken by surviving husband or wife.

Married Man or Woman With Child or Children

A. SEPARATE PROPERTY

Real Estate

All Other Property

Surviving husband or wife only inherits an estate for life in $1/_3$ of the land of the deceased. When such surviving husband or wife dies, all the real estate is owned by the deceased's child or children.

B. COMMUNITY PROPERTY

Real Estate

All Other Property

IF all surviving children are also children of the surviving spouse.

IF a surviving child is not also a child of the surviving spouse. Descendants of deceased children take their parent's share.

Unmarried Man or Woman or Widower or Widow With No Child or Children

(Father and Mother Surviving)

Entire Estate

| ½ father | ½ mother |

(Father or Mother & Brother or Sisters Surviving)

Entire Estate

| ½ father or mother | ½ brothers and sisters |

If only father or mother survives, then that parent takes $\frac{1}{2}$, and the other $\frac{1}{2}$ goes equally to all brothers and sisters. If there are no surviving brothers or sisters or their descendants, then all the estate goes to such surviving father or mother.

Widower or Widow With Child or Children

Real Estate

equally to all children

All Other Property

equally to all children

Children of deceased children take their parent's share.

(text continued from page 206)

will. You always have a choice of where your property goes after your death—simply write a will.

Can I leave my property to just one person?
"You can leave property to whomever you want."

Dear Mr. Alderman:
I have a granddaughter and a great-granddaughter. I want to leave all my property to my great-granddaughter. I have been told I cannot cut my granddaughter out of my will. Is this possible?

Under the law, you may leave your property to whomever you want. In Texas, there is no requirement that a spouse, child, or grandchild take any specific share of what you own.

I suggest you speak with an attorney about preparing your will in a manner that clearly spells out your intentions. This way you can ensure the will is not challenged as ambiguous or unclear. Shop around for an attorney who charges what you believe is a fair price. A few phone calls could save you a lot of money.

What happens to a joint bank account after death?
"It belongs to the survivor."

Dear Mr. Alderman:
My mother died recently. She had a joint bank account with my sister. My mother's will says my sister and I split everything. My sister says she is entitled to all the money in the bank account and that we split everything else. I say we split everything. Who is right?

Your sister. Your mother had a joint bank account with a right of survivorship. What this means is that the account is owned jointly by the two parties, and when one dies, the other automatically owns the entire account.

A will provides how the estate of the deceased will be distributed after her death. The estate, however, includes only property owned at the time of death. By operation of the bank agreement, the bank account was no longer owned by your mother and was the property of your sister.

Can I write my own will?
"Sure, but you may not want to."

Dear Mr. Alderman:
I have read a lot recently about how important it is to have a will. I have decided that I should have one, and I would like to write it myself. Is this legal? How should I do it?

It is perfectly legal for anyone to write his own will. If the will meets the requirements of the law, it will be just as valid as a will prepared by an attorney. But if you are going to write your own will, you must be careful. One small mistake can invalidate the entire will and cause real problems for your family. *For this reason, I strongly urge you to see a lawyer.*

There are two basic kinds of wills in Texas: a holographic will, which is written entirely in your own handwriting and signed; and a formal will, which can be handwritten, printed, or typed, and which must be signed and witnessed by two people.

If you write a holographic will, it is valid so long as it is completely handwritten and signed. It is not a valid holographic will if you type part of it or if you fill in blanks on a form. It also should be dated, and it should state that it replaces all other wills you may have written. A holographic will must clearly indicate it was intended as a will and should not have any printing, typing, or obliterations. For example, the document on page 211 would serve as a holographic will.

Holographic wills should be used only in emergency situations. Best advice: Don't rely on a holographic will. It must be letter-perfect, and it is too easy to make a mistake. If you feel you must write your own will, consider a formal will.

A formal will must be signed by the testator and witnessed by at least two witnesses. It can be written, typed, or part of a pre-printed form. For example, you can buy a form and fill in the proper blanks, or you could type it. You should also date your will, publish it (that is, declare it to be your will), and make sure everyone signs in the presence of everyone else. To give yourself added protection in other states, you should have three witnesses.

In addition to the proper signature, you should have what is known as a "self-proving affidavit." This allows your survivors to probate the will without having to go out and find the witnesses. A self-proving affidavit is simply a notary's statement that he has seen the people sign. At the end of this chapter I have included some model wills and a self-proving affidavit.

A holographic will should be letter-perfect.

> ### Last Will & Testament
>
> I, Jane Smith, a resident of Harris County, Texas, declare this to be my Last Will & Testament. I revoke all prior wills and codicils.
>
> First: I leave my 1990 Buick to my only brother, Jack Smith.
>
> Second: I leave my dog, Shasta, to Nancy Jones, who resides at 1324 West Oaks, Houston, Texas.
>
> Third: I leave the remainder of my estate to my parents, Susan Smith and Joe Smith, in equal shares. If they are not living, I leave the remainder of my property to the Society for the Prevention of Cruelty to Animals, Houston, Texas.
>
> Fourth: I nominate Larry James as independent executor of my will. If he is not living or does not want to be executor, I nominate Keith Long to act in his place. I direct that no bond be required of my executor.
>
> Executed at Houston, Texas, on July 2, 1997.
>
> Jane Smith

Although the law allows you to prepare your own will, I don't recommend it. One small mistake can totally invalidate the entire will. To be safe, you should have an attorney prepare your will, and you should not have to pay much money to have it done. For example, recently I telephoned 40 attorneys in Houston and asked how much they would charge to prepare a simple will for a single person. The prices ranged from $35 to over $600. I sent someone down to buy the $35 will and then had an expert look at it. It was a fine will and completely served the purposes of the person who bought it. *In other words, shop around. Most attorneys are competent to draft a simple will, and you may save yourself hundreds of dollars by making a few phone calls.*

What is an executor?
"The person in charge."

Dear Mr. Alderman:

My sister just passed away, and I was told I am the executor of her will. What does this mean? Does this mean that I won't inherit anything? Will it cost me any money? I don't want to sound cheap, but I am not a wealthy man.

When you die it is necessary for someone to gather up all your property, close your bank accounts, transfer title to your house, and then make sure everything is given to the people you designated in your will. This person is called an "executor" if it is a man and an "executrix" if it is a woman. Usually you appoint someone you trust, who you believe is competent to do what must be done as executor or executrix. By appointing you as executor, your sister was saying she believed you would be the best person to make sure her wishes are fulfilled.

There is no reason why the executor or executrix cannot also receive property under a will, and if the will provides, he or she does not have to post a bond, or pay any money, to serve.

But in order to put the will into effect, it has to be probated. Probate is a legal proceeding that gives the executor the power to act. To probate the will, you probably need an attorney. But probate is usually a routine matter, and you should shop around for an attorney. Be sure to compare prices and ask how the fee is computed. Some lawyers charge a percentage while others charge by the hour. You usually will be better off paying by the hour. I should also point out that the attorneys' fees are paid by the estate, not you, so you don't have to worry about this cost.

How can I avoid probating a will?
"You can't."

Dear Mr. Alderman:

I am getting on in years, and I want to leave my children property in my will without them having to go through probate. I don't have much property, and it seems a waste to spend a lot of money on probate costs. How can I make sure my will doesn't have to be probated?

You can't. As I said in the previous letter, "probate" is the legal term used to describe the process by which the terms of a will are given legal effect. Any property left to someone through a will has to go through some form of probate. Probate does not, however, have to be a long, expensive process. In fact, there is a new form of probate called "informal probate" that is designed for small estates. Informal probate should be very inexpensive.

If you wish to avoid any form of probate, you must either give the property outright, as a gift, or place it in trust before you die. You may want to speak with an attorney to find out what would be best for you in light of your concerns about probate and tax law. There are many forms of trusts, and before giving any gift you must consider the consequences of the gift tax law.

Who can be an executor?
"Nearly anyone."

Dear Mr. Alderman:

I am making out a will. A friend told me I couldn't make my son the executor of the will because he was going to inherit my property. I don't know who else to use. Can I name a bank?

The simple answer is to name your son. A person can be an executor of a will even if he is going to inherit under the will. The only people who may not serve as executors of a will are minors, incompetents, convicted felons, and others the court finds unsuitable. There are also some restrictions on when a nonresident or a corporation may act as an executor. A nonresident may only serve if he appoints a resident agent to accept service of process. A corporation may only serve if it is authorized to act as a fiduciary in this state.

The bottom line is that in most cases the executor is also a family member who will inherit some property under the will. Tell your friend he was misinformed.

Do I have to pay estate taxes?
"Only if you are rich."

Dear Mr. Alderman:

I am 83, and I have been told I should begin to give some of my property away to avoid paying estate taxes. I am married, and we don't have much money. We own a house worth about $75,000 and maybe another $50,000 in other property. In my will I leave every-thing to my wife, and if she dies before me, to our children. Will my heirs have to pay much in estate taxes?

First, I must make one thing clear. Estate taxes, which are collected by both the state and federal governments, are not paid by your heirs. They are paid out of your estate. In other words, the money is taken before your estate is distributed to your heirs. No estate taxes are due unless the estate is valued above a certain sum. In 1997 the sum is $600,000. This amount increases until 2006, when it will be $1 million. *In your case there would be no estate taxes.*

You also should know that no matter how large your estate is, no taxes have to be paid if the property goes to your spouse. For example, sup-pose your estate was worth $700,000; estate taxes would be due at your death. But if you left everything to your wife, no taxes would be paid. Of course, when she died, and left everything to your children, the taxes would have to be paid.

If you think your estate is going to have to pay estate taxes, you should see an attorney about estate planning. There are many things you can do to legally avoid paying estate taxes.

What is a life estate?
"Another type of ownership."

Dear Mr. Alderman:

Recently my father died. The lawyer in charge of things told me that my father left me his house but that he left a "life estate" to my step-mother, so I can't have it until she dies. I don't understand. If it is my house, why do I have to let her live there? I live in a small house, and it would be really nice to have a big place to live in. I don't want to sound cold, but my father had only been married to my stepmother for less than a year, and it doesn't seem fair. Is there anything I can do?

The answer is no. What the lawyer told you is right. If your stepmother has a life estate in the house, it is hers to do with as she pleases until she dies. It then becomes yours.

When you transfer property, there are many different ways of doing it. For example, you can give it outright, as in the case of a gift or the standard provision in a will. But this is not the only way to transfer property. *When you transfer property, you do not have to make an absolute transfer. The law allows you to transfer less than an unlimited full interest.* A common example would be when you rent an apartment. The landlord has transferred an interest in the property to you, but as a lessee your interest is limited by the terms of the lease. A life estate is another way to transfer property. When you get a life estate you get full rights in the property, but only for as long as you live. When you die, the property automatically goes to someone else.

So what rights does your stepmother have? Basically, she can do whatever she wants with the property—as if she owned it. But when she dies, it is yours. For instance, let's say she sold the property. All she has legal power to sell is her life estate, and therefore, when she died, whoever bought the property would no longer have title to it. It would be yours. The purchaser only has the same rights as your stepmother.

A life estate is a useful way of providing for one person during his or her lifetime, while making sure that ultimate title goes to someone else. Your father probably wanted to make sure your stepmother was comfortable for the rest of her life but that you ultimately got the house. That is exactly the result that will occur through the use of a life estate.

I just moved to Texas. Is my will still good?
"Maybe not."

Dear Mr. Alderman:
My wife and I have lived in Arkansas for over 20 years. We just moved to Texas to be near our grandchildren. We both have wills written by an Arkansas lawyer. Are they valid in Texas? We really would rather not have to spend the money to have new wills written.

The simple answer is, I don't know. To give you an answer I would have to be an expert on Arkansas law.

Even though this is the United States of America, every state has its own laws and is free to regulate its citizens as it sees fit. For example, in some states you can drink at age 18, while in others, it's 21; although you can gamble in Nevada and Atlantic City, gambling is illegal in most states.

The same thing is true with respect to wills. Every state has its own requirements for what must be included in a will and what happens if you don't have one or if you have one that is not valid. Although in most cases the requirements are the same, there is no guarantee that a will valid in one state is valid in another. *A will made up in another state is valid in Texas if it meets the requirements of Texas law.* The will is not valid, regardless of whether it is valid in the other state, if it does not comply with Texas law.

For example, Texas law requires that a will be witnessed by two people. If a will was made up in a state that required only one witness, and you had only one witness, it would not be valid when you moved to Texas. But if you make out a will in a state that requires three witnesses, it will satisfy Texas law as well. In other words, the only way to tell if the will is valid is to examine it to see if it complies with Texas law. Because I am not an expert on Arkansas law, I could not tell you if your Arkansas will is valid.

The best advice I can give you is to take your will to an attorney and let him or her look at it to see if it complies with Texas law. You also must make sure the will does what you want with your estate. As I said in the introduction to this section, you should shop around for an attorney before you see one. Wills are considered routine legal matters, and most attorneys are competent to handle them. You may save a lot of money with a few phone calls.

What happens to lottery winnings after I die?
"They go to your heirs."

Dear Mr. Alderman:
I have heard different reports about what happens to my lottery winnings if I die before they are paid out. Do my heirs collect the money, or does the state just get to keep the unpaid installments?

Every state with a lottery handles this problem in its own way. In some states, the money is paid only as long as the winner is alive. In others, including Texas, the money is considered an asset that will pass to your heirs as any other asset would.

State law dictates to whom your estate, including lottery winnings, goes after your death. If you want to ensure that your lottery winnings go to the person you want, with the least time and expense, make sure you have a will.

Can I abandon my property?
"Not if it is land."

Dear Mr. Alderman:
We own some property in the country that we bought as an "invest-ment." Unfortunately, it is now worthless. We have tried for years to sell it and cannot. Do we have to keep paying taxes? Can we stop paying and let them take the property?

Unfortunately, as long as you own the property you are responsible for the taxes. If you don't pay, the taxing authority has the right to go against either the property or you. You cannot force them to take the property as payment for back taxes, and you can't simply relinquish your ownership by abandoning the property.

The best thing to do is either sell the property or give it to another person or entity. Until then, you will be responsible for the taxes. Of course, you should also try to get your property reappraised in an effort to reduce your taxes.

What happens to my homestead after I die?
"Your heirs inherit it."

Dear Mr. Alderman:
Can a creditor take a person's homestead after his death? Are the heirs liable for any judgment against the deceased?

No. As you know, a person's homestead generally may not be taken by his creditors, even if they sue and win. The same rule applies after a person's death. The homestead will pass to the heirs free of the claims of creditors. Of course, the homestead will still be subject to any mortgage on the property.

A person's heirs also are not liable for any judgments against the deceased. The judgments must be paid from the estate, and if there is not enough money, they will go unpaid.

Are adopted children treated the same?
"Yes."

Dear Mr. Alderman:
Do adopted children inherit if a parent dies without a will?

Under Texas law, adopted children are treated the same as natural-born children for purposes of inheritance rights. This means they may inherit some or all of their parent's estate if the parent dies without a will.

Model Wills

As I said before, there is no one will that is right for everyone. You must consider who you want your property to go to after your death, and how you want that property to be transferred. For example, you may want property given to minors to be put in a trust until they reach a certain age.

The models that follow are just three examples of a will. One is for a single person, one is for a married person without children, and the last is for a married person with children. Read them carefully. If the model form does what you want to do with your property, then you should consider using it. You also can make changes to fit your needs. But I still urge you to contact a lawyer to draw up a will tailored to your special needs. These forms should be thought of as merely an emergency measure until you have a chance to see a lawyer.

Instructions

A "testator" is a man who makes out a will, and a "testatrix" is a woman. If you use these model wills, make sure you use the proper designation. Also, "executor" is used for a man, and "executrix" for a woman. Be sure to read the will carefully, and when you write yours *make sure you sign each page at the bottom and at the end of the will.* You should sign in the presence of three witnesses and a notary, and you should declare it to be your will before you sign. You also should have all the witnesses sign in the presence of each other and the notary. *Be sure to attach and complete the self-proving affidavit.*

Model will for single person.

LAST WILL AND TESTAMENT
OF
JANET GRANT

THE STATE OF TEXAS)
) KNOW ALL MEN
COUNTY OF HARRIS) BY THESE PRESENTS

THAT, I, JANET GRANT, a resident of HARRIS County, Texas, being of sound mind and disposing memory and more than eighteen years of age, do hereby make, publish and declare this to be my Last Will and Testament, hereby revoking all Wills and Codicils heretofore made by me.

ARTICLE I.
Declarations
Section 1.1 I declare that I am not now married.
Section 1.2 No children have ever been born to or adopted by me.
Section 1.3 It is my intention to dispose of all real and personal property which I have the right to dispose of by will.

ARTICLE II.
Executorship
Section 2.1 I appoint my father, FRED GRANT of HOUSTON, Texas, Independent Executor of this my Last Will and Testament and of my Estate. Should FRED GRANT, for any reason or at any time be unable or unwilling to qualify, or for any reason fail to qualify, or, after qualifying, for any reason fail to continue to act, I designate my friend TOM POST of HOUSTON, Texas, as successor or substitute Independent Executor under this will.

As used herein the term "Executor" shall mean the person then acting under either of the foregoing appointments.

Section 2.2 I direct that no bond or other security shall be required of my Executor and any Executor hereunder shall be independent of the supervision and direction of the Probate Court to the fullest extent permitted by law. I further direct that no action shall

_____
TESTATRIX

(continued on next page)

(continued from previous page)

be had in any court of probate jurisdiction in connection with this Will or in the administration or settlement of my Estate other than the probating of this Will and the return of any inventory, appraisement and list of claims due by or owing to my Estate.

Section 2.3 My Executor shall have, and may exercise without first obtaining the approval of any court, all of the powers of Independent Executors under the laws of the State of Texas.

ARTICLE III.
Bequests and Devises

Section 3.1 I give my diamond stick pin to my sister **SUSAN GRANT,** if she survives me by 30 days; if she does not, the gift shall lapse and become part of my estate.

Section 3.2 I hereby give, devise and bequeath the remainder of my estate, whether real, personal or mixed, and wherever situated to my parents, **FRED GRANT** and **MARTHA GRANT,** of **HOUSTON,** Texas, to share and share alike.

Section 3.3 In the event that either **FRED GRANT** or **MARTHA GRANT** does not survive me, I give, devise, and bequeath the remainder of my property of every kind, character and description, wherever situated, whether the same is real, personal or mixed, to the survivor.

Section 3.4 In the event that **FRED GRANT** and **MARTHA GRANT,** do not survive me, I give, devise and bequeath the remainder of my property to **TOM POST** of **HOUSTON,** Texas.

Section 3.5 In the event that none of the persons designated herein survive me, then I direct that my estate pass to my heirs at law.

Section 3.6 No one shall be deemed to have survived me unless that person survives at least 30 days after the date of my death.

IN WITNESS WHEREOF, I, **JANET GRANT,** testatrix, do hereby subscribe my name this the _____ day of _____, 19___, to this instrument and declare the same to be my Last Will and Testament, in the presence of _____ ,

_____

and _____

_____
TESTATRIX

(continued on next page)

(continued from previous page)

attesting witnesses at my request and in my presence and in the presence of each other.

The foregoing instrument was now here published as the Last Will and Testament of **JANET GRANT,** and signed and subscribed by her, the Testatrix, in our presence, and we, at her request and in her presence and in the presence of each other, signed and subscribed our names hereto as attesting witnesses.

Address: _____   _____

_____ Witness

Address: _____   _____

_____ Witness

Address: _____   _____

_____ Witness

(ADD SELF-PROVING AFFIDAVIT)

Model will for married person with no children.

LAST WILL AND TESTAMENT
OF
CATHY NAN SIMES

STATE OF TEXAS
COUNTY OF TRAVIS
KNOW ALL MEN BY THESE PRESENTS:

THAT I, CATHY NAN SIMES, of TRAVIS County, Texas, and being of sound mind and disposing memory and above the age of eighteen (18) years, do make, publish and declare this my Last Will and Testament, hereby revoking all other wills and codicils heretofore made by me.

I.

I declare that I am married to THOMAS SIMES and that all references in this Will to my spouse are references to him. I have no child or children, living or dead, born to me or adopted, at the date of the execution of this Will.

II.

I hereby nominate and appoint my spouse, THOMAS SIMES, as Independent Executor of the Will, and I direct that no bond shall be required of him. If my spouse, THOMAS SIMES, should pre-decease me, or for any reason fail to qualify or decline to act as executor, then I nominate and appoint JOHN TAPER, of AUSTIN, TEXAS, as Independent Executor of this Will, to serve without bond or compensation. If my spouse and JOHN TAPER both fail to qualify or decline to act as executor, I nominate and appoint ALICE BRADLEY of AUSTIN, TEXAS, as Independent Executrix of this Will, to serve without bond or compensation.

My executor/executrix shall have and possess all of the rights and powers and be subject to all of the duties and responsibilities conferred and imposed on an independent executor by the Texas Probate Code as the Code now provides or as it may be hereafter amended.

I direct that no action shall be taken in any court in relation to the settlement of my estate other than the probating and recording of the Will and the return of a statutory inventory and appraisement and list of claims of my estate.

_____
TESTATRIX

(continued on next page)

(continued from previous page)

III.

I give, devise, and bequeath to my beloved spouse, **THOMAS SIMES**, all of my property, real, personal, and mixed, and wheresoever located, of every sort and description of which I may die possessed, or to which I may be entitled at the time of my death, to have and to hold as his property absolutely.

IV.

If my spouse, **THOMAS SIMES**, should predecease me, or if he and I die as a result of a common disaster or under such circumstances that there is not sufficient evidence to determine the order of our deaths, or if my spouse, **THOMAS SIMES**, shall die within a period of 30 days after the date of my death, then all bequests, devises and provisions made herein to or for his benefit shall be void and my estate shall be administered and distributed in all respects as though my spouse, **THOMAS SIMES**, had not survived me.

V.

If my spouse, **THOMAS SIMES**, does not survive me, I give the sum of ten thousand dollars ($10,000) to **SANDY WRIGHT** of **HOUSTON, TEXAS**, if she survives me, and I give, devise, and bequeath my Hammond organ, automobile, jewelry and the residue of my estate to **JOHN TAPER** of **AUSTIN, TEXAS**, if he survives me.

VI.

In the event that **JOHN TAPER**, does not survive me, then I direct that my estate pass to my heirs at law.

VII.

No one shall be deemed to have survived me unless that person survives at least 30 days after the date of my death.

VIII.

If any beneficiary under this will in any manner, directly or indirectly, contests or attacks this will or any of its provisions, any share or interest in my estate given to the contesting beneficiary under this will is revoked and shall be disposed of in the same manner provided herein as if that contesting beneficiary had predeceased me without issue.

_____
TESTATRIX

(continued on next page)

(continued from previous page)

IX.

I declare that I have made and paid for funeral arrangements with **PLEASANT VALLEY REST, AUSTIN, TEXAS,** and I direct my executor/executrix to take all steps necessary to carry out such arrangements.

IN WITNESS WHEREOF, I, **CATHY NAN SIMES,** testatrix, do hereby subscribe my name this the _____ day of _____ , 19___ , to this instrument and declare the same to be my Last Will and Testament, in the presence of _____ ,

_____

and_____

attesting witnesses at my request and in my presence and in the presence of each other.

_____

TESTATRIX

The foregoing instrument was now here published as the Last Will and Testament of **CATHY NAN SIMES,** and signed and subscribed by her, the Testatrix, in our presence, and we, at her request and in her presence and in the presence of each other, signed and subscribed our names hereto as attesting witnesses.

Address:_____   _____

_____ Witness

Address:_____   _____

_____ Witness

Address:_____   _____

_____ Witness

(ADD SELF-PROVING AFFIDAVIT)

Model will for married person with children.

LAST WILL AND TESTAMENT
OF
JOSEPH RALPH SMITH

STATE OF TEXAS
COUNTY OF HIDALGO
KNOW ALL MEN BY THESE PRESENTS:

THAT I, JOSEPH RALPH SMITH of HIDALGO County, Texas, and being of sound mind and disposing memory and above the age of eighteen (18) years, do make, publish and declare this my Last Will and Testament, hereby revoking all other wills and codicils heretofore made by me.

I.

I declare that I am married to ROSIE JONNA SMITH, and that all references in this Will to my spouse are references to her. I have TWO children, now living, namely,

EMERSON SMITH	FEB. 18, 1978
	date of birth
BARBARA SMITH	OCT. 27, 1987
	date of birth

No other child or children, except as named above, were born to me at the date of execution of this Will and no child or children were adopted by me at the date of execution of this Will. All references in this Will to "my children" are to said named children and to any children hereafter born to or adopted by me.

II.

I hereby appoint my spouse, ROSIE JONNA SMITH, as Independent Executrix of my Will, and I direct that no bond shall be required of her. If for any reason she cannot, or refuses to act as Executrix, then I appoint GEORGE JAMES of DONNA, TEXAS, as Independent Executor of my Will, to serve without bond. If my spouse and GEORGE JAMES both fail or refuse to qualify, I appoint FIRST BANK OF DONNA as Independent Executor of my Will, to serve without bond. I direct that no action shall be had in any court in relation to the settlement of my estate other than the probating and recording of this Will and the return of a statutory inventory and appraisement and list of claims of my estate.

_____
TESTATOR

(continued on next page)

(continued from previous page)

III.

I give, devise, and bequeath to my beloved spouse, ROSIE JONNA SMITH, all of my property, real, personal, and mixed and wheresoever located of every sort and description of which I may die possessed, or to which I may be entitled at the time of my death to have and to hold as her property absolutely.

IV.

If my spouse, ROSIE JONNA SMITH, should predecease me, or if she and I die as a result of a common disaster or under such circumstances that there is not sufficient evidence to determine the order of our deaths, or if my spouse, ROSIE JONNA SMITH, shall die within a period of 30 days after the date of my death, then all bequests, devises, and provisions made herein to or for her benefit shall be void and my estate shall be administered and distributed in all respects as though my spouse, ROSIE JONNA SMITH, had not survived me.

V.

If my spouse does not survive me, I direct that my entire estate go to my surviving children, EMERSON SMITH and BARBARA SMITH, to share and share alike. If any child of mine is a minor at the time of my death, then I hereby deliver his/her estate to GEORGE JAMES as guardian of the estate of my child, GEORGE JAMES, to serve without bond. If for any reason GEORGE JAMES cannot act in such capacity, then I appoint LEE EARL, of DONNA, TEXAS, to act as guardian of the estate of my child and to serve without bond.

VI.

In the event that at any time it may be necessary to appoint a guardian for the person of any child of mine, then I nominate and appoint as such guardian GEORGE JAMES, and if for any reason he shall fail or cease so to serve I nominate and appoint in his place LEE EARL as guardian hereunder, and I direct that no guardian shall be required to furnish any bond.

VII.

In the event that any of my children shall predecease me or if he/she and I die as a result of a common disaster or under such

_____

TESTATOR

(continued on next page)

(continued from previous page)

circumstances that there is not sufficient evidence to determine the order of our deaths, then all bequests, devises, and provisions made herein to or for his/her benefit shall be void and my estate shall be administered and distributed in all respects as though my child/children had not survived me.

VIII.

In the event that none of the persons designated herein survive me, then I direct that my estate pass to my heirs at law.

IX.

No one shall be deemed to have survived me unless that person survives at least 30 days after the date of my death.

IN WITNESS WHEREOF, I, JOSEPH RALPH SMITH, testator, do hereby subscribe my name this the 21st day of JUNE, 1997, to this instrument and declare the same to be my Last Will and Testament, in the presence of ————————————
———————————— , ————————————
and————————————
attesting witnesses at my request and in my presence and in the presence of each other.

————————————
TESTATOR

The foregoing instrument was now here published as the Last Will and Testament of JOSEPH RALPH SMITH, and signed and subscribed by him, the Testator, in our presence, and we, at his request and in his presence and in the presence of each other, signed and subscribed our names hereto as attesting witnesses.
Address:

———————————— ————————————
———————————— Witness

Address: ———————————— ————————————
———————————— Witness

Address: ———————————— ————————————
———————————— Witness

(ADD SELF-PROVING AFFIDAVIT)

The Self-Proving Affidavit should be added at the end of any will.

SELF-PROVING AFFIDAVIT
For Will

STATE OF TEXAS
COUNTY OF _____

Before me, the undersigned authority, on this day personally appeared _____,
_____,
_____
and _____,
known to me to be testator/testatrix and the witnesses, respectively, whose names are subscribed to the annexed or foregoing instrument in their respective capacities, and all of said persons being by me duly sworn, the said _____,
testator/testatrix, declared to me and to the said witnesses in my presence that said instrument is his/her last will and testament, and that he/she had willingly made and executed it as his/her free act and deed for the purposes therein expressed; and the said witnesses, each on their oath, stated to me, in the presence and hearing of the said testator/testatrix, that the said testator/testatrix had declared to them that said instrument is his/her last will and testament, and that he/she executed same as such and wanted each of them to sign as a witness; and upon their oaths each witness stated further that they did sign the same as witnesses in the presence of the said testator/testatrix and at his/her request; that he/she was at the time eighteen years of age or over and was of sound mind, and that each of said witnesses was then at least fourteen years of age.

_____
Testator/Testatrix

Address:

_____
Witness

Address:

_____
Witness

Address:

_____
Witness

(continued on next page)

(continued from previous page)

SUBSCRIBED AND ACKNOWLEDGED before me by the said testator/testatrix, —————————————————————— , and subscribed and sworn to before me by the said —————————

———————————————— , ——————————————————— and ——————————————————————————— , witnesses, this ____ day of _____ , 19___.

—————————————————————
Notary Public

My commission expires:

—————————————————————

The Texas Legislature's suggested form for a directive to physicians, or living will.

DIRECTIVE TO PHYSICIANS

Directive made this _____ day of _____ (month, year).

I, _____ , being of sound mind willfully and voluntarily make known my desire that my life shall not be artificially prolonged under the circumstances set forth below, and do hereby declare:

1. If at any time I should have an incurable or irreversible condition caused by injury, disease, or illness certified to be a terminal condition by two physicians, and where the application of life-sustaining procedures would serve only to artificially prolong the moment of my death and where my attending physician determines that my death is imminent or will result within a relatively short time without application of life-sustaining procedures, I direct that such procedures be withheld or withdrawn, and that I be permitted to die naturally.

2. In the absence of my ability to give directions regarding the use of such life-sustaining procedures, it is my intention that this directive shall be honored by my family and physicians as the final expression of my legal right to refuse medical or surgical treatment and accept the consequences from such refusal.

3. I understand that Texas law allows me to designate another person to make a treatment decision for me if I should become comatose, incompetent, or otherwise mentally or physically incapable of communication. I hereby designate _____ who resides at _____ to make such a treatment decision for me if I should become incapable of communicating with my physician. If the person I have named above is unable to act on my behalf, I authorize the following person to do so:

    Name: _____

    Address:_____

I have discussed my wishes with these persons and trust their judgment.

(continued on next page)

(continued from previous page)

4. If I have been diagnosed as pregnant and that diagnosis is known to my physician, this directive shall have no force or effect during the course of my pregnancy.
5. This directive shall be in effect until it is revoked.
6. I understand the full import of this directive, and I am emotionally and mentally competent to make this directive.
7. I understand that I may revoke this directive at any time.

Signed _____

City _____ County _____ , TEXAS

I am not related to the declarant by blood or marriage; nor would I be entitled to any portion of the declarant's estate on his/her decease; nor am I the attending physician of the declarant or an employee of the attending physician; nor am I a patient in the health care facility in which the declarant is a patient, or any person who has a claim against any portion of the estate of the declarant upon his/her decease. Furthermore, if I am an employee of a health facility in which the declarant is a patient, I am not involved in providing direct patient care to the declarant nor am I directly involved in the financial affairs of the health facility.

Witness _____ Witness _____

The Statutory Durable Power of Attorney gives your designated agent the power to make decisions regarding your property and financial matters in the event that you are unable to do so.

STATUTORY DURABLE POWER OF ATTORNEY

NOTICE: THE POWERS GRANTED BY THIS DOCUMENT ARE BROAD AND SWEEPING. THEY ARE EXPLAINED IN THE DURABLE POWER OF ATTORNEY ACT, CHAPTER XII, TEXAS PROBATE CODE. IF YOU HAVE ANY QUESTIONS ABOUT THESE POWERS, OBTAIN COMPETENT LEGAL ADVICE. THIS DOCUMENT DOES NOT AUTHORIZE ANY-ONE TO MAKE MEDICAL AND OTHER HEALTH CARE DECISIONS FOR YOU. YOU MAY REVOKE THIS POWER OF ATTORNEY IF YOU LATER WISH TO DO SO.

I, _____ (insert your name and address), my social security number being __ __ __ - __ __ - __ __ __ __ (insert your proper SS#), appoint _____ (insert the name and address of person appointed) as my agent (attorney-in-fact) to act for me in any lawful way with respect to the following initialed subjects:

TO GRANT ALL OF THE FOLLOWING POWERS, INI-TIAL THE LINE IN FRONT OF (N) AND IGNORE THE LINES IN FRONT OF THE OTHER POWERS.

TO GRANT ONE OR MORE, BUT FEWER THAN ALL, OF THE FOLLOWING POWERS, INITIAL THE LINE IN FRONT OF EACH POWER YOU ARE GRANTING.

TO WITHHOLD A POWER, DO NOT INITIAL THE LINE IN FRONT OF IT. YOU MAY, BUT NEED NOT, CROSS OUT EACH POWER WITHHELD.

INITIAL

_____ (A) real property transactions;

_____ (B) tangible personal property transactions;

_____ (C) stock and bond transactions;

_____ (D) commodity and option transactions;

_____ (E) banking and other financial institution transactions;

_____ (F) business operating transactions;

(continued on next page)

(continued from previous page)

_____ (G) insurance and annuity transactions;

_____ (H) estate, trust, and other beneficiary transactions;

_____ (I) claims and litigation;

_____ (J) personal and family maintenance;

_____ (K) benefits from social security, Medicare, Medicaid, or other governmental programs or civil or military service;

_____ (L) retirement plan transactions;

_____ (M) tax matters;

_____ (N) ALL OF THE POWERS LISTED IN (A) THROUGH (M). YOU NEED NOT INITIAL ANY OTHER LINES IF YOU INITIAL LINE (N).

SPECIAL INSTRUCTIONS:

(IN THE FOLLOWING SPACE YOU MAY GIVE SPECIAL INSTRUCTIONS LIMITING OR EXTENDING THE POWERS GRANTED TO YOUR AGENT.)

_____

_____

_____

_____

_____

_____

UNLESS YOU DIRECT OTHERWISE ABOVE, THIS POWER OF ATTORNEY IS EFFECTIVE IMMEDIATELY AND WILL CONTINUE UNTIL IT IS REVOKED.

CHOOSE ONE OF THE FOLLOWING ALTERNATIVES BY CROSSING OUT THE ALTERNATIVE NOT CHOSEN:

(A) This power of attorney is not affected by my subsequent disability or incapacity.

(B) This power of attorney becomes effective upon my disability or incapacity.

YOU SHOULD CHOOSE ALTERNATIVE (A) IF THIS POWER OF ATTORNEY IS TO BECOME EFFECTIVE ON THE DATE IT IS EXECUTED.

(continued on next page)

234   Know Your Rights!

(continued from previous page)

IF NEITHER (A) OR (B) IS CROSSED OUT, IT WILL BE ASSUMED THAT YOU CHOSE ALTERNATIVE (A).

I agree that any third party who receives a copy of this document may act under it. Revocation of the Durable Power of Attorney is not effective as to a third party until the third party receives actual notice of the revocation. I agree to indemnify the third party for any claims that arise against the third party because of reliance on this power of attorney.

If any agent named by me dies, becomes legally disabled, resigns, or refuses to act, I name the following (each to act alone and successively, in the order named) as successor(s) to that agent:
_____ ,

Signed this _____ day of _____ , 19___ .
_____
(your signature)
State of _____
County of _____

This document was acknowledged before me on

_____ _____ (date) by

_____
(name of principal)

_____
                                    (signature of notarial officer)
(Seal, if any, of
notary)_____
                    (printed name)

                    My commission expires: _____

THE ATTORNEY IN FACT OR AGENT, BY ACCEPTING OR ACTING UNDER THE APPOINTMENT, ASSUMES THE FIDUCIARY AND OTHER LEGAL RESPONSIBILITIES OF AN AGENT.

INDEX